FOOD SECURITY AND PANCHAYATI RAJ

About the Editor

Pradeep Chaturvedi, is a well known development expert involved in Food Security process for the last 15 years, since World Food Day was established in 1981. His expertise lies in project planning, implementation and management with emphasis on technology transfer and skill building. A number of pioneering projects and studies of national and international significance have been conducted under his guidance. At present, Mr. Chaturvedi is also working as a Consultant to FAO's Regional Wood Energy Development Programme for Asia.

He contributed significantly in the preparatory meetings to FAO's International Conference on Nutrition in 1992; and is currently involved in the preparatory process to the World Food Summit during November 13-17, 1996 at Rome. Mr. Chaturvedi has especially concentrated on motivating NGOs in India and Asia-Pacific regions.

Mr. Chaturvedi is a Graduate in Engineering. He is a Fellow of the Institution of Engineers (India) and the Recipient of FAO's World Food Day Silver Medal 1991.

Mr. Chaturvedi has edited and authored 16 books related to sustainable development, and renewable energy and energy conservation: and has contributed papers at a number of national and international conferences.

FOOD SECURITY AND PANCHAYATI RAJ

Edited by

PRADEEP CHATURVEDI
Secretary General
Indian Association for the Advancement of Science

Foreword by

DR. M.S. SWAMINATHAN

Published for

IAAS INDIAN ASSOCIATION FOR THE ADVANCEMENT OF SCIENCE

and

FOOD & AGRICULTURE ORGANISATION OF THE UNITED NATIONS

by

CONCEPT PUBLISHING COMPANY, NEW DELHI - 110059

ISBN 81-7022-616-3

First Published 1997

Published and Printed by
Ashok Kumar Mittal
Concept Publishing Company
A/15-16, Commercial Block, Mohan Garden,
NEW DELHI - 110059 (India)
Phones: 5554042, 5504042
Fax No. 091-11-5598898

DEDICATED
TO

WORLD FOOD SUMMIT

FOREWORD

Contemporary development experience has shown that inspite of the spectacular progress made in many areas of human endeavour, we are yet to overcome successfully the problems arising from environmental degradation, growing economic inequity, including the feminisation of poverty, population expansion and jobless economic growth. The 1996 Human Development Report of UNDP contains the following data in relation to the widening rich-poor divide.

— The poorest 20 per cent of the world's people saw their share of global income decline for 2.3 per cent to 1.4 per cent in the past 30 years. During the same period, the share of the richest 20 per cent rose from 70 to 85 per cent.
— The assets of the world's 358 billionaires exceeded the combined annual income of countries with 45 per cent of the world's people.
— If present trends continue, economic disparities between the industrial and developing nations will move from inequitable to inhuman.

The most serious manifestation of poverty is under- and mal-nutrition, which in the case of under-five children leads to a permanent impairment of their innate genetic potential for physical and mental development. This is why all countries should work towards building both at the individual and national levels a sustainable food and nutrition security system which will ensure:

— that every individual has the physical, economic, social and environmental access to balanced diet that includes the necessary macro- and micro-nutrients, safe drinking water, sanitation, environmental hygiene, primary health care and education so as to lead a healthy and productive life.
— that food originates from efficient and environmentally benign

production technologies that conserve and enhance the natural resource base of crop and animal husbandry, forestry, inland and marine fisheries.

New measures of human development are also being constantly standardised for enabling political leaders and policy makers in deciding on priorities for resource allocation. For example, the 1996 Human Development Report of UNDP has suggested a *Capability Poverty Measure* based on indices relating to underweight children, unattended births and female adult literacy. In many countries including ours, capability poverty far exceeds income poverty in terms of severity. This situation stresses the need for a micro-level attention to problems relating to the quality of human life.

India will be commemorating the 50th anniversary of its independence from Colonial rule in August, 1997. Planned deployment of financial and natural resources for "development" began in 1950 when India launched its first 5-Year Plan. The Ninth Five Year Plan will begin in April, 1997 and it will be designed to take the country to the new millennium. During the last 50 years, India's population has increased by over 600 million and the country will have a population of over a billion within the next 5 years. Population growth coupled with environmentally unsustainable pathways of economic progress have resulted in making past achievements in agriculture, industry and social development pale into insignificance in relation to current and future challenges.

It is in this context that an Expert Group appointed by the Government of India in 1993 under my Chairmanship to develop a draft National Population Policy suggested a paradigm shift in developmental planning. The Group pointed out that development strategies must address the totality of the way, people live, work and think: People must have a central role in deciding how they live. Population policies should therefore be viewed in the broader context of social development. For this purpose, the Group proposed that elected Members of Village Panchayats and town and city Nagarpalikas should develop their own planning tool, which was termed "Socio-demographic Charter".

The local level socio-demographic charter was to be based on a "pro-nature, pro-poor, pro-women and pro-democratic choice" orientation to developmental planning. Such a plan prepared by elected representatives of village and towns/cities would help to articulate priorities and strategies according to local needs and circumstances. Thus, complex socio-economic problems like poverty, population growth, gender inequity and unemployment can be viewed and dealt with in a disaggregated manner. Seemingly insurmountable problems then become solvable.

At our Research Centre in Madras training modules have been prepared for enabling elected members of Panchayats and Nagarpalikas to prepare socio-demographic charters for their respective areas. Socio-political empowerment without associated administrative, financial and legal empowerment can only lead to frustration and unfulfilled expectations. Therefore, the socio-demographic charter should include mechanisms for achieving a proper match between programmes and resources.

I hope the modules will find widespread application. They have been designed in a manner that generic and location-specific issues can both be dealt with by the village/town planning groups. This is important, since there is a wide variation within the country in indicators like TFR, IMR and sex ratio. India is among the few countries which have a sex ratio highly adverse to women. This is why the Training Module incorporates a Gender Code which will help local communities to adopt measures which can lead to gender equality as well as help to monitor the progress being made in this direction.

This book on "Food Security and Panchayatiraj" is a timely contribution. We will have functional Panchayats all over the country before the end of this year. This will provide uncommon opportunities for mobilising peoples' power for solving the chronic problems of endemic hunger and deprivation. The elected bodies require planning tools for articulating their priorities and strategies. Such a planning tool will help them to examine social and economic problems in an integrated and holistic manner.

I hope the Panchayatiraj Institutions will help us to enter the new century with the confidence that children will be born in our country for happiness and not just for existence. Mr. Pradeep Chaturvedi deserves our gratitude for this excellent publication. The Indian Association for the Advancement of Science and the Food and Agricultural Organisation of the United Nations have rendered invaluable service to the cause of orienting Panchayatiraj Institutions to achieving food security at the level of every child, man and woman.

M.S. SWAMINATHAN

PREFACE

Progress made in agriculture in India in the recent decades is quite impressive. However, despite the increased production and per capita availability of foodgrains, a substantial portion of the rural population continues to be poor and under-nourished due to lack of purchasing power. Although green revolution technologies did help in increasing production and productivity, it has not succeeded in alleviating poverty at the grass-root level.

At the World Food Summit convened by the Director-General of FAO, on 13-17 November 1996, at Rome, the Heads of Governments would meet to find solutions to eradicate hunger and poverty globally. Each country is expected to devise ways to ensure food security and nutrition for its nation. In this connection, after discussion with concerned Ministries like Agriculture, Food & Rural Development of the Government of India; NGOs; and many eminent experts, a consensus was reached to hold a National Conference on "Panchayati Raj--The Key to Food Security and Nutrition" at New Delhi on 2-3 July, 1996.

The National Conference evinced keen interest and was attended by Secretaries of the concerned Ministries, representatives of UN Agencies in the country, various NGOs and Chiefs of Panchayats.

The outcome of the National Conference and Recommendations are of great relevance to the new concept of decentralized grass-root level planning and its implementation to ensure food security at village level. The organizers, therefore, decided to publish all the Papers in the form of present volume. M/s Concept Publishing Company, who have specialised on publications relating to Panchayats have cooperated in publication and circulation of this Book.

I am sure the Book will be a good reference volume on Food Security in India through Panchayats.

New Delhi
October 16, 1996

PETER ROSENEGGER
FAO Representative in India & Bhutan

INTRODUCTION

The Indian Association for the Advancement of Science, IAAS, has been involved with the World Food Day activities since 1982. This long association with FAO offered us an opportunity to study different aspects of 'food security' at national and international levels. World Food Summit provides a unique opportunity to synthesise all our experience and bring together different like minded agencies to discuss different options for attaining 'food security'.

'Food Security' entails three basic issues, viz., availability, stability and accessibility. 'Food Security' is defined as a situation where everyone has access, at all times, to the food needed for an active and healthy life. At the household level, food security implies having physical and economic access to food that are adequate in terms of quantity, quality and safety. Poverty has been stressed to be the root cause of malnutrition leading to poor food security. Two identified possible routes for achieving food security are: (i) to produce own food; and (ii) to access food through food trade. That means either create food production capability or else offer an opportunity for better income and employment generation so that the poor can have access to food.

The two-day National Conference on "Panchayati Raj--The Key to Food Security and Nutrition" was organized with the objective to develop a strategy for micro-level food security and nutrition for the poor through the Panchayati Raj System; and to identify major areas crucial and requiring pioneering effort to develop the same.

The thrust of the conference was on the following:

(i) Reasons for lack of food security.
(ii) Potential of village panchayat system as an important mechanism for ensuring food security at the village level.

Background papers clearly indicated as to what needs to be done to attain food security. Panchayati Raj, being a unique elected self governance system, it was considered appropriate to focus on how the Panchayati Raj can be effective in food security. To ensure that the outcome was as true to the ground realities as possible the focus centred around the 13 representative Pradhans (Chiefs) of panchayats from different parts of the country. The Conference also had presentations from the Secretaries and senior officials of the concerned ministries; Members of Planning Commission (past and present); Scientists from research institutes; experts from socio-economic institutes; State government officials; leading NGOs and experts involved in micro and macro level planning, besides Pradhans (Chiefs) of panchayats. The Conference also had presentation on the FAO's sponsored Study on District Planning: Lessons from India (a Planning Guide); and Capacity Building in the Block Level Panchayats for Micro Level Planning and Training for the same with the intervention of NICNET.

To facilitate clear understanding about observations on different issues ralting to the World Food Summit, the Papers have been grouped as follows:

I. Panchayati Raj Institutions--New Features.
II. Food Security--Current Situation; Nutritional Aspects, Household Food Security, Public Distribution System.
III. Agricultural Growth and Poverty Alleviation.
IV. Experiences of NGOs and other Agencies working with PRIs.
V. Decentralized Micro-level Planning and its Implementation
VI. Training Requirements for Micro-level Planning.

Untiring efforts of Mr. V. Kumar, Consultant, FAO, and Mr. O.P. Dewan, Information Officer, FAO, duly supported by Ms. P.M. Sujatha and Mr. Ashok Malhotra were helpful in giving shape to the Report.

The Conclusions and Recommendations have been given in the beginning with a view to facilitate readers to have a glimpse of the outcome of the Conference.

I am sure the joint effort in organizing the Conference by Indian Association for the Advancement of Science, FAO office, Delhi, Indian Farmers Fertilizer Cooperative, UN Inter Agency Group on Food Security, has brought the expected outcome; and that the Papers published in the present volume will be of long term interest to the works.

PRADEEP CHATURVEDI
Secretary-General
Indian Assn. for the Adv. of Science

New Delhi
October 16, 1996

CONTENTS

PANCHAYATI RAJ INSTITUTIONS—NEW FEATURES

ONE

ROLE OF PANCHAYATS IN ATTAINING FOOD SECURITY FOR THE POOR

VINAY SHANKAR

Ensuring food security would involve adequate food production, storage, distribution and, above all, capacity, particularly of the poor, in terms of money incomes to buy. The effort, therefore, has to be directed to create avenues of employment in the rural areas so that every villager earns enough money to live a life of dignity, the most important component of which is the ability to purchase food for himself and his family.

It has all along been felt, and for some time, with increasing inferiority, that there is a need for much greater decentralization of governance to ensure participation of the people in the management of affairs affecting them not only in the process of decision making but also in planning and management of programmes of development. India has had a tradition of self-governance, and panchayats have been in existence since the *Vedic* times. They were institutions of self-governance, exercising enormous formal and informal power and enjoying exalted status. They lost their importance particularly during the time when the country was under British rule as the foreign ruler wanted to exercise greater control in order to retain and foster its rule, and thus centralised the administration. During the freedom struggle, the Indian leaders, particularly Mahatma Gandhi championed the cause of panchayats and visualised Gram Swaraj. In keeping with these sentiments, Article 40 of the Indian Constitution provides that the State shall take steps to organize village panchayats and endow with them with such powers and authority as may be necessary to enable them to function as units of self-government.

Achieving democratic decentralization has all along been exercising our mind since Independence and a number of Committees have examined the manner in which this could be achieved. The State Governments have tried different models of Panchayati Raj Institutions (PRIs), but effective decentralization could not be achieved. After considerable deliberations on the subject by a Committee under the Chairmanship of Dr. G.V.K. Rao, its recommendations on PRIs were accepted and the Government decided to amend the Constitution providing for the setting up of a three-tier PRI structure. Accordingly, the Constitution was amended in 1992. Every State has now enacted a law providing for a Gram Sabha and panchayats at the levels of village, the intermediate (normally development block) and the district. These panchayats have to be given powers to prepare plans and schemes of socio-economic development and implement them. In this task, they are to enjoy autonomy.

On the lines of the Central Finance Commission, the States have set up State Finance Commissions to advise the States on the issue of devolution of funds to the PRIs. Apart from responsibility and authority for preparing and implementing schemes of socio-economic development, the panchayats have also been given powers of self-governance. In the country there are nearly a quarter million panchayats with three million elected members. It will thus be seen that in India there is now a significant framework of self-governance in place. The devolution of responsibility, authority, powers and resources to these institutions is still in the stage of evolution. However, the momentum is picking up and the process seems irreversible.

As already mentioned, as essential element of food security is employment of all able bodied persons in the villages capable of giving them sufficient incomes to acquire food and meet their other basic needs. During the last five years a frontal attack on poverty has been launched jointly by the Central and State Governments and the Central Government alone would have spent Rs. 350 billion in the five years on poverty alleviation programmes in the rural areas. The State Governments have also contributed to these programmes. The result has been that the incidence of poverty has come down sharply and the objective is that within the next few years poverty should be eradicated. While implementing the programmes of poverty alleviation, the attempt has been to ensure that not only employment is generated but durable assets are also created and the minimum needs of the rural people are met. These include provision of drinking water, housing for the poor, construction of assets such as village roads, school buildings, etc.

As we move towards a situation of genuine self-governance, sharp reduction of poverty, satisfaction of minimum needs and provision of rural infrastructure, it is interesting to examine what role the PRIs can play in food production, marketing, storage and distribution.

The country consists of areas which are agriculturally developed and those which have lagged behind. In agriculturally developed areas, there is a situation of surplus and generally the infrastructure like roads, agricultural markets, distribution channels are well established. The problem in these areas is to ensure that the farmers get remunerative price for their surplus, the consumer gets the food at appropriate prices, and the distribution costs are kept as low as possible. In the food deficit areas, there is greater incidence of poverty and the infrastructure of roads, agricultural markets, etc. are less developed. In these areas the poor farmers are compelled to sell their produce after harvesting, at unremunerative prices and later buy the grain from the market at higher prices.

In India, after Independence, a series of reforms have been introduced to achieve the goals of the marketing system. Some of these reforms include setting up of regulated agricultural markets, cooperative marketing societies and above, introducing State trading for which the Food Corporation of India (FCI) was set up. Marketing reforms have vastly changed the marketing scene for the better in India since Independence. However, there are still deficiencies--pre-harvest or immediate post-harvest sales at low prices, little grading at the village level, tie-in-sales and high marketing margins. These can perhaps be attributed to inadequate infrastructure of transport, grading, storage facilities, marketing credit, market intelligence, etc. Deficiency perhaps also lay in putting greater emphasis on centralised wholesale markets rather on primary markets and village level functionaries. In the centralised wholesale markets the capital intensity for these facilities is high and the chance of their percolating to small markets, small farmers and village petty traders whose services may be equally important as of wholesale buyers. It is obvious that since the issue of food security is a complex one and has inter-relationships with so many socio-economic factors, agricultural marketing needs to be an integral party of the broader developmental policy. In the new dispensation, the PRIs have been given the responsibility and authority to make their own developmental plans and make investment decisions to an extent.

Since PRIs are institutions of self-governance, they should not engage in commercial activity. Their role should more appropriately be to encourage and support systems in the cooperative, private and voluntary sectors which would meet the needs of their village and the district in the matter of food security, among other things. Apart from undertaking and supporting schemes which will result in economic development and adequate money incomes to the villagers, particularly the poor, they need to encourage food production, preventing pre-harvest and post-harvest losses, checking losses in storage, taking steps to prevent distress sales of food specially by the poor, estimating the gap between demand and local production and ensuring that the deficit will be met through normal trading channels particularly the public distribution system (PDS). In India, there is a network of fair price shops under the PDS where the foodgrains and other essential commodities are available at the rates prescribed by the Government. The PRIs have a role to perform in the efficient functioning of the PDS. They have the authority to inspect and supervise and also to see that the items are available in the required quantity and that they satisfy the quality standards.

In India, the PRIs can play a role complementary to that of the State trading organization i.e. the FCI. It being a national organization, it has necessarily to take macro-view of its objectives, strategies, activities, etc. The village and block level interests and concerns get overlooked. Its operations from a centre have to cover a large geographical area and it deals in items which have national importance. Although systems have been developed to meet needs of every fair-price shop, smaller scale operations can be taken over by local entrepreneurs, cooperatives with due encouragement of panchayats. They need to strive for setting up godowns for the storage of foodgrains.

The farmers store foodgrains in their own dwelling house. Bamboo and mud silos are traditional storages of foodgrains. However, these are not damp proof and rodent proof. Hence, there is a need for rural godowns. A programme was taken up by the Department of Rural Development, Government of India under which 3,813 godowns were constructed in 21 States with a capacity of 21.26 lakh tonnes. Many of these godowns are not fully utilised because of ignorance on the part of the farmers, locational difficulties and non-availability of pledged loans to farmers from banks. The panchayats should play an active role in overcoming these difficulties. The Panchayats could also encourage mobile storage facilities. It has been estimated that a storage capacity of 8 lakh tonnes additionally should be created in the rural areas.

The panchayats have also to play an important role in procurement, storage and marketing of agricultural produce, particularly the foodgrains. These activities could include the following:

(a) Development of rural periodic markets;
(b) Introduction of grading at producers level;

(c) Proper preparation of produce for market;
(d) Construction of link roads;
(e) Farm level storage;
(f) Farmer and consumer education; and
(g) Marketing intelligence.

In the country, the agricultural markets are regulated through a State level legislation. While the jurisdiction of the agricultural markets extends to every village, the facilities are almost entirely concentrated in the market yards, which are located in bigger towns. Therefore, the rural markets play a complementary role. These rural markets are multi-purpose in the sense that they provide facilities for marketing of all kinds of goods including foodgrains. Although the regulated agricultural markets can and also perform the functions mentioned above, and there could be a possibility of duplication, but they are too distant for many villages. By proper coordination the duplication can be avoided.

I, therefore, feel that as Constitutionally recognized institutions of self-governance, the panchayats have a role which cuts across all sectors and institutions in the districts, and it is their obligation to ensure efficient functioning of the institutions, particularly those dealing with meeting the basic needs in the districts. Food being the most basic of all necessities should naturally enjoy a high priority in the activities of the panchayats. As the PRIs are still in an evolutionary stage, the exact modalities and scope of role of panchayats in food security will have to be worked out in different States of the country. As the conditions vary from State to State, a number of n. odels will emerge. This is a new and exciting field and there is very considerable scope for research and experimentation.

TWO

PANCHAYATI RAJ STRUCTURE AND ITS LINKAGE TO DEVELOPMENT

GEORGE MATHEW

From ancient times villages in India had a tradition of self-management. The system of five (*paanch* in Hindi) people conducting the affairs of the village was known as panchayats. Today a member in the village self-governing bodies in most parts of the country is known as a Panch. These traditional forms of village governance were mostly caste-based, and static without any relation to the larger systems. They were not elected but inherited.

Many students of ancient and medieval Indian society had admired the system even calling it, 'Little Republics'. During the British period in 1882, the then Viceroy Lord Ripon introduced 'Local Self-Government' in India. The District Boards which were established as a result were mostly nominated and their functions were municipal. But the idea of self-government took root in Indian psyche and the creed of Mahatma Gandhi was 'Grama Swaraj'; that is, villages should be self-sufficient, self-regulating and autonomous units but interdependent. Although it found prime of place in the national movement for independence, when the Constitution was written for independent India, village self-governing systems, the panchayats, found place only in the Directive Principles (Article 40) as 'units of self-government'. It was left to the States in the Union of India to establish panchayats. It was not mandatory since it was not in the statutes.

Panchayats: 1950-1992

Thus independent India's federal system had two-tiers—Union of India and the States—and, in fact, it is one of the basic features of the Indian the

Constitution. In 1959, following Balwantrai Mehta Committee's recommendation, the States established the panchayats but they were mainly considered as 'instrumentalities' for ensuring people's participation in development. Even this showed signs of decline and collapse from the mid-1960s. Only Maharashtra and Gujarat had active panchayat system till 1977. Attempts to establish panchayats in most of the States failed mainly because of three main reasons: (1) insufficient finance, (2) irregular elections, and (3) inadequate devolution of powers.

In 1978, a new generation panchayat system came up. The Asoka Mehta Committee recommended that panchayats must be political institutions. West Bengal (1978), followed by Karnataka in 1983 and later Andhra Pradesh introduced this kind of panchayats. During this period, because of the success of panchayats in these States, the idea of a "District Government also came up. Towards the end of 1980's, it was the common belief that unless panchayats are made part of statutes which is mandatory, the majority of State governments will not devolve powers to districts and below. Moreover, excessive concentration of power at the Centre resulted in cracks in the federal structure. After two unsuccessful attempts in 1989 and 1990, the Indian Parliament in December 1992 passed the 73rd Constitutional Amendment and on 24 April 1993 panchayats became part IX of the Constitution. The 74th Constitutional Amendment Act, Simultaneously passed by Parliament, pertains to urban areas. 26 per cent of India's population is urban.

Significance of the Constitutional Amendments

So far Indian democracy in practice was a superstructure. The roots of democracy had not gone deep into the base for want of suitable structures. Elections to Parliament and State Assemblies were regularly held every five years but it meant very little in terms of a meaningful democratic functioning or creating democratic culture at the grass-roots level. Although in 1959, the then Prime Minister of India, Jawaharlal Nehru, and the Minister for Panchayati Raj and Community Development, Shri S.K. Dey, fervently supported establishment of vibrant panchayats in all the States, elections were irregular and some States did not hold elections for 15 to 20 years on one excuse or other. With the 73rd and 74th Constitutional Amendments, every five years elections will be held to the three tiers of the panchayats and municipalities. For panchayats the three levels are the village panchayats at the lowest level, the block panchayats at the intermediary level, and the district (country) panchayats at the top. Three types of Municipalities are (1) Municipal Corporation, (2) Municipal Council, and (3) Nagar Panchayat. Thus, India will have about 475 district panchayats (India has 505 districts of which 30 do not come under panchayats because some are urban and others are tribal districts), about 5,100 block panchayats and about 2,25,000 village panchayats. There are around 90 Municipal Corporations, 1,500 Municipal Councils and 1,800 Nagar Panchayats in the country. The rural bodies along with their urban counterparts—the Municipalities—will be electing about 3 million representatives.

Main Features of the 73rd and 74th Amendments

The striking features of the 73rd and 74th Constitution Amendment Acts are:

1. Panchayats and Municipalities will be "institutions of self-government".
2. Gram Sabhas in villages and Ward Committees in Municipalities comprising all the adult members registered as voters in the area will be the basic units of the Democratic system.
3. There shall be a three-tier system of panchayats at village, intermediate block/taluk and district levels. Smaller States with population below 2 million will have the option not to have an intermediate level panchayat.
4. Seats in panchayats at all the three levels shall be filled by direct election.
5. In all the panchayats, seats would be reserved for Scheduled Castes (SCs) and chairpersons of the panchayats at all levels also shall be reserved for SCs and STs in proportion of their population in the State.
6. One-third of the total number of seats will be reserved for women. One-third of the seats reserved for SCs and STs will also be reserved for women. One-third offices of chairpersons of panchayats at all levels shall also be reserved for women.
7. Every panchayat shall have a uniform five year term and elections to constitute new bodies shall be completed before the expiry of the term. In the event of dissolution, elections will be compulsorily held within six months.
8. An independent Election Commission will be established in each State for superintendence, direction and control of the electoral

process and preparation of electoral rolls for panchayats and municipalities.

9. Specific responsibilities will be entrusted to the panchayats to prepare plans for economic development and social justice in respect of 29 subjects listed in the Eleventh Schedule. The 74th Amendment provides for a District Planning Committee to consolidate the plans prepared by the panchayats and municipalities.
10. The panchayats will receive adequate funds for carrying out their functions. Grants from State governments will constitute an important source of funding but State governments are also expected to assign the revenue of certain taxes to the panchayat. In some cases, the panchayat will also be permitted to collect and retain the revenue it raises.
11. In each State a Finance Commission will be established to determine the principles on the basis of which adequate financial resources would be ensured for panchayats and municipalities.

Thus the journey (1882-1992) from the "local self-government" idea of Lord Ripon through "units of self-government" to the "institutions of self-government" concept in the 73rd Constitutional Amendment took more than a century. This evolution in the federal polity of the country must be specially underlined.

Nowhere the 'institutions of self-government' is defined. It may be recalled here that only three conformity legislations, viz., those of West Bengal, Tripura and Bihar, unequivocally mention that the objective of their panchayat legislations is to endow panchayats with functions and powers so as to enable them to function as vibrant institutions of self-government. The other extreme is that of Haryana. The Haryana Act categorically says that the panchayat system is meant for the better administration of the rural areas.

However, the 'institutions of self-government' have been interpreted in two ways:

First by saying that panchayats are institutions of self-government, the Constitution endows it with autonomy and powers of government. So governance by elected representatives of the people, according to the Constitutional provisions, is an important element which distinguishes the post-73rd Constitution Amendment panchayats from the previous ones. Therefore, *de facto* it is the third-tier of governance.

The second interpretation is that it is only strengthening

'administrative federalism' and nothing more than that. Prof. S. Guhan in an illuminating paper presented in Delhi argues that the provisions of the 73rd Amendment strengthens 'administrative federalism' in order to facilitate and encourage administrative and financial delegation from the States to local bodies. "Their administrative powers and responsibilities and the financial resources to exercise these powers and to discharge the responsibilities are entirely derived from legislation that will have to be passed by the State" says Guhan. They have no legislative or judicial powers and, therefore, in Guhan's view just conferring constitutional status or having regular elections do not confer third level of governance.

Prof. Guhan's argument is technically valid. However, in countries where local bodies exist, they are given powers of delegated legislations, e.g. budget, bye-laws and regulations. They also enjoy considerable powers of regulations attached to their functional responsibilites. Police and judicial powers could also rest with the panchayats. There is a lot of thinking going on in this direction after the 73rd Amendment.

The moves to make the local bodies really the third level of governance in India has been incremental; there has not been quantum jump. The fact that district planning responsibilities are now given to the local bodies is a major step in the right directions. In the prevailing ethos, some States have gone ahead in transferring powers to the panchayats in an unprecedented way.

ELECTIONS AT THE GRASS-ROOTS LEVEL: SINE QUA NON FOR STRONG DEMOCRACY

The elections to the Panchayats in India have been an excellent barometer of functioning democracy. Although it began without the participation of political parties, now at all levels they do participate officially. The polling percentage is also very high. The fact that elections were not held for several years or decades at this level since Independence has been detrimental to the growth of a vibrant democratic system.

The study of "Panchayat Election Process and Election Issues in the Karnataka Panchayat Elections—1995" conducted by the Institute of Social Sciences reveals some interesting findings of the democratic process.

37.2 per cent people, whom we interviewed, came to know about the panchayat elections from the newspapers. Almost an equal number (34.6 per cent) said their first information was from radio and television. Only 13 per cent learnt about the elections from political parties. About 12 per cent were told about it by friends, neighbours or relatives and 2.7 per cent knew forthcoming event in the market place.

This is an interesting indication about the changing rural Kannada. Print media has taken over the information network in the Karnataka villages and modern electronic media is catching up. The traditional source of information, like market place and neighbourhood is receding to background.

What were the Main Issues in the Panchayat Elections ?

Non-performance of members of the 1987-90 panchayats was the issue in elections according to 24 per cent respondents. For 21 per cent, political parties, their ideology was important. 17.6 per cent said corruption decided the outcome. Removal of poverty, Dalit and Women's issues took a back seat. Only 2.9 per cent and 2.5 per cent, respectively said 'Hindutava' and 'Babri Masjid' were election issues.

This show Panchayati Raj is becoming a political institution and not merely a development institution.

About the election campaign, door-to-door visits have received maximum rating (48.8 per cent), 22.6 per cent said handbills were the main campaign method. 13.2 per cent said loud speakers were used by the candidates. Only 7.6 per cent reported public meetings and 8.4 per cent wall-posters and wall-writings.

Why did a Villager Vote for a Particular Candidate ?

44.9 per cent voted because he/she was a 'good person', 10.1 per cent voted because of party considerations. It is especially important to note that only 1.3 per cent voted because the candidate belonged to his or her caste.

To the question, whether caste affinity was an important factor in the elections, only 35.7 per cent said yes. For an overwhelming majority 63.2 per cent caste of the candidate was not an issue at all. The above two observations are important because it shows decisively that caste factor is playing a lesser role because of the grass-roots democratic process.

Almost half of the respondents (45.8 per cent) believe that alcohol had an influence on the elections. According to 28.5 per cent respondents, money played a part. About 6 per cent believe presenting clothes, food-grains, etc. were ways of influencing the electorate. 16 per cent respondents testified that candidates offered sumptuous meals in the evenings to swing villagers to their favour. The rich and influential in the villages were treated with beer and 'foreign' liquor but poor were given only local made liquor like *arrack*.

About a specific question as to whether money power influenced the Panchayati Raj elections majority (54.3 per cent) said they did. But the sizeable number (413 per cent) believed that at the panchayat level influence of money power is not there at all.

This is an important indicator about fairness of elections at the lôcal bodies.

Was there Violence during Elections ?

95 per cent said there was no violence. It was interesting that among 5 per cent who said there was violence, 3.2 per cent reported group clashes, and 0.2 per cent stone pelting. There was no report of murder. This is again a credit worthy achievement of Karnataka that it could conduct panchayat elections as part of a normal democratic process.

How did they Look at the Period 1991-95 when Panchayats were under Administrators ?

75.3 per cent of the respondents had no opinion. 4.3 per cent said there was high corruption. For 3.2 per cent, administrators ruled without any partiality, for 3.6 per cent, administrators displayed a careless attitude and 3.2 per cent said during that time people had no access to the panchayats.

81.5 per cent said that the elections were completely fair. Only 14.6 per cent reported "some problems". It is interesting to note that only less than 1 per cent (0.8 per cent) said there was booth capturing and kidnapping. 5.8 per cent reported that there was rigging.

The two panchayat elections in 9 years (the earlier one being 1987) have taken Karnataka's grassroots level democracy on the road to a mature and vibrant system. West Bengal held the 4th panchayat elections in May. 1993 after the new panchayati raj system was introduced in the State since 1978. Uninterrupted 15 years even before the Constitution Amendment. After observing the 1993 elections I had written:

> Travelling through the countryside during the run up days of the panchayat elections, one thing was most discernible. Panchayats have taken firm roots in the State. A Bengali villager cannot now imagine his life without the panchayats. Parliament, the Assembly, even the District Parishads are far away in his scheme of things.

> But the Gram Panchayat and the Panchayat Samiti at the block level are day to day realities; much of his life revolves around these democratic institutions. So he has a stake in the elections which come every five years. It also explains the high percentage of polling. This time more than 75 per cent voters exercised their franchise.
>
> The graffiti, the flags, the wall posters which decorate the dusty village roads and houses or tea shops convey not only a message but also a lot of meaning about democracy and the democratic process in a multi-party setting. If a visitor asks a candidate of the opposition party whether the previous Panchayat had done any good to the village his/her answer will be positive and will catalogue a series of developmental work done. Then why oppose? The answer is, things could be better. That is the spirit of democracy at the grass-roots level.

The role of political parties in the Panchayat elections is crucial. The earlier concept of consensus (in effect consent to whatever the powerful was saying or doing) is giving way to people aligning on party lines to call into question every action that is less than transparent. If one party becomes protector of the oppressed, for whatever reason, another party becomes the guardian of the oppressor. As of now, open participation of political parties in the panchayat elections is the best way to challenge the age-old autocracy of caste or family. With regular elections every five years, the churning process will continue in the villages of India.

Women in Local Governance

The unique feature of one-third representation for women in local bodies and one-third of offices of Chairpersons at all levels in rural and urban bodies opens up tremendous possibilities for rapid social change in India's villages, helping towards good local governance.

The Constitution (Seventy-third Amendment) Act, 1992, Article 243D (3) reads:

> Not less than one-third (including the number of seats reserved for women belonging to the Scheduled Castes and the Scheduled Tribes) of the total number of seats to be filled by direct election in every Panchayat shall be reserved for women and such seats may be allotted by rotation to different constituencies in a Panchayat.

And Clause (4) of the Act has the following provision:

> not less than one-third of the total number of offices of Chairpersons in the Panchayats at each level shall be reserved for women:
>
> Provided also that the number of offices reserved under this clause shall be allotted by rotation to different Panchayats at each level.

These two provisions will result in about one million women getting elected to the panchayats and municipalities. It is important to note that in several States more than the mandatory 33.3 per cent women got elected to the Panchayats.

In order to make women's participation in society and politics a reality, enormous work remains to be done, given their present socio-economic condition. If we take the age-specific death rate for children between 0 to 4 years, the male infant mortality rate is 33.6 per cent, while the female infant mortality rate touches 36.8 per cent, as per the 1987 data. The sex ratio (1991) is one of the lowest in the world with 927 females for every one thousand males. The female literacy rate (1991) is only 39.42 per cent when compared to 63.86 per cent for males. The work-force participation rate (1991) for males is 51.56 per cent and for females, less than half, that is, 22.73 per cent. Although all the above-mentioned indicators bear a certain degree of relationship, two key socio-economic indicators in particular—the literacy rate and the work-force participation rate-amply testify to the male bias in Indian society.

The question to be tackled is: Is the removal of these hurdles a must for women's participation in society and the polity? Or will their participation in societal affairs through the local bodies remove those handicaps which exist at present? There is no clear-cut answer except to say that a beginning must be made. The present Constitutional provision gives a historic opportunity. If positive action could be taken and the momentum kept up. sooner than later, 50 per cent of elected positions in the Panchayati Raj Institutions must be reserved for women, and the State legislatures and Parliament should follow this principle. In fact, recently the State government of Karnataka has announced 25 per cent reservation for women are elected members of the State Assembly.

A study of the latest Panchayat elections in West Bengal and Karnataka, conducted by the Institute of Social Sciences, has found that women responded in full measure to the opportunity provided to them. In West Bengal, on an average nearly three candidate contested every seat reserved for women at the village panchayat and panchayat committee levels with the number going up to four at the district panchayat level. Out of 24,855 seats reserved for women in three tiers, only 561, or little over 2 per cent, went uncontested. Fifty per cent respondents were of the view that reservation for women in panchayats was a step in correct direction. They whole-heartedly welcomed it. The study in Karnataka reveals that 80.3 per cent respondents welcomed the 33 per cent reservation for women. Why do they support the move? 28 per cent believe that it must be done for the sake of gender equality. For some, women elected representatives will be less corrupt. In the same study 6 per cent oppose reservation for women because they are illiterate, they have no capability. They cannot function effectively as people's representatives. West Bengal and Karnataka have high level of political awareness and longstanding experience in grassroots level democracy. This explains the encouraging response in favour of women. But for many States, especially in the northern Hindi heartland, they still have a long way to go in this respect.

Devolution of Powers

The basic principle on which the Panchayati Raj system has been envisaged in India is that whatever can be done best at a lower level must necessarily be done at that level and not at the upper level and only those things which cannot be done at the lower level must go to a higher level.

But it must be stated here that the first five year term of the new Panchayats and Municipalities is a period in which lot of trial and error will take place. This time must be considered as a 'gestation period' because it is not easy to change the mind-set that has set in during the last five decades of Independence. The political system without strong local governments has affected the working of the civil service as well as politicians at the State and Central level. Therefore, in the State Panchayat Acts after 1993 one finds that the States have accepted the letter of the 73rd or 74th Amendments rather than their spirit. Genuine devolution of powers will take place only through strong demands from below—the Village Assembly (Gram Sabha), Village Panchayats and District Panchayats as well as enlightened citizen's organisations. Transfer of activities and functions to panchayats is taking place very slowly. Even in an enlightened State like West Bengal, whenever staff is placed under Panchayats, court injunctions come against such actions and the Minister in-charge of Panchayats stated recently that hundreds of such court injunctions are existing against the department orders. But in order that the officers and people accept the new situation, West Bengal has effected changes in the designations. For instance, the Block Medical Officer is now known as Samiti Medical Officer.

Another problem is that although States have enacted conformity acts, many States have not formulated rules and bye-laws for the day-to-day functioning. Added to this, the necessary infrastructural facilities are lacking for Panchayats in many States. Therefore, looking at the experience in the last two years, one must have guarded optimism about Panchayat Raj.

The Ground Realities

Although all States have accepted the Constitutional Amendments giving the rural and urban local governments a new status the ground realities are far from satisfactory. There are several factors:

(a) The reluctance of State-level politicians to recognize the importance of the lower levels of governance—their autonomy, their powers and their areas of functioning. The Ministers, the MLAs and senior political leaders are worried that the power they enjoyed so far will diminish if panchayats and municipalities become powerful. They also do not like leadership emerging from lower levels which could pose challenges to them in due course. It may be remembered here that the active and functioning local bodies are considered 'nurseries' for leadership. Therefore, they put all hurdles in the way of panchayats blossoming into full-fledged local governments. The latest example is that of the State of Orissa. When the new government came to power in early 1995, it dissolved the duly elected panchayats and municipalities. It is learnt that the reason for this action was that the ruling party MLAs were impatient to get full control of large sums of money coming to the panchayats through Central Government schemes for rural development. If panchayats function properly with large numbers controlled by opposition parties as well, and people become aware of their rights through regular participation in the panchayat programmes and activities, it will result in the decline of the unique position MLAs enjoy. And that is not welcomed by the MLAs and ministers. Latest from Orissa is that the State Election Commission has indefinitely postponed the elections on the pretext of ensuing monsoon. All political parties have joined together and gave a memorandum to the State Election Commission to this effect.

(b) The government officials and government employees prefer to work with a distant control mechanism—that is, the State capital. They do not want to be closely supervised as it happens under panchayati raj. Therefore, their non-cooperative attitude with elected panchayat members is a major issue the States have to tackle. An interesting example is that the All India Federation of Primary School Teachers had passed resolutions and held meetings expressing their unwillingness to work under panchayats.

The other related issue is that the officials who work at the district level and below may be reluctant to take orders from the elected panchayat executives like District Panchayat President, Block Samiti President or Village Panchayat President. The low social background of most of the elected representatives accentuates the problem. Therefore, India needs a new democratic culture to make the local governments strong.

(c) Low level of political consciousness in many parts of the country is another factor which will pull the new panchayati raj backward. The Bimaru States (*Bimaru* in Hindi means prone to sickness)-Bihar, Madhya Pradesh, Rajasthan and Uttar Pradesh with 340 million population (1991 Census) have a low panchayat raj performance rating. The main reason is low level of political awareness, prevalence of feudal authority and feudal values. Unless serious efforts are made to break the present apathy towards new political institutions like the Panchayati Raj, they themselves will continue as oppressive instruments. Low level of literacy, especially of women, patriarchal system, etc., will work against weaker sections in the villages and especially women. Majority of people suffering from the shackles of traditional oppressive power structures will take time to gather sufficient strength to participate effectively in the new opportunities provided through the Panchayats. Serious conflicts have taken place in the villages because of the new Panchayats during elections and afterwards in their functioning. This conflict dimension will continue.

Madhya Pradesh was the first State to conduct elections to the panchayats after the 73rd Constitution Amendment. After more than a year of the elections to the Panchayats in Madhya Pradesh reports appeared in newspapers that all is not well with their functioning. Students of the Indian social scene had anticipated such negative trends. When newspapers reported chain of events from different parts of the State that a lady Sarpanch was stripped naked, another lady Sarpanch was gang raped, upa-sarpanch was tortured, a Dalit panchayat member was beaten up, it was important to investigate and study the social forces at work behind these incidents.

The research faculty at the Institute of Social Sciences spent several weeks in the villages, stayed with the villagers, observed the day-to-day life and goings on in the hamlets, collected basic data about the area, interacted with a large numher of persons and reconstructed the stories with as much factual evidence as possible.

It was clear from our investigations that a panchayat is a microcosm of the society of which the village forms a part. The noble ideals of "institutions of self-government" as expounded by the 73rd Constitution Amendment cannot be translated into reality in the present iniquitous society. The beautiful picture of Panchayati Raj cannot be drawn on the canvas of stringent caste system, feudal values, gender inequality, inhuman poverty conditions and the wide chasm existing between the rich and the deprived.

Therefore, the legitimate question was: Could rural India wait till all these conditions are set right? For instance, education for all must be achieved, land reforms implemented, women must achieve equal status with men and economic growth should go in step with social development. But given the present pace of change, how long it will take? Can Indian villages wait for their local governments till the ground realities are conducive? Therefore, a realistic approach was: Panchayats must be made, and should themselves become instruments of social transformation through a vibrant political process at the local level. This is what we have attempted through the 73rd Constitution Amendment.

The Madhya Pradesh incidents revealed the ground realities in our villages. The situation generates its own protests. These are positive signs of the first step towards the awakening of Indian villages through the Panchayati Raj.

Implementation of the Constitutional Amendment by the States

The States of Tamil Nadu, Bihar and Orissa have no elected Panchayats. Eight hill districts of Uttar Pradesh, Chandigarh, Lakshadweep and Pondicherry also have not held elections to Panchayats. Goa and Manipur are yet to hold elections to the Zilla Panchayats. That is, about 145.4 million rural population (23 per cent) have no elected panchayats. The chief ministers, ministers and ruling party MLAs in the above-mentioned States have not displayed the necessary political will to hold elections to the Panchayats, and under one pretext or other, they were dragging their feet. Their actions have reached the point of flouting the Constitution. Several Public Interest Litigations are pending before the High Courts against these States for not holding elections on time. Vested interests are using writ petitions in the courts to delay holding elections. 85 writ petitions were pending before Madras High Court during the AIADMK government's rule. The DMK government which assumed office in May this year has committed itself for holding the Panchayat elections by September 1996.

West Bengal, Karnataka and Madhya Pradesh are in the forefront with political will to implement the Panchayati Raj. The other States have gone about it without much enthusiasm. It is left to the NGOs and people's organisations to force the issue in these States so that the State governments give whole-hearted support to it. In the present situation, judicial intervention through Public Interest Litigation (PIL) is also a possibility to make Panchayati Raj work.

Decision-Making in Panchayats: Who Will Do It ?

In the Hindi heart-land where social, economic and political backwardness is a reality, for weaker sections to assert their rights will take some time. Women are proxy, SCs and STs have to obey the commands of the mighty and powerful. Studies of functioning of Panchayats from Madhya Pradesh reveal the limitations as well as possibilities of State intervention without the necessary social support systems. State legislations for positive discrimination of Scheduled Castes, Scheduled Tribes, Backward Classes and women or making the local bodies "Institutions of Self-Government" are only a necessary condition. The State has introduced changes in governance where the societies had any social reform movement, land reforms or the fruits of education. In this context a convenient way to retain power in the hands of traditionally powerful is to put up proxy candidates in accordance with the letter of the law, but keep the control in the hands of the dominant castes, always men. Men are the main actors in wards reserved for women or in Panchayats even where the Sarpanches are women. The incapacity of the dominated to assert their rights is at the root of the problem. Moreover, neither the respect due to the office nor the respect for the person is accorded in most Panchayats. The elected office is bereft of power. The officials who are to guard the dignity of elected persons also succumb to local politics and power play.

Implication of Panchayati Raj/Municipalities as the Third Tier of Governance on India's Federal Structure

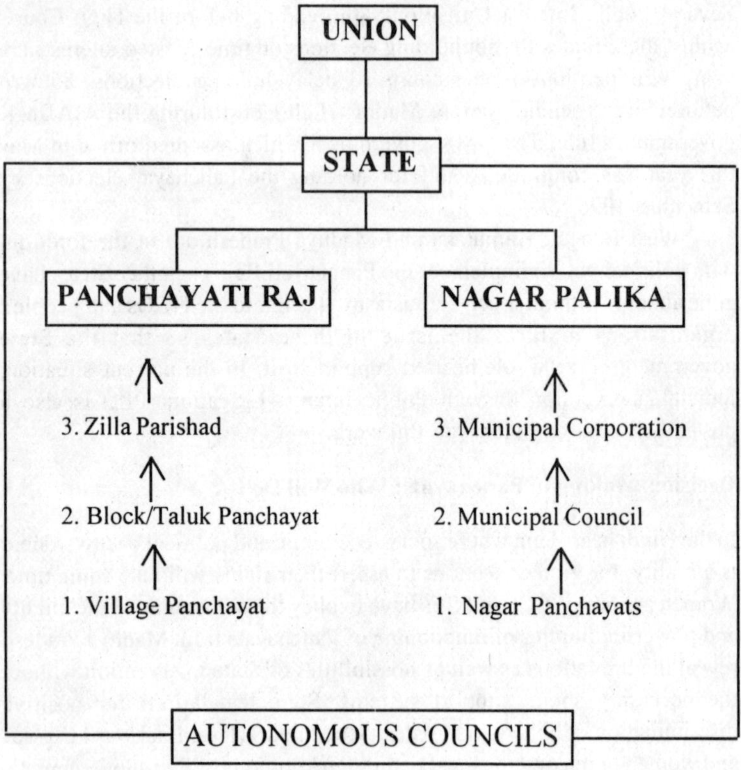

However, even in these areas there are pockets where genuine democratic functioning is taking place. For instance, militancy of the 'Dalits' (oppressed) is playing a crucial role in many places. NGOs, women's organisations (Mahila Samakhya in U.P., for example) are worth mentioning in this regard. In some areas vigilant officials and political party workers and media persons function as watch dogs to ensure equitable decision-making. In the days to come the present decision-making process will definitely change for the better.

Other States where awareness is better, women and other low caste panchayat representatives have been able to take decisions and participate effectively. Proper party functioning contributes to it. In Karnataka, women's participation in Panchayats in the 1987-91 period had helped to improve attendance in schools, regular classes by teachers, development of sanitation and health facilities, augmentation of drinking water supply, and so on. Women representatives are considered less corrupt, hard working and demanding.

11th and 12th Schedules and Decision-Making

The 29 subjects in the 11th Schedule and 18 subjects in the 12th Schedule are more or less mentioned by all State Acts as being transferred to the Panchayats. The respective departments will have to tgransfer their functions with staff to the appropriate Panchayat levels. In the event financial decision-making will be by the respective panchayats—whether it be village or Block or District. Prevailing rules for each department must be changed to make it function under the Panchayats or Municipalities. This is a slow process. Strong demands from the elected panchayats only can speed up the process. A lot of thinking and homework is being done so as to bring, in practical terms, the working of the line departments under panchayats. The exercise in this regard on education by the Central Advisory Board of Education (CABE) Committee and UNICEF-ISS is worth mentioning here. Now the State governments are giving priority for bringing the departments of education and health under the panchayats. Forests and environment are other areas. The existing departmental rules have to be changed and new rules have to be introduced. As mentioned earlier, the unwillingness of the officials to go to panchayats and lack of political will are delaying the change. However, States like Madhya Pradesh, Karnataka and West Bengal have gone a long way in this regard. It is hoped that others will follow suit.

The International Agencies are also keen that the Panchayats must become powerful and District Panchayats must be in a position to receive aid and monitor the implementation of projects.

Panchayats and Finance

The State Finance Commissions (SFCs) have been constituted in all the States according to the provisions of the Constitutional Amendment. The SFCs of West Bengal, Punjab, Kerala and Madhya Pradesh have submitted their reports to the Governors making recommendations for distribution of funds between the State and Panchayats. The Governors will give these reports to the State governments to be placed before the Assemblies. Only after the Assemblies adopt the report, do they become binding for the States. The other 18 State Finance Commissions are expected to submit their reports by March/April 1996.

The Tenth Finance Commission of the Central Government, which submitted its report last year has recommended an ad hoc per capita grant of Rs. 100 for rural population (based on 1971 Census figures) for the period 1996-2000. This grant-in-aid works out to Rs. 1095.23 crores per year. These allocations are meant to be only as an "additionality over and above the amounts flowing to the local bodies from State governments". In addition, the Panchayat Ministers' Committee has recommended that all State governments make 5 per cent of their tax and non-tax collection available to the Panchayats.

The Panchayats and Municipalities will have the following sources of funds: (1) Allocations by Central Government through the Central Finance Commission, (2) Allocations by the State government, (3) Central government rural development schemes like Jawahar Rozgar Yojana (JRY), and (4) Taxes and other revenues which the local bodies themselves could raise.

It has been found that when people realize that local bodies function responsibly and democratically, their capacity to raise resources also increases substantially (e.g. Karnataka).

District Planning (Article 243 ZD) is required to maintain an organic link with the State and national planning. It also envisages a bottom-up planning exercise, building blocks comprising the plans of village panchayats, block/taluka level panchayats, district panchayats as well as minicipal bodies. West Bengal already had a District Planning Committee Act, which envisages a District Council chaired by the leader of the Opposition. West Bengal develops to panchayats more than 50 per cent of the State plan funds. The panchayats at different tiers are empowered to prepare development plan for the five-year term and annual plan for development of human resources infrastructure and civic amenities. State government is transferring functions and powers along with funds and personnel. Panchayats at all tiers have been empowered to approve their own budget and bye-laws. They have also been empowered to borrow from financial institutions. Previously such matters required prior approval of higher tiers or the State government. This means panchayats have functional liberty without any interference.

In terms of resource mobilisation also West Bengal panchayats are way ahead. Apart from the usual tax revenue, a portion of the professional tax collected by the State government is allocated to Gram Panchayats. Cess on PWD roads, minor and major, mineral collected by the State government are paid to the Zilla Parishad after deducting collection charges. Another important measure worth mentioning here is that if the collection of small savings, stamp duty and registration fee, amusement tax, motor vehicle tax, royalty/cess from major and minor minerals exceeds the target, 50 per cent of the additional collection is ploughed back to the district for development. District Planning Committee decides its utilisation. During 1994-95, Rs. 1,65,84,000 was returned to the districts under this scheme.

Panchayats and NGO Sector

India has large number of Non-Governmental Organisation (NGOs), strengthening the civil society. When local bodies were not in existence, they did substantial work in helping to air the problems of people and community. NGOs are working to enhance people's capacity for self-governance and self-advancement. They were involved in developmental activities as well. After the 73rd and 74th Constitutional Amendments a large number of NGOs in India are playing a catalytic role in creating enabling conditions for the success of the panchayats such as.

(1) Awareness building about the new legislation, new phase of panchayats. They provide information through pamphlets, wall posters, video cassettes (documentaries). One day conferences, camps for two days or more are held at District and Block levels.

(2) Training elected representatives about the powers and responsibilities. Several NGOs, institutions and State-run institutes have prepared training modules for the elected representatives. The period of training ranges from 2 to 5 days. Training priority is for those who are elected for the first time as well as women, SCs and STs. Lectures, group discussions, skits (role plays), video films form part of the training. It is a welcome sign that government officials, retired personnel, academic persons take active part in these training programmes. Backward States like Bihar, Rajasthan, Madhya Pradesh are attracting such programmes in a big way. But there is urgent need to critically look at the training programme taking place in various States—their contents, course dynamics

and participation.

(3) Involving in local elections, putting up candidates in the Panchayat and municipal elections or supporting independents or political parties. In a large number of States where elections were held in 1994 and 1995, the NGOs had put up candidates. In Andhra Pradesh, Himachal Pradesh, Rajasthan, Uttar Pradesh, Madhya Pradesh, sizeable number of panchayat members are with NGO background. But in highly political States like Kerala, West Bengal and Karnataka their impact in elections is relatively less. The study of Panchayat elections in Karnataka found that for 78.3 per cent respondents, NGOs did not play an active role in the elections. 2.6 per cent said NGOs supported political parties openly, 2 per cent said NGOs held independent election campaigns, 1.7 per cent said they conducted workshops and meetings and 1.5 per cent said NGOs put up candidates. The future trend seems to me that people may not appreciate political role of NGOs at the higher levels (district, block), but it may happen at the lowest village panchayat level because of close face-to-face interaction and less influence of party lines in the villages.

(4) NGOs have another important role in assisting panchayats in planning and implementation of social development strategies and programmes. They have the capacity in many cases to bring new knowledge and technology to the rural community and prepare the way for their wider adoption. Panchayats need professional support and NGOs are in a position to visualize the need, guide them and obtain the requisite services. Kerala Sastra Sahitya Parishad's (KSSP) work is one such example. In future, this role will enhance.

Thus it has been found that NGO work could be complementary to the Panchayats. There have been instances of conflicts also. The experience of Samaj Pragati Sahyog (SPS), a non-government organisation, working in Dewas District in Madhya Pradesh is a case in point. The Sarpanches of the area have made the presence of a voluntary organisation a major issue as they fear the NGO will encroach into their area of responsibility. This happens when the local bodies reduce themselves to the position of NGOs. In the new phase, NGO sector-civil society—has an important role in strengthening the local bodies, equipping the weaker sections like Scheduled Castes (SCs), Scheduled Tribes (STs) and women to participate fully in the grassroots democratic institutions. The NGOs in cooperation with the Panchayats could give new orientation for the developmental activities in rural areas.

Tribals and Panchayats

The 5th and 6th Schedules in the Constitution give special status and privileges to tribal areas. A high level committee under the chairmanship of Mr. D.S. Bhuria, Member of Parliament, set up by the Union Government to suggest proposals to extend the 73rd Constitution Amendment to the Scheduled areas has recommended: (i) constituting village assembly in all tribal villages because community should be the basic unit of self-governance in tribal areas, (ii) reserving a majority in all levels of the elected bodies for members of the Scheduled Tribes, (iii) only a tribal could become a sarpanch (president).

In reality, in tribal majority areas, non-tribals are controlling the affairs, dominating the scene and destroying the tribal tradition. Tribal land is appropriated by non-tribals. Therefore, leaders like B.D. Sharma (former Commissioner of Scheduled Castes and Scheduled Tribes) oppose extension of 73rd Amendment to tribal areas because tribal communities have lived as effective institutions for centuries and they cannot be considered as an administrative unit. The matter—Tribals and 73rd Constitution Amendment—is still unsettled; it is being debated.

Conclusion

Expectations about the new Panchayati Raj have been raised both among the ordinary people and elected representatives. Throughout the country its implementation in the last two years has been uneven. Tremendous possibilities have opened up. Village society is differentiated, inequitable and traditional. But, it cannot be denied that elected bodies at the local level have, and in future will give, a voice to the disadvantaged and give them a say in resource management—however, limited it may be. Several State governments are adopting a double standard. Cound the Central Government force the States to implement it? Then State governments could say that the Centre is interfering in the affairs of the State. But sanctity of the Indian Constitution and Judicial Courts' interventions are presently working as a driving force to implement Panchayati Raj. These two factors must be undergirded with people's awareness, political will by parties and governments, cooperation of the bureaucracy and empowerment of women and oppressed sections of Indian society. This takes time, may be three or four elections will change the present scenario for the better. But the journey has begun.

THREE

PANCHAYATI RAJ INSTITUTIONS
The Emerging Scenario

K.P.A. MENON

Ten years back when I was once invited to address a distinguished audience at IARI during the Convocation Week I decided to deal with the topic of resource-based planning at the local level since that had been a subject of special interest to me for more than two decades I could not, however, get sufficient courage to make a logical presentation of the theme involving the local governments that are concerned with local level plans utilising the local resources for the optimum benefit of the local people for a very simple reason that one could not be sure or confident about the very existence of local governments in all the States. This was the sad situation in spite of the fact that some of the State governments had taken various imaginative and often innovative steps for the establishment of the Panchayati Raj Institutions (PRIs) at various levels, guided to a great extent by the recommendations of the Asoka Mehta Committee. In a large number of States elections to PRIs were not being held regularly and no indication was forthcoming about the seriousness of the State governments or State legislatures in activising the PRIs that were languishing for lack of funds and, what was more serious, their own unawareness of the role that was to be played by them. Organisation of Village Panchayats had been accepted as the sacred duty of the State governments and the provision itself embodied under Article 40 was quite mandatory that "The State shall take steps to organize village panchayats and endow them with such powers and authority as may be a necessary to enable them to function as units of self government". Though the expression used was that the State *shall take steps* it was an unfortunate fact that there was no judicial remedy available to the citizens to compell the State governments to respect such provisions of the Constitution that envisaged the establishment of local governments, provision of free and compulsory education for children, participation of workers in the management of industries etc. As such I decided to give my talk on Administrative Decentralisation and Resource based Planning. The British Government had taken certain steps for de-centralising the administration upto the level of districts and below. With the initiation of the Community Development Programme the block had become an important unit for development administration. Everything else was vague below that level. Today when I am dealing with the same problem of micro-level planning I could be a little more confident about linking local governments with local resource based plans for the benefit of the local people. The amendments to the Constitution have made it quite clear that local governments are to be a part of the Indian political system and the State government cannot shy away from the responsibility of organising PRI's at different levels.

A Rationale for Local Government

While Democracy has been functioning in some form or other in various parts of the globe no one seems to be quite sure that the government is in the hands in the people who are best qualified to govern or that such government is being done for the benefit of the people. Plato had visualised a ruling class elite known as *Guardians* who were to remain detached from everything else in the world including family life, to devote themselves exclusively to the task of governing the people, for ensuring the prosperity of the State along with the happiness of individuals. After more than two millenniums of experimentation, people seem to have been convinced by the arguments advanced by Abraham Lincoln that democracy is meant to be the government of the people, by the people and for the people. Lincoln was certainly aware of the fact that the goals of democracy had remained unrealised even in the State where it had been functioning through parliamentary institutions for more than six centuries. Any one holding the reins of government will naturally claim, he was governing for the people but the people were being taken for granted in most cases. How could it be a government of the people without their voice ever being heard by those who were taking decisions on their behalf ? How could it be by the people when many of the representatives did not actually belong to the people. It is to be remembered that, in the oldest functioning democracy of the West only a small percentage of the people had been enjoying the voting rights when Abraham Lincoln made this Statement.

The United States of America had already established a new form of government in which people could get a better opportunity of governing themselves. The federal form of government allowed the States to function with a good deal of authority and autonomy in matters that concerned the citizens of the State and, at the same time have a powerful voice at the centre in matters that had been made the specific responsibility of the Central government. Still it would have been a travesty of facts if one were to assume that the government though avowedly designed for the benefit of the people, was of the people or by the people. The people were far removed from the government and the level at which decisions were being taken. People were, in most cases being taken for granted and they, in turn acquiesced in whatever happened because there was no other way. An experiment was, however, going on simultaneously for fuller and more effective participation of the people through different forms of local governments.

This takes us to the question of what exactly is meant by local government. According to J.J. Clarke "Local Government is that part of the government of a nation or State which deals mainly with such matters as concern the inhabitants of the particular district or place, together with those matters which Parliament has deemed it desirable should be administered by Local authorities, subordinate to the Central government".

According to A. de Tocqueville "Local assemblies of citizens constitute the strength of free peoples. Town meetings are to liberty what primary schools are to science; they bring it within the people's reach. They teach men how to use and enjoy it. A nation may establish a system of free government but without the spirit of municipal institutions it cannot have the spirit of liberty".

Much earlier John Stuart Mill had made it clear "It is obvious, to begin with, that all business purely local, all which concerns a single locality, should devolve upon the local authorities". Professor Herman Finer has mentioned in his treatise on English Local Government that local government also falls into the same category as such devises as federalism and proportional representation". They are safeguards against the tyranny of the wholesale herd that has a tendency of destroying original individuals and groups. Local Governments are thus an essential ingredient of a dynamic democratic society and a stabilising force.

Local Governments in the East and West

It has been mentioned about the United Kingdom that the local government had not evolved out of the national government but it was just the other way. It is a historical process that local governments or small principalities got merged or enlarged forming bigger units of the government. In this way the number of governments started becoming smaller and we know about the heptarchy followed by the three kingdoms of Northumbria, Mercia and Wessex. The English kingdom later on evolved from Wessex and units like Wales and Scotland were added much later.

What has been mentioned about the United Kingdom is much more true in respect of India. During the early Vedic period the expanded families became clans or *gotras* and self contained units were formed by the clans coming together. With better communications and the progress of trade and commerce larger units started coming up. There is a reference to sixteen *Janapadas* during the Later Vedic period and four of them came into greater prominence. Out of these four, Magadha became the predominant unit and the Mauryan empire got established in the Indo-Gangatic plain during the Buddhist period. It was this Magadhan empire which became one of the famous political units of the world during the period of the Mauryans when it covered the bulk of South India as well. What is, however, unique about India's political history is that the village institutions, by whatever name they were known in the South or North continued to exist without being disturbed for centuries and millenniums. According to Sir Chanes Matcalf "These village institutions were "Little Republics that seemed to last where nothing else ever lasted". Dynasty after dynasty might have ruled over particular regions of India, empires might have come into existence and disappeared, invaders might have established alien governments in the form of Sultanates or empires, but at the grassroot level the village institutions continued their existence discharging most of the functions that intimately touched the lives of the people. This position continued during the medieval period and the rule of the Mughal Emperors but the position changed with the advent of the East India Company and British dominance. The rulers deliberately neglected and discouraged and PRIs that had played a prominent role in the social and cultural life of the people of India. We get detailed accounts regarding the functioning of the village institutions in different regions of the country during different periods. The spirit of democracy and collective thinking prevailed in most cases and, at the same time innovative steps were also being taken for effective administration along with economic development. For instance, during the Chola period local governments played a prominent role in the southern parts of India, now covered by Tamil Nadu and other States. The committee system of local administration had been accepted with safeguards against monopoly of power. There were restrictions regarding the same person holding office time and again along with a broad based forum for discussion. Drawing from the lessons of past history Mahatma Gandhi and other leaders started making plans for the revival of PRIs after the attainment of independence which still seemed to be a far-off goal during the struggle for independence. Though local government was not given a constitutional status under India's new Constitution the PRIs got prominent mention under the Directive Principles. Their establishment was, however, left to the State governments. This was indeed a logical step because the Constitution makers wanted to refrain from advocating a rigid system. It would not have been an unhealthy trend to have local and regional variations for local governments and State governments were at liberty to establish the kind of system that best suited their own State and local conditions. Subsequently, based upon the recommendations of the Balwantrai Mehta Committee, the three tier system of Panchayats was accepted by most of the States. The not so edifying history of PRIs after independence is a subject that has been dealt with by a large number of committees. Asoka Mehta Committee Report was indeed an important landmark, whose recommendations were taken advantage of by a few State for re-organising the PRIs and making the local government more active and meaningful. Otherwise, it would appear that there was a general apathy towards the PRIs among most of the State governments. Not only that, some States who had taken some progressive steps for establishing an effective system of local government through PRIs started backtracking and establishing rival centres of power. It was becoming quite clear that democracy at the higher levels was not willing to share powers with the lower levels. Inspite of such aberrations it became quite apparent to the right thinking people that the establishment of PRIs was essential and unavoidable for having a faster pace of economic development and for the removal of poverty.

Local governments have started coming into greater prominence in most of the developed countries. In the United Kingdom itself local government had existed for many centuries in the form of institutions like county, borough and parish. With the industrial revolution thickly populated industrial areas started springing up which called for better roads, better sanitation and other facilities. The national government had to come into the picture with varieties of legislations from time to time and a new system developed with different forms of local government at different levels and with varying status like the County, the County Borough, the Urban District, the Rural District and the Parish at grass-root level. A separate pattern had to be developed for the capital city of

London. I am making a reference to this because some of these developments may be of interest to a country like ours where some kind of industrial revolution is changing the face of the country in certain regions and localities. An important future of the local government institutions of the United Kingdom is the system of functioning through committees. The members of the committee are not experts in the respective spheres but men endowed with sound common sense and experience. The officials and experts of the government have their presence in the committees without dominating them though they are always in a position to give a lot of guidance.

The local government system as it exists today in France dates back to the Napoleanic period. Before the Revolution of 1789, there was practically no system of local government in France. Though the revolutionary assembly tried to establish local government, institutions like the Departments, Arrondissements, Cantons and Communes, they did not functioned effectively. The local units enjoyed lot of democratic powers no doubt but things did not progress. It was Napolean, who established an efficient system of local administration with a Prefect playing a dominant role in the Departmental government. This system, though not highly democratic has stood the test of time and it is often mentioned that in the form of the Prefect the shadow of Napolean still stalks in every nook and corner of the country. Attempts have been made recently to make these institutions more democratic.

The Department is an important unit of local administration with eighty-nine such units of varying sizes in the country. They could be the 'Hors class' or of the First, Second and Third class according to the area, population and importance. The Arrondissements and Cantons are not units of local government but geographical units of administration only. The Commune is the unit of local government at the grass-root level. It functions through the Mayor and a Municipal Council. Much of the work of the Commune is done by the committees that it appoints. In the Department itself, the Prefect as the representative of the French government, appointed by the Minister for Interior Affairs had a lot of authority over the working of the democratic body. The council could discuss only such matters that were placed before it by the Prefect. If the council goes into political matters, the Prefect could very well intervene and declare such proceedings as illegal. The position has been changed to a great extent by recent legislations but even in the earlier system things had not worked out as badly as one might apprehend. The local government institutions of France have really stood the test of time. Even when there were rapid changes at the national level, the governments have functioned effectively in France with people getting all the essential services through the agency of the local governments.

The local government of the United States is not of a uniform pattern. On one hand they have the system of the Mayor and the council with the variation of 'Strong Mayor' and Weak Council or vice-versa. There is another system known as the Commission government with a number of Commissioners having collective responsibilities over the city council. Started for the first time in 1901 after a national disaster in the form of a tidal wave that almost submerged the city of Galveston it gained in popularity for some time. In this system, the Commissioners function like the Board of Directors of a Corporate body. This was not found suitable for areas with large population. Finally, there is the Council and Manager system in which the City Manager is entrusted with large responsibilities. In all the systems that prevail in the USA, the Committees play a prominent role but they have gone by an assumption, that there cannot be a uniform pattern of local administration for a mammoth city and smaller units of local government.

As already mentioned India had its own tradition of local government that stood the test of time for more than two millenniums. Unfortunately it could not stand upto the pressures of the modern industrialised world. It is not surprising because no attempt was made by the rulers to revitalise the "Local Republics" and to orient them towards their new responsibilities. There were solitary exceptions like Lord Ripon who advocated the system of local government both for tackling problems of local interest and as a training ground in administration. A question might arise whether the experience gained by the Western countries is of much relevance in the Indian context. Since our country has adopted the ideals of a modern welfare State with a democratic and federal system of government of the western *genre* it goes without saying that the experience gained by the western countries could be taken advantage of by our planners, policy makers and administrators in this field. In fact we have been greatly influenced by such developments in establishing local governmental institutions of different types with varying degrees of authority. For instance there are Municipal Corporations that function as autonomous units independent of the district administration directly under the State government. The dual administration that has been introduced in metropolitan cities like Delhi bears a close resemblance to the administration of the Department of Seine on the basis of the principle that "Paris belongs to France", which is like an admission "Delhi belongs to India". There are certain principles that have been generally accepted by the western democracies that appear to have a good deal of relevance under Indian conditions as well.

1. Local Government has to be organised in order to meet local and regional needs. The needs of a highly urbanised area is bound to be quite at variance from those of an agricultural district which may again be quite different from those of an island area of some norms, the State legislatures will have to take practical steps for organising local governmental institutions that can meet the local needs.
2. All vital decisions affecting the lives of the local people will have to be taken by the people themselves through their elected representatives. The local administration consisting of officials, scientists and experts will work under the local government and as a part of it. The local government should, however, ensure that there is no unnecessary interference in their working. Asoka Mehta Committee has given some clear guidelines, the relevance of the Chief Executive Officer of the Zilla Parishad stating pattern that could be developed at different levels.
3. The modern era calls for the services of professionals of different types for a faster pace of economic development. This has to be kept in mind while the local governments are being organised for planning and implementing programmes of economic developments, social welfare and cultural advancement.

Current Scenario and Future Prospects of PRIs in India

It cannot be claimed that PRIs have started functioning effectively in all the States or even in the bulk of them. In the wake of the constitutional amendment a number of States have already passed the legislations necessary to bring into existence PRIs as statutory bodies as contemplated by the new provisions of the Constitution. Unfortunately one does not get an impression that political will is behind the local government institutions in all the States. Even now there are States showing a definite disinclination for taking the leap forward that would commit them both for the establishment of the PRIs at different levels and for taking a definite commitment of holding elections at regular intervals. It should, however, be kept in mind that the disinclination is only on the part of the political leadership of the States. It is to be expected that the voice of the people will ultimately prevail and no political party can, without damaging its bona fides and standing before the people afford to evade the issue for any length of time. It was quite apparent during the period when the amendment to the Constitution was being discussed that the country, as a whole was solidly behind the government in this regard.

While the PRIs have come to stay under the changed situation created by the constitutional amendment their effectiveness will depend upon how serious the State governments are in activising and utilising these institutions. Powers to impose taxes is not inherit in the PRIs. They can levy and collect taxes only to the extent they are authorised by the State legislatures. Similarly, State government can assign to the PRIs a share of taxes and other revenues of the State and make grants-in-aid for carrying on varieties of functions coming within the purview of the PRIs. There is a provision for a Finance Commission whose establishment is mandatory no doubt, but to what extent such a commission will come in support of the PRIs depends to a great extent on the attitudes of the State government who establishes such a finance commission with member of their own choice. It will, however, appear that the atmosphere has changed for the better and, if not anything else political compulsions will ultimately work in favour of the PRIs getting a better deal.

Article 243G of the Constitution mentions that the legislature of a State may, by law, endow the Panchayats with such powers and authority as may be necessary to enable them to function as institutions of self-government and such law may contain provisions for the devolution of powers and responsibilities upon Panchayats at the appropriate level, subject to such conditions as may be specified therein, with respect to:

(a) The preparation of plans for economic development and social justice;
(b) The implementation of schemes for economic development and social justice as may be entrusted to them including those in relation to the matters as may be listed in the Eleventh Schedule.

This Article is followed by two other Articles 243 H and 243 I relating to powers to impose taxes and the constitution of a Finance Commission to review the financial position. It will be quite clear that the constitution makers are aware of the fact that such responsibilities cannot be discharged without the availability of adequate financial resources. Since, however, provisions for devolution of power and responsibilities is an optional clause we come back once again to the problem of the State's political leadership as reflected through the State legislature.

In the context of the constitutional safeguards that have been provided there is every reason to hope that PRIs at different levels will start functioning more effectively in the not so distant future. Finance Commissions both at the national and State levels are apprised of the situation relating to paucity of funds. Much will depend upon the earnestness and sincerity will which the State Governments implement the programme. Art. 243G enjoins upon the State governments to endow the Panchayats with certain powers that are necessary to function as institutions of self-government. The PRIs are expected to play a vital role both in the preparation of plans for economic and social development and in their implementation. The twenty-nine items enumerated in the Eleventh Schedule include agriculture and allied activities very prominently. Therefore, it goes without saying that the PRIs are expected to play a dominant role in food production and the sphere of food security.

Independent India's first Prime Minister Jawaharlal Nehru had once described India as a rich country with poor people. Nothing could be more true about our country which is one of the richest in resources and yet more than 50% of the people are living in poverty. It is indeed a Statement of great significance, containing its own commentary. We remain poor only because the resources are not utilised. In many cases we are not utilising the resources because we are not even aware of their existence. Going one step further, there are the liabilities of today which could be the assets for tomorrow. Giving one specific example, the compost and waste material of the city, which is one of its great liabilities could be an excellent asset for crop production in the rural areas if there is a proper interaction between the rural and urban areas. That is why Asoka Mehta Committee had made a specific mention of the rural-urban continuum. A low lying and water logged area of a village could be a present liability giving a poor insignificant yield of paddy and breeding mosquitoes to boot. If this is converted into a pond it could be a durable asset for undertaking pisci-culture, having a duckery and various other activities. The waste material of one process could be the growth element for some other activity. I recollect an experiment initiated under the leadership of a former Chief Minister of West Bengal who advocated the farmers of his constituency to give up the cultivation of the main paddy crop and switch over to the same crop in other seasons. Though the suggestion was ridiculed in the beginning, his persistence paid rich dividends. The area is now one of the richest producers of the off season paddy and the landscape itself has changed beyond recognition. The flood water is being welcomed along with the rich silt that is carried by it and converted into an asset in the following season. These are only illustrative examples and should serve as eye-openers to us.

Resource Based Plan

An attempt was made in a systematic manner for having resource based planning in what was then described as an Integrated Rural Department Project in 1975. The resource inventory was prepared for some selected districts like Chandrapur in Maharashtra and Cannanore (Kannur) in Kerala. It was noticed that the scientist did not have to work in a vacuum. The soil and water resources would naturally form the starting point for any project for agricultural development. Sunlight is also of great importance. The scientists, therefore, started with the collection of meteorological data relating to rainfall, temperature, humidity, wind speed, sunshine hours etc. Soil survey reports were collected along with a complete list of all water bodies, ground water availability, drainages etc. Information was gathered on crops and cropping patterns and matters relating to animal husbandry, fisheries. Data on infrastructure facilities available were collected along with data on population, education and health status etc. Though such an exercise has later on been conducted for many districts there has been no spectacular progress. This really exposes both the strength and the weakness of the programme and should be helpful to us when we are thinking about local level resource based plan.

Unit of Local Level Planning

This matter has been discussed by various experts and expert committees many times without any of them going into the last details. What is now needed is the implementation of the programme right upto the grass-root level. Some time after the Balwantrai Mehta Committee Report was accepted a few State started making effective use of the Panchayat Samitis at block level. Some States started doing such work more at the district level and there were some who tried it at lower levels also. It has been emphasized by the Asoka Mehta Committee that the district level plan and the plans at the lower levels are to the complementary to each other. They even felt that a planning team may not be available at the level of the village or Mandal Panchayat. The expert team of the district was expected to help the Panchayat at the lower levels for preparing local level plans. It has also been made clear that Micro Level Planning may not be possible nor necessary for each village. The committee laid special emphasis on the role of Mandal Panchayat and it appears that plans should be made for a group of villages rather than for individual villages.

It is not that each village should not be individually involved in the process of planning. The Gram Sabhas are expected to meet at least two times in a year and they will be in a position not only to pose their problems but even suggest the solutions in a general way. Subsequently the plan will have to be formulated for a viable area comprising a group of villages. The position may be different for certain areas like the deserts of Rajasthan or the cold deserts of the Himalayas where the villages are situated too far apart. This would be considered micro-level planning in a real sense whether it is a single isolated village or a group of villages preferably covered by the same watershed. Such micro-level plans will have to be dovetailed into the district level plan or the plan of a sub-district with proper initiative from both sides. There are many projects like medium irrigation schemes, waste land reclamation etc. that will have to be undertaken at the district level and the major irrigation schemes may be for much bigger units. These are all accepted in principle but there has not been any effective planning and implementation with proper co-ordination so far. I am only giving an indication of the direction in which we have to move without going into the details in this short chapter.

Resource Hunt and Resource Mobilisation

It goes without saying that one cannot be expected to achieve an objective without adequate resources being made available. When it comes to the question of resources many people start with the allocations that are being made under different plan and non-plan schemes for a particular area and all other schemes meant for economic development. If there is inadequacy of funds attempts are made to get more funds from other sources. When the State government is short of funds they look up to the central government and sometimes to financial institutions within and outside the country. Projects are often made for World Bank financing or assistance from U.N.D.P. and such other International bodies. Ultimately comes the realisation that the funds available are not adequate enough for achieving the objective. Under these circumstances one is compelled to resign oneself to the unpalatable situation where the objective cannot be achieved due to lack of funds. This is what I have described as "Resource Hunt" which ultimately ends with the realisation that the hunt has not been successful.

Panchayats have always being claiming that they are short of funds. This happens for two reasons. First of all, they do not have the required power of imposing taxes in many cases. Secondly, the State governments do not place sufficient funds at the disposal of the local governments. It is expected that the position will improve in respect of both the constraints. With the allocation of responsibilities under the amended Constitution it is expected that the State government will be making higher allocations to the PRIs for implementing various programmes of economic development. Many of the Central schemes may also be implemented through the agency of the PRIs. Hopefully, more funds will be made available to them. It should, however, be remembered that there is no increase of resources for development in this process. The programmes that were being implemented by some governmental agency is being handed over to the PRIs alongwith required fund. The position will become different if the Panchayats are given the powers of taxation and such powers are properly utilised. The second part of the proposition is more important because it has often been noticed that the local governments are often shy of utilising even the existing powers of taxation due to various pressures or unwillingness to take unpopular decisions. It is however, possible, from another point of view, to make more resources available by re-organisation of the system itself. Giving one example, land revenue resource have become a minor resource for the State governments in terms of percentage. It was once pointed out a Chief Minister that the land revenue collection is not even able to cover the cost of collection. If this responsibility is handed over to the village Panchayats, the cost of collection could come down to less than 1/10th of the revenue collected. It would also become a stable source of revenue to the PRIs. There are many such avenues that could be effectively tapped. If the PRIs are to be entrusted with important responsibilities, the question of making adequate resources should also receive immediate and proper attention.

So far I have been dealing with resource hunt which is in my view different from resource identification. There are four basic resources that are essential for agricultural production—soil, water, air and sunlight. These four resources are put to use by another important resource in the form of human entrepreneurial skill for creating wealth, agricultural wealth to start with. Financial resources are no doubt necessary for activising the five resources that have been enumerated but even with a specified quantum of financial resources more assets could be created with proper and scientific utilization of the four resources through the agency of human skill. In the scheme formulated at one point of time through the agency of the Indian Council of Agriculture Research an attempt was made to identify all the available resources of a specified area and a detailed inventory was made of those resources.

From the experience gathered so far one could come to the following conclusions:

(a) There are many resources that are not being utilised and, in many cases, their existence as a possible resources is not even acknowledged.

(b) By changing production pattern it is possible to get more agricultural wealth due of the resources that were already being utilised. For example taking to a more appropriate crop in dry land area the yield per unit area could be doubled or trebled. Introduction of new cropping patterns could bring about revolutionary changes as in the case of rice cultivation in Punjab and Haryana and the wheat revolution of West Bengal followed by Bangladesh.

(c) The liability of today could be an asset of tomorrow. For instance desilting of a blocked drainage could increase the productivity in two ways by better irrigation and fertility of soil from the silt that could be utilized as an organic manure. Again, a water-logged area could be taken out of paddy cultivation and converted into a fish pond or irrigation tank. Here again the removed silt could be a further asset.

(d) There could be a matching of unutilised human labour resources to potential assets with the availability of money capital. Schemes of wasteland reclamation, soil conservation, drainage improvement etc. could be attampted through employment schemes specially when the public distribution system is over-full.

It had also became quite evident that district is not the appropriate unit for Micro Level planning. After the resources inventories were prepared it appeared that large resources were required for full utilization of the resources. Two decades ago one could not think about a district plan involving an outlay of 200 to 300 crores and it appeared that one will be only scratching at the surface with an allocation of one or two crores.

It is, therefore, imperative that this exercise of resources identification should be further disaggregated to the block level and levels below that. Here we come to the role that could be played by PRI's. If the resources inventory of a small local area of one to five villages were available to the local authority of the area with representatives of the local people they could apply their minds to the utilisation of the available resources, comparatively small in numerical terms, with the financial resources that are available or could to make available. These include:

(a) Allocation under different plan schemes for programmes like irrigation, soil conservation, communication etc.
(b) Allocation under I.R.D.P., Employment programmes and other programmes for the poor.
(c) Bankable schemes that could be drawn on community basis or individual basis.
(d) What could be coming out of people's own resources when they are convinced that any investment made by them would mean creation of assets in a cost-effective manner. This will become possible with the proper interaction of the technical experts and scientists with the local people. The local government is expected to bring them together.

The Machinery for Planning

The level at which local level planning should be undertaken and the machinery that is needed for formulating the plans have been discussed by various committees including the Asoka Mehta Committee on Panchayati Raj Institutions, the Dantwala Committee etc. It has been admitted that the district will be an important unit for planning but Micro Plans will be formulated at levels further down. The block is also being considered as an important unit for undertaking this exercise but the real Micro Level Planning will be, in most cases, for a group of villages.

The Planning exercise cannot be effective if it is undertaken in isolation at any particular level—grassroot level, Block level or district level. The plans at different levels are to be taken as complementary and supplementary to one another. It may also be necessary for the planning machinery at the higher level to get involved in the planning process at the lower levels. Since the senior experts of the different departments are stationed at the district level it is expected that they would give guidance and help to the planning machinery at the lower levels. It is, however, necessary that expertise in planning should be built at the different levels of PRI's.

This brings us the question of creating the expertise needed for Micro-level Planning. Planning is a process that cannot be left to the untrained amateur. It is not that we require a high profile academician or scientist to do the planning, but it does call for some special skill and expertise that could be acquired through education and training. All the States have their own Agricultural Universities though some of the smaller States may be tagged on to some common university in the region. There are other institutes and training centres concerned with various facets of economic development. State Governments have their own Administrative Staff Colleges and such other institutions. Many of these could be involved in the process of training the trainers as well as the planning officers and other members of the planning team. Some of the Agricultural Universities have started new faculties dealing with such matters like study and training in Co-operation, Business Management etc. Special courses could be designed for micro-level planning at various levels. The work could be undertaken by other universities and colleges as well. Many of these institutions could also have itinerary teams that could impart training to the staff at the block level or even the level of village Panchayats. The responsibility for organising the training needs of a whole district could possibly to entrusted to the Chief Executive of a district level Panchayat.

Role of PRIs in Transfer of Technology

Innumerable schemes relating to the transfer of technology have been formulated and implemented all over the country during the last four decades and more. Programmes like the Lab-to-Land Programme and institutions like the Extension Training Centres and Krishi Vijnan Kendras have given a clean demonstration of how agricultural production could be stepped up by the use of appropriate technology. Inspite of larger allocation being made for such programmes during successive Five Year Plans, their value has been of a demonstrative character. It cannot also be claimed that they have reached the people at large. The position can undergo a revolutionary change if such programmes are undertaken at the level of the Village Panchayats—the Mandal or by any other name it is called. One State has already established Krishi Bhawans at the level of village Panchayat level. If these could be converted into Krishi and Vijnan Kendra, centres of agricultural science and technology as well as centres of demonstration the impact could be considerable. It has to be accepted that the problem of food production and food security can be tackled only at the village level and the involvement of the village Panchayat is inescapable in all such programmes.

FOUR

PANCHAYATI RAJ AND FOOD SECURITY

L.C. JAIN

Food Security

Let us first define our notion of food security. Whose food is to be secured and by whom?

If there are adequate food stocks in the economy at the aggregate level to meet the demand, we do have the means to ensure food security. Our ability to do so is reinforced, if in addition to adequate stocks, we also have at the distribution end market mechanisms supplemented by efficient public distribution system (PDS) to carry the stocks to the consumption centre-urban and rural.

But while these are necessary conditions for ensuring food security, they are by no means sufficient to clear the hunger of the poors. Studies in India have shown that access of the poorer households to food depends on three vital conditions (a) purchasing power in their hands; (b) local production or proximate production of foodgrains for more *assured access* than offered by market mechanism and/or PDS; and available stock accessible foodgrains being of the variety/type preferred by the poorer households in their respective regions.

There is an obvious interconnection between these three (a) to (c) conditions. If local production of foodgrains is expanded/maximised, it will expand work and income i.e. purchasing power for the poorer underemployed/unemployed persons; and there is greater likelihood of the production pattern being more in accord with local consumption preferences.

Underlying the above view is that the central concern or focus of policy of food security is the poorer sections. That is the answer to the questions whose food security?

Next question is: Who is to ensure such security ? The State of The Community or both. Generally, the finger points towards the State. But we have enough experience by now to recognise the limitations of what the State can do. It can more easily gather adequate stocks at the aggregate level by imports or procurement from market surplus regions/districts; it can warehouse them and also despatch them to deficit areas. But its limitations are that it is able to do so only in respect of procurement of select grains (e.g. wheat, rice) which are in surplus in a limited number of districts (no more than about 15 to 20 per cent of the total of about 450 districts).

Thus, the procurement of foodgrains, by the State generates more and more purchasing income/power in the surplus/producing districts and little in the deficit/consuming districts. An illustration is that in the recent years foodgrain stocks of central government have risen to record levels while per capita consumption of foodgrains has declined. Secondly, type of foodgrains offered to deficit area consumers are not necessarily those preferred. And, equally importantly, the despatch and ultimate arrival of the foodgrains, from centrally administered stocks, is subject to frequent delays. Studies of PDS have shown repeated visits by consumers to PDS outlets only to be told "stocks have not yet arrived" or "supply is inadequate", let alone the question of what type of grains, their quality and price. The stomachs can brook no delay. They have to be fed twice a day at least.

The State clearly cannot produce satisfaction if the conditions, referred to above, surrounding the poorer consumers are to be met even partially.

If, there was no alternative, then of course, all these limitations will have to be swallowed willy-nilly.

But there is an alternative not in terms of replacing the role the State is playing or can play, but developing an additional source of strengthening food security by the community and at each local level.

Panchayati Raj

That is where Panchayati Raj enters the scene.

Briefly stated, Panchayats (as mandated by the recent 73rd Amendment to the Constitution), provide a *local institution*, accountable and accessible to each village population. In the words of the 73rd Amendment, the Village Panchayat has "to prepare an area plan for economic development and social justice" for its respective population

That is a micro plan. In the context, the main economic activity at village level is and will be for the foreseeable future, agriculture based on the given resources of soil, water, vegetation, livestock and manpower. Cropping pattern is invariably in accord with location—specific agro-climatic and soil conditions and local consumption pattern.

But much of the area (three fourths of cultivable area) is rain fed, dry-farming, with yields which are low but need not be so low. Agricultural scientists are agreed that with some moderate investment on land levelling and moisture retention through reduction of run-off, production and productivity in these areas can be improved significantly. These rain-fed areas are also the areas where a high proportion of the poor and underemployed/unemployed are concentrated, and where infant mortality rate is higher than average.

Besides, the size of operational holdings in small and becoming smaller by the day; and the absolute number of operational holdings is expanding relentlessly. (See Annexure). This is an obvious constraint in raising yields and production. But in the absence of a local institution (such as the panchayat) not even an attempt has been made to overcome this and other constraints in realizing the potential for higher yields/ production which the agricultural scientists are agree, exists-ready to be picked up. Even with the Panchayats, it is not going to be easy to realize the potential, but without their minding each village and within that each operational holding, it is well nigh impossible to do so as evident from the failure of the agricultural exclusion machinery in the past four decades.

Conclusion

A local representative institution and micro-planning are thus a must to raise local production which in turn offers the best food security to the poor.

It is here that there is a strong nexus between Panchayati Raj and food security for the poor. What can we, FAO and all, do to aid the Panchayats in this endeavour, should be high on our agenda.

ANNEXURE

NUMBER AND SIZE OF OPERATIONAL HOLDINGS

Over three decades 1960-61 to 1990-91, the area operated by operational holdings in India increased from 131.46 million hectares to 165.60 million hectares. In the same thirty years period the number of operational holdings increased from 48.88 million to 105.29 million.

As a consequence there was a substantial increase in the area operated by marginal and small holdings both in absolute terms and proportionally.

In this thirty years period, the area occupied by marginal holdings increased nearly three-fold from 8.78 million hectares to 24.62 million hectares, and in the case of small holdings the corresponding increase was about 75 per cent from 16 million hectares to 28.71 million hectares.

Between the marginal and small holdings which in 1960-61 occupied only 18 per cent of the total area of all operational holdings, by 1990-91 had come to occupy about 33 per cent of the total area. These changes have impacted significantly on average size of operational holdings. Overall the average size declined in these three decades from 2.69 hectares to 1.57 hectares.

The decline in average size of holding occurred in all classes of holdings: marginal, small, semi-medium, medium and large. While the decline in the case of marginal holdings at 10 per cent was the most pronounced in the large holdings, the decline at one per cent was the lowest of all classes.

It is also noteworthy that as the decadal data in this 30 years, there is a continuing trend in respect of increasing number of operational holdings, decline in the average size of holding and expansion in the absolute occupied by marginal and small operational holdings.

TABLE 1 : Operational Holdings (1970-71 to 1990-91)

	Number (lakh)		Area (Lakh ha.)		Average Size (hec)	
	70-71	90-91	70-71	90-91	70-71	90-91
AP	54.2	92.9	135.8	144.6	2.51	1.56
Bihar	75.8	117.1	114.8	109.0	1.51	0.93
MP	53.0	84.0	211.9	221.1	4.00	2.63
Mah.	49.5	94.7	211.8	209.3	4.28	2.21
TN	53.1	80.0	77.1	74.7	1.45	0.93
UP	156.4	200.7	181.6	179.9	1.16	0.90
Total Six States	442.0	669.4	933.0	938.6	14.91	9.16
All India	710.1	1052.9	1621.4	1656.0	2.28	1.57

Note: States primarily dependent on agri. on food crops. Crops : Yield per hec.

TABLE 2 : Main Food Crops— (Variations in the years 1970-71 to 1993-94)

Crops	Yields kg per Hectare		
	1970-71	1990-91	1993-94 (quintal/hec)
Rice	1123	1740	18.8
Wheat	1307	2280	23.7
Jowar	467	814	8.9
Gram	663	702	6.5
Maize	1279	1518	15.8

Source: Centre for Monitoring Indian Economy (CMIE).

TABLE 3 : Yield of Main Food Crops : Variation District-wise (1988-91)

District in the State	Rice	Kg./hec	Jowar	Kg./Hec	Bajra	Kg./hec	Maize	Kg./hec	Wheat	(kg/hec)
AP										
High	W. Godavari	2,727	Ananthapur	1083	Chittoor	1452	Karimnagar	2600	Warangal	1000
Low	Adilabad	1563	Nalgonda	360	Nalgonda	312	Adilabad	904	Mahbubnagar	553
Gujarat										
High	Rajkot	3000	Panch Mahals	1422	Jhe Dangs	1667	Banas Kantha	1732	Junagadh	3046
Low	Bharuch	722	Surendranagar	176	Banas Kanta	629	Mehsana	1332	Bharuch	751
M.P.										
High	Bhind	1917	Chhindwara	1531	Gwalior	1215	Chindwara	2914	Hoshangabad	3176
Low	Satna	466	Shivpuri	499	West Nimar	347	Rewa	869	Durg	537
Maharashtra										
High	Kolhapur	2462	Kolhapur	2104	Kolhapur	1000	Kolhapur	2109	Kolhapur	1623
Low	Akola	567	Bandra	319	Sangli	211	Latur	600	Bhandara	575
Punjab										
High	Ludhiana	3712			Faridkot	1000	Amritsar	1872	Ludhiana	4205
Low	Amritsar	1769			Firozpur	750	Firozpur	1000	Hoshiarpur	2821
T.N.										
High	Madurai	3851	Madurai	1593	Chengalpatti	1883	Thanjavur	2201	North Arcot	1000
Low	Coimbatore	592	Coimbatore	519	MGR Rama-nathapuram	586	Tirunelveli Kattabomman Chidambaranar	500	Salem	625

Source: CMIE.

FIVE

KEY NOTE ADDRESS

SARITA J. DAS

I consider it a privilege to have been asked to deliver the Key Note Address at this very significant National Conference on the theme "Panchayati Raj' the Key to Food Security and Nutrition". This Conference will serve to focus attention on the issue of food security and, as chairperson of the National World Food Day Committee, I would like to sincerely thank the FAO, the Indian Farmers Fertiliser Cooperative (IFFCO), the Indian Association of the Advancement of Science (IAAS) and the Ministries of Food, Rural Development, whose painstaking efforts have made this Conference possible.

The World Food Summit would be held in November 1996. This Summit will bring back, to the forefront of the international agenda, the issue of universal food security. The Summit aims to identify specific problems being faced related to food security and the actions that are to be taken by National Governments and the international community to mitigate these problems. It is evident that today's world is interlinked in terms of institutions, economies and societies and these linkages have transcended national boundaries. The situation, therefore, calls for a global approach and a commitment on the part of the comity of nations to address themselves squarely to the question of food security.

We, in the developing world, are more sharply aware of the problems and the misery that lack of access to food can create. About 800 million people today in the developing world do not have enough food to meet their basic needs and many more experience prolonged hunger, malnutrition and other deficiency related diseases. As populations keep growing, it would be necessary to step up global food production. In addition, it will be increasingly imperative to ensure that people are given access to the food they need. Employment and incomes, therefore, would also have to be generated in order to ensure access to food. A number of measures would have to be taken by national governments, international community and international agencies to confront these challenges. If we do not act concertedly with determination and political commitment, it may have grave consequences. We have no time to lose.

Over the years, India has developed a sound food security system and we can legitimately be proud of our achievements in this regard. We are not complacent and our efforts are directed towards further strengthening and refining this system. We have endeavoured to protect the interests of both the grower as well as to consumer through our policies. Through the Public Distribution System and the revamped Public Distribution System, we have ensured that consumers, especially the vulnerable groups living in remote and inaccessible areas, have access to food at reasonable prices. Similarly, our food reserves or bufferstocks are maintained with the intention of intervening effectively in adverse situations. I would not like to dwell on this aspect at length since this distinguished gathering is already aware of these details. Suffice it to say that the resilience that we have built up over the years has stood us in good stead on the food security front and that our efforts would be directed to further improvements in the system.

This Conference would be addressing itself to the role that Panchayati Raj Institutions could play in the food security system. The 73rd Constitution Amendment (1992) has infused a new dynamism and purpose in local self-government institutions. While Panchayati Raj institutions have been in existence for long, they did not acquire the status of being viable and responsive people's bodies for various reasons. The constitutional status now accorded to these bodies will provide them with certainty, continuity and strength. It is a revolution in the history of Panchayati Raj Institutions in our country. This would empower rural people to determine their own destiny and will enhance their capabilities and involvement in the process of "planning from below". A large measure of decentralisation in the implementation of development activities will, therefore, be available, with popular participation. The financial provisions of the amendment are aimed at ensuring the financial viability of these institutions which is necessary to render them effective. The empowerment of scheduled castes and scheduled tribes by reservation of seats for them as also for women, has been ensured through the amendment. It is obvious, given the provisions of the 73rd amendment, that major changes are in the offing and that a new day in the history of Panchayati Raj movement has dawned.

How are we to involve the Panchayati Raj System in Food Security? What are their perceptions of food security? What would be the role they could play in ensuring access to adequate, safe and nutritious food? How can the Panchayati Raj System be effectively involved in development of strategies for micro-level food security? These are but a few of the issues that this Conference would address. These issues are complex and solutions will not emerge easily. There are many dimensions involved and there will be differing perceptions of the roles of different players. But the discussions at the Conference will serve to focus attention on key issues, generate a debate and a new awareness of the view points and perceptions of different groups. What is important is that we must ensure continuous and focused attention on problems relating to food security, both in the national and international context. It will not be possible for us to overcome these challenges if we do not devote ourselves adequately to comprehending the issues involved, in order to identify local, national, regional and global solutions.

I am confident that this National Conference will serve the purpose of initiating a meaningful debate on strategies to secure micro-level food security and nutrition for the poor.

PANCHAYATI RAJ AND COOPERATIVES: The Twin Keys to Food Security and Nutrition: Madhya Pradesh Experience

DHARMENDRA NATH

Public Distribution System including Support Price Purchase Programme in Madhya Pradesh is based very largely on Panchayati Raj and Cooperatives. They provide the cutting edge for both operations.

Food Procurement is initially done by primary cooperatives called Service Cooperative Societies working as agents of State Procurement Agency. State Level Agency transfers the procured stocks to Central Procurement Agency for storage and issue as required. Most of the procurement is at Support Price Level though at times looking to overall demand supply situation procurement at prices higher than Support Price is also done. Credit for purchase and gunnies for storage and other support measures are organised by the Central Procurement Agency and are passed down to the Service Cooperative Society through the State Procurement Agency. Local Panchayati Raj institutions keep a watchful eye on the whole programme and Local Food Administration takes their help in disseminating information and seeking local support.

Public Distribution System in Madhya Pradesh is anchored in cooperative movement. All retail outlets called Fair Price Shops are in the cooperative sector. These are at the level of Service Cooperative Society, the same body which does grass-root level procurement. A group of 15-20 such Societies are connected with a Lead Society. Lead Society of the area collects stocks from Issue Centres of the State Distribution Agency, transports them and delivers them to the primaries. Lead Society has credit linkage with District Central Cooperative banks and is in a position to channel credit from Central Cooperative bank to the primaries. The whole chain is subject to Cooperative audit. This arrangement has been put in place since 1992 as it is an improvement over the earlier system and provides a distribution chain in rural areas unmatched by any other. Prior to this the retail outlets called Fair Price Shops were individually run and they were lifting and transporting the stocks directly from the Issue Centres. Their access to credit was uncertain and it varied. There were many complaints against the working of the old system mainly relating to diversification of stocks and overcharging of price etc. The cooperative chain has provided a much better substitute. Being part of the Cooperative chain provision of any subsidy and reimbursement of any losses is easy to manage.

It would be seen that Price Support System and Public Distribution System are two cross currents of the same stream. In case of procurement stocks flow upwards from Service Cooperative Societies to Central Procurement Agency and in case of distribution the stocks flow in the reverse direction. The same system serves not only the requirements of the consumers but also those of the producers by offering remunerative prices to them. In fact not only marketing but credit and other agricultural input requirements of farmers are also catered to by the system. It would be seen that the system serves the requirement of Food Security in the short run by making the stocks available and in the long run by supporting production.

Supervision of the whole Public Distribution System has been very largely placed in the hands of Panchayati Raj bodies. At the district level there is a Supervisory Committee presided over by the President of the District Panchayat and at the block (Janpad) level there is a parallel Committee presided over by the Janpad President. Thus while cooperatives do the actual handling and business of Public Distribution System its supervision and monitoring is in the hands of Panchayati Raj institutions which also have the power of inspection of Fair Price Shops at all levels. To further strengthen the linkage between Panchayati Raj institutions and Public Distribution System Local Food Administration officers are required to attend the meetings of the District/Janpad Panchayats.

In addition to supervision and monitoring Panchayati Raj System has other significant responsibilities also in the management of Public Distribution System, Village Level Panchayat is the authority to issue entitlement cards called Ration Cards for its area. Secondly, block level Panchayat i.e. Janpad Panchayat is the authority to allot Fair Price Shops in its area. This not only ensures better use of local level knowledge but it also ensures the necessary local level adjustments in the programme. This part of Panchayati Raj involvement has been introduced in the State since also ensures the necessary local level adjustments in the programme. This part of Panchayati Raj involvement has been introduced in the State since late 1994. It is still in an experimental stage but the idea is to streamline the system and to make for smooth working as one goes along.

As a further step in the same direction village level Panchayats have been entrusted with the responsibility of executing nutrition programmes for pre-school and school-going children etc. This involves preparing and serving ready to eat food, stocks for which are drawn from Public Distribution System or elsewhere.

In an effort to reach the stocks to the remoter areas and small village hamlets etc. the agency of Mobile Fair Price Shops has been introduced over the years. These are truck mounted and/or run by the State Distribution Agency directly. The vehicles which are six tonners or ten tonners make daily trips to the villages to be covered, particularly to villages having weekly temporary markets (called *hats*). Visit to *hats* is very useful since large numbers of people from the surrounding areas visit the place on that day to buy or sell and they are in a position to conveniently use the services of the Mobile Shops on that day. This thrust of Public Distribution System in remoter areas is clearly an effort to accommodate the requirements of the more needy sections of population and is an attempt at better targetting of the System. To make it more worthwhile these Mobile Shops carry not only the normal items but also additional consumer items likely to be required like salt, kerosene, matches, soap etc. Their operation requires additional subsidy and that is one reason why they are run directly by the State Agency.

Public Distribution System in the State covers at present all sections of population urban or rural, rich or poor. It is a matter of public policy as to how to target better in favour of the poor and the malnourished. However, if a sharper focussing is required the ground work has been prepared in the State in the form of Voters' Identity Cards which carry colour coding indicating family income level. Families with income of below Rs. 6,000 per annum have been given Cards with a red colour line and those with family income of less than Rs. 11,000 have been given Cards with green colour line. This arrangement will come in handy whenever it is decided to restrict Public Distribution System to certain income levels. It is interesting to note that family income levels have been fixed at the village Panchayat level.

SEVEN

PANCHAYATI RAJ: The Key to Food Security and Nutrition

ARKAPRABHA DEV

West Bengal having a geographical area of 88.75 lakh hectares accommodates 67.98 million people (1991 Census) rendering a population density of about 766 per sq. km. Sixty-three per cent of the total geographical area has already been brought under cultivation. Net cultivated area in the State is about 54.5 lakh hectares and total number of cultivators as per agricultural census report of 1985 is 61.3 lakh and per cultivator availability of net sown area comes to about 0.88 hectares. The net irrigated area is 20 lakh hectares. Due to continuous division and fragmentation of cultivated land, larger capital investment for development in the agricultural sector is gradually becoming unremunerative.

West Bengal agriculture is dominated by small and marginal farmers ranging from 81.94 per cent in different regions with average of 90 per cent who share 60 per cent of land. 70 per cent holding below one hectare. The small and marginal farmers play a key role in agricultural production process of the State.

West Bengal has 17 Agricultural districts comprising 52 Administrative subdivisions, 341 Development Blocks, 331 Panchayat Samitis and 3,246 Gram Panchayats. The Literacy percentage is above 57 per cent. The total number of household is 97,49,182.

For scientific management of regional resources and for formulation of need based agricultural plans, the districts of West Bengal have been included in three regions viz., (1) Eastern Himalayan Region, Zone-II, (2) Lower Gangetic Plain Region, Zone - III, (3) Eastern Plateau and Hill Region, Zone - VII, out of 15 Agro-climatic regions of the country.

The extension machinery is geared up to advocate multiple cropping in larger areas through better land management, utilisation of irrigation resources and adoption of recommended package of practices to boost up production. It has so far been possible to raise the overall cropping intensity in the State to 162 per cent and gross cropped area to 76.4 lakh hectare and there is further possibility to improve upon it. The per capita production of foodgrains is 193 kg.

Against this background and having cropping intensity of 162 per cent, the State could produce 132 lakh tonne of foodgrains (rice, wheat, pulses and minor cereals), 50 lakh tonnes of Potato, 55 lakh tonnes of vegetables and about 14 lakh tonnes of fruits constituting the food crops. Among non-food crops, producing 59.3 lakh bales of jute, the State ranked first in the country. Excepting cereals, the production of other food crops is just to meet up half the requirement of the State. Weather induced fluctuation lead to production peaks and troughs of these crops, particularly rice. The net result renders the majority of people to remain underfed not to speak of balanced diet.

There is, therefore, need for sustainable agriculture aiming not only to maintain present production profile but increase future production keeping pace with the increasing demographic pressure. The issue of shrinkages of arable land due to industrialisation and urbanisation has also to be kept in mind while planning further development in agricultural sector.

Consensus developed long back to address the issue in its proper perspective which led to launching of various agricultural development schemes. Land Reforms leading mainly to land redistribution constituted the first step in this endeavour but lack of adequate support to the "Land gift" beneficiaries limited the development. Subsequently a number of developmental schemes were implemented taking all-round development of the agriculture sector, but still these programme procedures did not make any provision for directly addressing the farmers problems *in situ*.

Development of technology for agricultural advancement is not a problem now, rather the problem is its transfer to and adoption by the farmers. The technology developed at the research institution pass through extension personnel, mass media and institutional sources percolating down to the village level farmers. All these added to partial failure in achieving the desired yield in agricultural development.

Real progress is, however, visualised through planning and implementation of agricultural development programme based on local resources, scope, capacities, problems and needs. The Panchayat which is the local governing body constituted by village people has vital role to play. The rural mass builds up a strong personal relationship with each other by virtue of their long association and homogeneity in social, thinking. Information from institutional agencies are taken by less number of farmers who generally come from the lower strata of the villages and who have little or no literacy, small holdings and less income. This group of people interact better and prefer to derive information from the co-villagers. The Panchayat Samitis being represented by the villagers are expected to address the village issues better, giving the farmers opportunities to participate in the developmental programme. This creates a sense of involvement, responsibilities and encourage the farmers to achieve their goal utilising the total resources. Thus Panchayat that exists at the village level, can support the rural poor farmers to accelerate their economic growth.

EIGHT

FINANCING OF VILLAGE PANCHAYATS IN UTTAR PRADESH: Need for Review

FAHIMUDDIN

The Seventy-Third Constitution Amendment Act, 1993 can be termed as a watershed in the realm of decentralization in India. Under this amendment all States except those with population below 20 lakhs and some special areas like Hill areas, etc. listed in Article 243-M of this amendment must have a three-tier Panchayati Raj structure at the village, intermediate and district levels. The underlying philosophy of Panchayati Raj is embodied in the concept of Local Self-Governance (LSG): each spatial unit to be self-governing and ultimate arbiter of planning and development.

The U.P. Scenario

Uttar Pradesh is one of the few States in the country which enacted Panchayati Raj Act as early as 1947 providing for the establishment of village panchayats. It has amended this original Act on April 22, 1994 in order to bring it in conformity with the provisions of 73rd Constitution Amendment Act, 1993. The Government of U.P. has also constituted a Finance Commission to review the financial position of the panchayats and to make recommendations to improve it.

Functions and Finances of Village Panchayats

The village Panchayats in Uttar Pradesh have to perform a vide range of activities, some of them are statutorily compulsory and some discretionary. These functions include all aspects of social and economic development except law and order. To perform such a wide range of activities, the village panchayats should have corresponding financial resources. The sources of income of village panchayats in U.P. can broadly be divided into four categories. These are taxes and fees, grants-in-aid, income from local economic enterprises and public contributions. The taxes are house tax, vehicle tax on cycle, rickshaw or animal driven carts, the profession tax on persons or firms doing business in the village, the miscellaneous tax like pilgrim tax, etc. and fee for water supply, stamp duty and grants-in-aid both matching and ad-hoc. Village panchayats in U.P. may also get money from local economic enterprises like common land, village forest, etc. There is also a provision by which public can make contributions in the form of cash, kind and labour.

Resource Mobilization

So many sources of finance available to village panchayats in U.P. give the impression that the financial position of village panchayats in U.P. leaves nothing more to be desired and there appears to be more or less match between the functions of village Panchayats and financial resources available to them. However, the reality is altogether different. It has been estimated that around one-third of total village Panchayats of the country are in U.P. Out of these only 89 have an income of more than Rs. 10,000 per annum and the income of 60,608 panchayats is less than Rs. 1,000 per year. The total income of village Panchayats from taxes and fees-optional or compulsory was Rs. 542.85 lakh in 1993-94. This income total at the State level, no doubt, is good indicator to show the position of Panchayats in terms of resource mobilization. However, the State totals are meaningless on account of wide variation in the size and population of individual Panchayats. The better indicator, in this regard, is the per capita income of village Panchayats at the State level. On this criteria, the income level of village Panchayats in U.P. comes only Rs. 0.60 during 1993-94.

Sources of Revenue Generation

As mentioned earlier that village Panchayats in U.P. are empowered to levy large numbers of taxes besides grants-in-aid for various development activities. However, our case study of two sample village Panchayats of Sitapur district, U.P. indicates that own resource generation constituted only 6 to 8 per cent of the total revenue received during 1989-90 and 1993-94. The Jawahar Rozgar Yojana (JRY) is the main source of income as the share of JRY in total receipt constituted as high as 94 per cent. Thus, given the current pattern of availability of finances to village panchayats, a very limited scope of discretion is available to village panchayats for planning of locally perceived needs.

Instability in Funds Availability

The village Panchayats in U.P., at present, are mobilizing negligible finances both from own sources and government grants-in-aid. Moreover, the availability of finance is very erratic. In case of our sample, the analysis shows that in 1989-90 Rs. 79 was the per capita receipt from all sources which increased to Rs. 117 in 1992-93. Again in 1993-94, the total receipt declined to Rs. 22. In this way, it becomes evident that the per capita receipt of village Panchayats in U.P. is very meagre and that too is extremely unstable.

Potentials of Income Sources

We have examined the taxation power and generation of financial resources of village Panchayats in U.P. from different sources. It is evident that in U.P., the village Panchayats have been empowered to levy taxes which included a long list of items. However, it has become clear that yield from these resources are not sufficient enough to provide a sense of fiscal independence in village Panchayats. The reasons for this situation can be attributed to the following:

1. The taxation power is too wide and incapable of being meaningfully utilized.
2. Most of the prescribed taxable sources may not be existing at the Panchayat level or may be partially, to yield reasonable revenue.
3. There may be reluctance on the part of village Panchayats to levy taxes due to proximity to people or due to lack of organizational capabilities in levy and collection of taxes.

In order to test the above assumptions, we have tried to find out that how many sources of taxation are really available at the Panchayat level. It is evident that out of ten prescribed sources, only four sources namely, Panchayat tax, tax on animals, vehicles and shops are available which can be levied upon if the village Panchayats desires to do so. Moreover, out of these four existing sources of taxation, only Panchayat tax is being imposed in both the sample village Panchayats and tax on animals, vehicles and shops are not being imposed at all.

We also tried to understand why the existing sources of revenue are not being taxed at all. The replies given by the sample village Panchayats reveal that proximity to people is major cause followed by the lack of competence to manage tax collection.

Potential and Actual Collection

It is generally postulated that village Panchayats do not put serious efforts to collect taxes. As a result, a substantial gap remains between potential and actual collection. We have tried to verify the validity of this assumption that how far the gap remains between the potential and actual collection of a tax and if whole of the potential is tapped, does it provide reasonable amount of returns to village Panchayats? We have examined this by analysing the case of Panchayat tax—the only tax in U.P. the village Panchayats are reported to be levying and collecting. Our analysis shows that roughly 30 per cent of the potential of Panchayat tax is not being tapped in our sample. This problem seems to be more serious in case of the village Panchayat which is large in size and comparatively better endowed with resources as against small-size less resource base Panchayat. The other important question arises that how much revenue a village Panchayat can generate if it taps all potentials? Will it be a meaningful yield? Our estimate shows that roughly Rs. 1,400 per village Panchayat per annum can be generated if all taxable items are exploited. In absolute sense this amount appears to be negligible and comes to Rs. 2 per capita in a year. With such a paltry per capita annual receipt what a Panchayat can seriously plan for development is difficult to imagine.

Panchayat Tax Collection in U.P. : A Myth Not Reality

The Directorate of Panchayati Raj, Government of U.P. claims that around Rs. 5 crore were collected from Panchayat tax in U.P. during 1992-93. However, an indepth discussion with district Panchayati Raj officials and Chairpersons of sample village panchayats revealed that the Panchayat tax is never collected from the village people. When the Directorate of Panchayati Raj exerts pressure, the village Panchayats set apart some money received under different government programmes and show it as a collection of Panchayat tax by making financial manipulations. Thus a part of the money provided to village Panchayats by government, mostly under JRY, is used to show the collection of Panchayat tax in U.P. and the figures of Panchayat tax do not represent the real collection by the village Panchayats.

Policy Guidelines

The following policy suggestions are recommended for financing of village Panchayats in Uttar Pradesh:

1. The village Panchayats in Uttar Pradesh have been empowered with long list of taxation. As we have found that this list does not conform with realities existing at bottom level of Panchayats because most of the items of taxation do not exist at all. Hence it would be necessary and rational policy in future to avoid giving too long and unrealistic list of power of taxation to village Panchayats in Uttar Pradesh.
2. The village Panchayats in Uttar Pradesh are incapable of meaningful utilizing the taxation power given to them due to physical proximity to people or lack of organisational capabilities. A clear attitude of reluctance is evident on the part of village Panchayats in both the cases of imposition and realisation of taxes. Therefore, the responsibility to levy and collect taxes, Panchayat tax in particular, should not be entrusted upon village Panchayats during their current term of Five Years. The Revenue Department of Uttar Pradesh which collects land revenue should be asked to realise the Panchayat tax. The amount thus collected may be transferred back to village Panchayats after making some deductions in the form of collection charge. This does not mean that a donor-donee relationship should be encouraged between State and village Panchayats in U.P. and village Panchayats should be completely absolved of responsibility to raise resources for their own planning. However, in the absence of awareness of need and importance of generation of own finances on the part of village Panchayats, nothing is to result in reality. Since the present term of village Panchayats in U.P. has just begun and will continue for five years, the Government must plan for a complete package of awareness programme for the elected members of all three tiers of Panchayats. The government should also involve NGOs in this programme because State machinery may not be able to manage such a vast programme. If such an orientation is successfully given to village Panchayats, they will develop a sense of resource management and strive to generate own resources by all means at their command including imposition of taxes. The government should also devolve the formula of matching grants to village

Panchayats. It will further induce them to raise their own resources in order to get matching money from the government.

3. As long as planning is sectoral, limited scope can be found for planning and development of locally perceived priorities. Increasingly more untied funds should be consciously and conscientiously provided to village Panchayats.
4. Remunerative enterprises suitable to village Panchayats may be taken up by the village Panchayats in Uttar Pradesh to enhance their financial position. We may learn from the experiences of other States in this regard. Vengal Rao Committee has commended the then Madras Government scheme of planting trees on tank bunds which brought ample income to village Panchayats. Some Panchayats in coastal Andhara Pradesh had also earned good profit from similar enterprises.
5. A rational formula is to be adopted to lay down the procedures of sharing of taxes and cess like Motor Vehicle Tax, income of Agricultural Marketing Societies and cess on land revenue, etc. between State and village Panchayats. Some of the areas of U.P. has experienced substantial commercialisation of its agriculture. A tax on commercial crops like sugarcane and potato etc. may be imposed by the village Panchayats with proper planning of its collection. However, it is to be ensured that the special development programmes should not adversely be affected, for example the development programme of oilseeds and fisheries, etc.
6. Keeping in view the present status of village Panchayats in U.P., the greater emphasis is needed for quite some time in future to devolve financial resources from State Government to village Panchayats. Panchayat Finance Commission of U.P. should look into the rational of not investing village Panchayats with more powers to tax. There is a need of greater devolution of untied resources to State from Centre in order that the State may devolve more untied resources to Panchayats. It is also to be ensured that other tiers of Panchayat system do not deprive village Panchayat of its functions and finances.

NINE

MYTHS AND REALITIES OF THE PANCHAYATI RAJ SYSTEM FOR DECENTRALIZATION OF PLANNING

NARINDAR S. RANDHAWA

I. Implications of Experiences of Panchayati Raj Institutions

Panchayati Raj was launched in the State with the Punjab Gram Panchayat Act, 1952. The District Boards established under the Punjab District Board Act, 1883, continued to function and they were replaced by the Panchayati Samiti and Zila Parishad Act, 1961. It accomplished a three-tier Panchayati Raj System—District, Block, and Village.

Several attempts have been made to evaluate the functioning of the Panchayati Raj System for the country and for the State of Punjab from time to time. To name some —Ashoka Mehta Committee (1978); and the Expert Group led by Dantwala. The Punjab Government also appointed study teams, namely, Rajindra Singh Study Team, Badal Study Team, Harcharan Singh Committee and the Departmental Officers Committee. These all-India and Punjab State evaluations concluded that the functioning of the Panchayati Raj System fell far short of the expectations. Some studies stressed decentralized planning at the district level. It is relevant here to quote the finding of the Badal committee:

> Panchayati Raj was introduced in this State more as a result of the National Policy of the Central Government rather than as an act of faith and as a means to bring about effective decentalization. Although comprehensive legislation was brought about through Panchayati Raj Acts, yet these institutions suffered from lack of funds and genuine transfer of power and responsibility".

The failures of the Panchayati Raj System for more than four decades incited the interest in their revival. The Rajiv Gandhi Government introduced Sixty-Fourth Constitutional Amendment Bill on 15 May, 1989. It culminated into the Seventy-Third Constitutional Amendment Act, 1992, on the Panchayats.

The Seventy-Third Amendment resulted into following extremely significant provisions:

— making Panchayati Raj Institutions as an organ of the Constitutional scheme of the country,
— in addition to the Central, State and Concurrent list of subjects, the fourth list of subjects for Panchayati Raj Institutions was added;
— a separate Election Commission for Panchayati Raj Institutions; and
— a Finance Commission for Panchayati Raj Institutions.

The decentralization of planning for economic and social development and its implementation where relevant was at the core in the earlier attempts on the Panchayati Raj system. It was given further thrust by Article 243-G powers, authority and responsibilities of Panchayats in the Seventy-Third Amendment:

> "Subject to the provisions of the Constitution, the Legislature of a State may, by law, endow the Panchayats with such powers and authority as may be necessary to enable them to function as institutions of self-government and such law may contain provisions for the devolution of powers and responsibilities upon Panchayats at the appropriate level, subject to such conditions as may be specified therein, with respect to:
>
> (a) the preparation of plans for economic development and social justice;
> (b) the implementation of schemes for economic development and social justice as may be entrusted to them including those in relation to the matters listed in the Eleventh Schedule".

It is well known that hardly any progress has been made on the achievements of the above core objectives. The past experience of 45 years reveals, the following main impediments in the proper functioning of the Panchayati Raj system:

(i) Lack of proper understanding of the scope and methodology of integrated-multilevel-decentralized planning at the district, block, village levels, and tasks needed to be performed.
(ii) Restrictions imposed by the government on the panchayats in the performance of their functions.
(iii) Existence of parallel bodies to perform the same functions.
(iv) Lack of technical knowledge and dearth of suitable personnel.
(v) Inadequate financial resources.
(vi) Politicization of the system.
(vii) Unwillingness to grant authority and power provided under the Act to Panchayati Raj Institutions at district, block and village levels by the politicians and bureaucracy.

Unless the above impediments are not removed, the history of failures of the last 45 years will definitely repeat itself.

The Punjab Panchayati Raj Act, 1994, came into force on 21 April 1994 and has been operational for more than two years. Steps taken so far to alleviate the above constraints should be examined.

Article 202: Emergency powers of the State Government contains:

> "If at any time the State Government is satisfied that situation has arisen that purposes of this Act cannot be carried out in accordance with its provision, the State Government may, by notification--
>
> (a) declare that the functions of a Panchayat shall, to such extent as may be specified in the notification, be exercised by such person or authority as it may direct; or
> (b) assume to it all or any of the powers vested in or exercisable by the Panchayat; and
>
> such a notification may contain such incidental and consequential provisions as may appear to the State Government to be necessary or desirable for giving effect to the objects of the notification: Provided that such a notification shall not remain in force for a period of more than six months".

The major difference made in the Seventy-Third Amendment is a time limit imposed on such a notification. This damoclean threat, though time bound, of intervention by the State Government, if used excessively and frequently, can lead to politicization of the Panchayati Raj system and convert the democratic system into an organ of the State power, instead of being a representative of the people.

There are strong fears of the possibility of misuse of powers by the government of various shades. A glaring example is the existence of parallel body of planning at the district level (district planning boards) where the Minister from the area could wield a great influence and can use the discretion excessively, rendering the main aim of planning--to get maximum economic and social returns and benefits from the limited resources--inoperative. Why could the district level planning functions be entrusted to the Zilla Parishads?

The three-tier institutions-district, block, village--have been given a herculean task of planning and implementation of the items relevant for them. There are 29 subjects included in the 11th schedule (Article 243-G) of the Seventy-Third Amendment Act, 1992. They cover almost all the production activities, education, health, welfare, poverty alleviation, infrastructure, public distribution system, maintenance of community etc. These subjects at the State level are being dealt by several ministries/ departments/sections/corporations. The Panchayati Raj Institutions have not been provided any suitable persons to consolidate activities for all these 29 subjects for formulating a meaningful simple, and action-oriented plan. They are expected to depend on the technical staff of the government available at different levels. Is a Sarpanch expected to perform all these functions--a wild dream. Same is the case of Block Samitis and Zila Parishads. *A beginning, therefore, should be made to define the scope and type of plans which are expected to be formulated under the integrated multilevel-decentralized-planning system at district, block and village levels.* Accordingly a core of technical manpower required should be estimated and provided, which should interact with the concerned functionaries of various departments of the government.

The Punjab Government constituted the Punjab Finance Commission under the Punjab Finance Commission for Panchayats and Municipality Act, 1994, on 22 April, 1994--a very timely and prompt action. It is understood that the commisison has submitted its report which is under review of the government. Power vests with those who control the purse. Therefore, severe constraints of inadequate financial resource are yet in force.

There is an extreme resistance to develop authority and power to lower level. The system of retaining power and authority as far as possible at the State level is still in vague. Therefore, there has not yet been any perceptible improvement in the delegation of authority to the Panchayati Raj system as is envisaged in the Seventy-Third Amendment and the State Panchayati Raj Act, 1994.

In nutshell, we are yet in a standstill situation after a period of two years of attempting to rejuvenate Panchayati Raj system. Hardly any perceptible steps have been implemented at the field level. How much should it take long to get the Panchayati Raj system moving towards a full swing? It is time to give a serious thought to it. We should not let the chemistry of events, finds a solution itself. The solution, thus, emerging may not be appropriate. Let not the history of past 45 years of failures repeat, it will be too costly, unwise, and dangerous.

There is, however, one exception—a significant step forward has been taken to increase the awareness and knowledge of the representatives of the Panchayati Raj institutions in respect to:

- provisions under the Seventy-Third Amendment made in the Act, 1992;
- scope and implications of planning and implementation at district, block and village level;
- impediments in the functioning of Panchayati Raj system and evolving suggestions to make the system more participatory, effective and efficient; and
- procedures and contact points to utilize the provisions under the poverty alleviation and other welfare programmes.

The first step was the CRRID/Rajiv Gandhi Foundation Sub-Regional Workshop on Panchayati Raj Institutions, November 24-26, 1994, Chandigarh. The Workshop was attended by about 95 participants, predominantly the representatives of the Panchayati Raj system, some ministers, professionals and politicians. The core paper was Multilevel Planning for Successful Implementation of the Panchayati Raj and Economic Liberalization by N.S. Randhawa and G.S. Kalkat.

As a follow up of this Workshop, it was opportune that Shri Rashpal Malhotra, Director, CRRID, was able to secure a project on "Training and Education of Panchayati Raj Representatives in Punjab" supported by the Central as well as the Punjab Governments. A CRRID Team comprising Shri Kesar Singh, Shri Sukhwinder Singh Johal, and the author, is now conducting Block level workshops. These workshops have already been completed in the Hoshiarpur, Kapurthala and Fatehgarh Sahib districts.

The project in its first phase will cover eight districts of Punjab.

II. Salient Indications from Block Level Workshops for Training and Education of Representatives of the Panchayati Raj Institutions

The workshops at the block level conducted in the three districts have exploded some myths and unfolded some stark realities with regard to the functioning of the Panchayati Raj Institutions. For instance:

(1) A deep seated feeling of *despondency* was noticed. It was expressed time and again that the government system has already so much deteriorated in regard to rampant corruption, malpractices and nepotism that no way appears to be in sight to break this vicious circle—*helplessness*. It was also feared that it could get worst in the future. A very dangerous mindset is in the society and leading to the emphasis on self interest, even using unfair means to match the falling value, system of the politicians and bureaucracy. *It should be a warning sign to the society.*

(2) Shamlat lands (common lands) are main source of the non-tax income of the Gram Panchayats constituting 30 per cent of their incomes. The house tax forms only a very small proportion. These lands are going out of control of Gram Panchayat speedily. There is a widespread practice of their illegal possession, sometimes with the connivance of concerned officers. Litigation to regain control of such lands requires substantial funds and efforts by the Panchayats. Generally such funds are not available with them. Consequently illegal possession of such lands continues and expands, leading to dwindling of the major source of income of the Gram Panchayats. It is an *alarming situation needing urgent attention.*

(3) The system has become extremely politicized. Hardly a neutral Panchayat exists. There are basic compulsions for Panchayats to align themselves to the political parties right from the Panchayat elections.

(4) There is a tremendous financial burden on Sarpanches, in addition to multifarious claims on their time, to provide services and help to the members in respect of litigation, the police cases etc. They are often required to make contributions to the elections of higher political echelon, namely, MLAs and MPs, in their respective areas. They have to provide hospitality to and entertainment of

visiting government functionaries and to give forced donations to the officially supported causes. An estimate of Rs. 1 lac a year is in circulation. Sarpanches have no funds to meet such expenses. These expenses got to be met by them from their own resources or through pilferrages from the incomes, grants and from the funds of schemes/programmes being implemented by them.

Another serious implication is that such heavy expenses bias the system to the better off, as the poor cannot afford to bear such expenses, unless they resort to corrupt and nefarious practices.

One wonders if Sarpanches are undergoing such heavy financial costs and devoting substantial time to the Panchayati Raj system, why they yearn to be. There are several motivations which are embodied in the system itself. The well-to-do Sarpanches find this system to wield power for their personal use as well as Panchayats. Some of them have business enterprises such as contractors and factories and the contacts they make in the government circles through their position, also yield them good dividends. It gives them a political clout. Being sarpanches, they are in touch with upward political hierarchy from which, they draw power and benefits. The selfless service creed which we used to be proud of, if it still exists in some cases, is vanishing fast--*a turbulent scenario.*

(5) Decentralization as practiced in Panchayati Raj system is simply *an illusion*. Panchayati Raj system is being used by the government functionaries as a conduit for poverty alleviation and other welfare programmes/schemes, centrally sponsored or supported by the State government, namely Integrated Rural Development Programme (IRDP), Jawahar Rozgar Yojana (JRY), Employment Assurance Scheme (EAS), Special Area Programmes etc. The government through the bureaucracy has found it convenient to use the Panchayati Raj system in various degrees to implement such programmes/schemes without devolution of authority. This type of arrangement is termed as a *deconcentration*. It does not generally include decentralization of power or authority. It is a process of transferring some functions to the lower levels to decrease the work load of the main authority and to facilitate its functioning without the participation of lower levels in formulating of programmes/schemes and granting them authority--an illusion of decentralization. Thus these institutions provide only supportive and not participatory role.

Even under the prevailing decentralization system, there are wide spread leakages in the channels through which funds move to the beneficiaries under the various poverty alleviation programmes. Rajiv Gandhi in one of the his public addresses lamented that out of a rupee spent on various anti-poverty programmes, 15 paise reached the beneficiaries, the rest 85 paise being eaten up in the process. The studies done on evaluation of these programmes bear the testimony to these tendencies of vast cracks in the delivery system. The CRRID's recent evaluation of IRDP is also indicative of this widespread phenomenon. The continuation of such substantial pilferages over a period of time, have made the beneficiaries very resentful of the system as they feel that they are being cheated out of their rightful entitlement.

In the real decentralization, the devolution in the Integrated-Multilevel-Planning framework, should be the delegation of authority to the lower levels, allowing discretion for decision making corresponding to the decentralization of functions. Though it is a frequent political rhetoric on decentralization in many developing countries, it is seldom fully adopted. The case of India/ Punjab is not an exception. In simple words, decentralization is the replacement of top-down planning approach by planning from below.

The decentralization has now become more imperative with the progress in economic liberalization. With the change over from the socialistic pattern of society of the economy and mixed planning system, the emphasis under liberalization is on privatization to generate growth impulses. The private sector will need prompt action and delegation of authority to the lower level is, thus, a necessity. The diverse policy and planning requirements at various levels, call for a mechanism (including State) that is decentralized enough to cope with the intricacies of the market oriented economy.

(6) Primary education (I to VIII) is one of the three most important basic conditions to accelerate growth and improve the structure of the society. The other two main basic conditions are macro-economic stability and low income inequality. Human capital built through education provides educated and disciplined labour force, make investment more productive, facilitate the transfer and adoption of advanced technology from abroad and within the country, and enhances entrepreneurship. In our education system, primary education receives the lowest priority. It is suffering from several handicaps such as lack of infrastructure (building, black

boards, teaching material, etc.), dearth of teachers particularly with proper mindset, several vacancies not filled specific house rent allowance for teachers in cities/towns, biases the teachers preference towards cities/towns, above all lower priority in allocations of funds to the primary education sub-sector.

(7) The Punjab Congress Legislature party has accused the bureaucracy openly as a main cause of the reverses of the Congress in the recent parliamentary elections. Is not bureaucracy expected to be politically neutral? A Burmese proverb recently quoted by Aung San Suu Kyi (leader of the Pro-Democracy Movement in Myanmar) is very relevant here: "If the roof is not sound, the whole house become vulnerable to leaks. That is to say, if soundness is lacking at the top there are bound to be problems all along the line until the very bottom". The members of the Indian administrative service are supposed to be *creme de la creme* of Indian Intelligentsia (though this version has changed in the recent period because of opening up of more remunerative and challenging opportunities)—extremely intelligent chosen through a competitive system. They are the upper most layer of bureaucracy. With the deteriorating political system, they have to bend themselves under the political pressures. Experience has taught them to be flexible and accommodative than principled and rightist. Those who did not oblige, the politicians, have to bear the adverse consequences. Then why point an accusing finger to the bureaucracy than mending the own house.

(8) The Panchayati Raj system is at the cross-roads. We are to choose a path for progress and development, devoid of corruption, nepotism and venality. For this purpose instead of putting a blame on bureaucracy squarely, political system requires extreme reforms particularly in the code of conduct. A strong and honest leadership at the top is a necessary condition, but it is not sufficient to attain this goal. The other power echelons of the system are to follow the tenets of the leadership. It is a herculean task, but achievable. Nostalgically I am reminded of S. Partap Singh Kairon's achievements during his tenure as Development Minister and later as Chief Minister. Did not he cleaned up the bureaucracy, and motivated them to move on, which put the Punjab on the growth path through consolidation of land holding, rural electrification, supply of power to tubewells, installing surface drainage system, establishing network of rural roads and making effective

arrangement for supply of agriculture inputs. This is to name only some of them. There is a strong lesson in it.

(9) Finally, *awakened Panchayati Raj institutions* could become a very forceful and defining factor in determining success and failure of the various political parties. It is in their own interest that issues concerning them are suitably incorporated in their manifestoes and are truthfully implemented when they come in power.

FOOD SECURITY—CURRENT SITUATION, NUTRITIONAL ASPECTS, HOUSEHOLD FOOD SECURITY, PUBLIC DISTRIBUTION SYSTEM

TEN

FOOD-LIVELIHOOD SECURITY AT THE COMMUNITY LEVEL AND ROLE OF PANCHAYATI RAJ INSTITUTIONS

NEELA MUKHERJEE

Introduction

Food-livelihood security is the key issue for many village communities in India where poor households at the subsistence level, are exposed to acute food-livelihood insecurity in their day-to-day living. In the absence of any institutional safety net, the poor households, not having many choices around, try to hedge against such insecurity, in ways more than one, by going without food and adequate nutrition, by begging, by increasing their borrowings and debt, by mortagaging and selling their little assets, by migrating to other lands, etc. Many such communities face food insecurity on a recurrent basis which adversely affects their nutrition levels, mental and physical health and general sense of well-being. It increases risks and uncertainties in their day-to-day living, impoverishes them and diminishes their capacity of having sustainable livelihoods.

In an age of shifting paradigm of development from 'top down' to 'bottom up', recognition of local level realities is foremost on the agenda of development perspectives. Panchayati Raj Institutions (PRIs) is a way of projecting that reality through local institutional framework for progressing towards community-based sustainable development. PRI stands face to face with grassroot reality and hence is placed in a comparatively advantageous position than other development institutions to influence development from bottom and also generate waves of development from within. It is in this context that PRIs hold the key to progress towards food-livelihood security for its community members on a sustainable basis.

Issues in Food Security

The indigenous knowledge about the varied dimensions of food-livelihood security lies with the local communities. It is they who best know the issues in question, the degree of insecurity involved, nature and frequency, the extent of deprivation, the factors determining it, the coping strategies adopted, and the ways to minimise or resolve such crises. Hence, it is important that they constitute the key actors to any policy intervention at the local level. It is the local level Panchayat which can initiate and implement plants along with the local community for appropriate interventions in approaching food-livelihood security at the local level.

The Dynamics of Food-livelihood Insecurity

The first issue is learning about local community's perceptions on food-livelihood insecurity in a participatory framework. It is they who possess the knowledge to describe the problem best. Generally, it is most convenient for us (as outsiders to local community) to apply a definition of our own to understand the concept of food-livelihood security. By applying a simplistic definition to a multi-dimensional issue, we run the risk of missing vital aspects of such an issue and also distorting local facets of the problems at hand. It is important that we approach local communities who are exposed to considerable insecurity of food-livelihood and ask them to explain the nature of such a multi-dimensional problem. Experience shows that they are not only able to explain the complex problem but also arrive at solutions and recommendations to the problem concerned. Such solutions and recommendations emerging at the local level can then become steps to identify effective ways to tackle the problem of food-livelihood insecurity through local institutions.

Learning from Local Community: The Debilitating Impact of Food-livelihood Insecurity—A Case Study of Arjuni Mouza

The factors determining food-livelihood security can vary from village to village. As long as such factors are not identified by local community, the local dynamics of food-livelihood security remains hidden and not revealed. For instance, in Arjuni Mouza (smallest unit of a sub-division) in Midnapore district of West Bengal, India, where, participatory management in forestry (joint forest management) failed, only recently in 1994, the root cause, as suggested by the villagers is to do with their food-livelihood insecurity. Many of the villagers as landless labourers face acute shortage of food from time to time. The period and timing of such illicit felling of local forest was closely linked to the period when such insecurity was at its peak. Both groups of village men and women were approached in order to learn more about such insecurity.

A group of village women while discussing about food availability and livelihood, did a food calendar on the ground which highlighted critical results. There was a strong factor of 'seasonality' in food-livelihood insecurity of poor people in this area. However, in 1994, the poor community was confronted with acute food shortage, more pronounced than the earlier years.

From the discussions based on the food calendar it was clear that from Vaisakha (mid-April to mid-May) to Sravana (mid-July to mid-August), the poor people in that area worked hard and did farming work for better-off farmers with which they bought food and also saved a little for the difficult months which followed. In Sravana there was greater availability of work due to buoyant farming activities when almost all members of households were generally occupied.

The worst part of the year was during Bhadra to Kartika (mid-August to mid-November) which were critical months since no agricultural or other work was available except for catching fish and selling them in local markets. Such livelihood strategy was quite uncertain and risky since opportunities for catching fish were not available on a daily basis and the returns from such catch was mostly marginal with its low sale price. Some villagers pointed out that during mid-August of 1994 insecurity of food and livelihood was relatively acute as compared to other years and some of those people who were at the brink of starvation resorted to illicit felling of local trees from the forest and sold them in the local markets for meagre amounts. Such felling culminated ultimately into mass felling in a short period of time when the local forest became virtually free for all.

The food calendar indicated that whereas some work was available for the poor in Agrahayana (mid-November to mid-December) in nearby villages, when both men and women found employment, Pausa (mid-December to mid-January), the month to follow was good only for men's work. The poor households did some savings in both the months of Agrahayana and Pausa and also bought corn at cheaper price and stored it for the difficult months which followed. In Magha (mid-January to mid-February) the poor caught fish and sold them as a livelihood, while in Phalguna (mid-February to mid-March) they sold firewood and were able to earn a meagre living. However, in Chaitra (mid-March to mid-April) life became more difficult when income earning opportunities were practically nil and hence purchasing power for food was in short supply.

In an area facing recurrent cycles of food-livelihood insecurity one relevant question is why then the local forest remained intact prior to mid-1994. The village women helped in explaining the same through the help of the seasonal food calendar and compared it with an earlier one that they had done in 1993.

Food Calendar by Village Women in 1993

A food calendar prepared by village women in 1993, highlights three aspects of local community life. One, the knowledge of rural women in the procurement of food; two, their rolé in such procurement of food; and three, the seasonality of food availability, its shortage and the dependence of the villagers on food from commons, forests and 'micro environments'.

A group of village women prepared a food calendar on the ground with 12 stones to represent 12 months. The column heads showed the different kinds/sources of food, while the row heads depicted the different months of the year. Then, with the help of both stones and pebbles they showed their main basket of consumption, the items being rice, potato and pulses where the number of stones indicated the quantum of food. Later they used different kinds of leaves, sticks and twigs of trees to show their supplementary items of consumption such as vegetables, wild leaves, roots, fruits, meat of wild animals, fish, snails and wild water plants. However, weights of the supplementary items were not indicated, availability of which varied from day to day even within a month.

Seasonal Food Variations

The food calendar of 1993, as shown in Chart 10.1 has some important features in terms of food availability. First, the basket of food consumed can be divided into two groups: principal food items (rice, potatoes and pulses) and secondary food items (leaves, fish, fruits and wild animals). And both have critical roles to play in village life. Second, rice consumption reaches a peak in Magha (mid-January to mid-February) after which it declines until Chaitra (mid-March to mid April), to remain stationary until Asvina (mid-September to mid-October), following which it further declines by almost half of the earlier period.

Third, eating of potatoes follow approximately the same trend as rice for the months of Magha and Phalguna and then declines sharply and

CHART 10.1: **Seasonal Food Calendar**

Item/ Month	No. of Stones			Vegetables	Fruits	Food from other sources	Others from Wild
	Rice	Potato	Pulses				
Magha (mid-Jan to mid-Feb)	15	13	3	Cabbage			Wild Borums Wild Rabbits
Phalguna (mid-Feb to Mid-March)	9	11	2	Spinach			'Neem' leaves
Chaitra (mid-March to mid-April)	4	4	2	Pumpkin		Fish and wild water plants	
Vaisakha (mid-April to mid-May)	4	3	1	'Pui' leaves (Herbs)	*Mango *Jack fruit	Fish, Snails and wild water plant	
Jyaistha (mid-May to mid-June)	4	4	2	'Lota' leaves (Herbs)	*Mango *Jack fruit	Fish and wild water plants	
Asada (mid-June to mid-July)	4	3	3	'Jhinga'			
Sravana (mid-July to mid-August)	4	4	5	Papaya			
Bhadra (mid-Aug to mid-Sep)	4	3	3	Green Banana		Fish and Snails	

CHART 10.1 *(Contd.)*

Item/ Month	No. of Stones			Vegetables	Fruits	Food from other sources	Others from Wild
	Rice	Potato	Pulses				
Asvina (mid-Sept to mid-Oct)	4	3	2				
Kartika (mid-Oct to mid-Nov)	2	4	3	Raddish Leaves			
Agrahayana (mid-Nov to mid-Dec)	2	4	5	Tomato			
Pausa (mid-Dec to mid-Jan)	2	9	6	Brinjal			Wild Rabbits

Note: The number specified under Rice, Potato and Pulses represent the number of stones showed by villagers.
*Show fruits of trees growing near-by.

Women village analysis-Namita Mallik, Binapani Dandapat, Pratima Bhakta, Sushila Mallik.

Date: 4.2.1993, Village Krishna Rakshit Chak, Midnapore.

ays at a lower level during the period from Chaitra (mid-March to mid-pril) to Agrahayana (mid-November to mid-December) and picks up ;ain in Pausa (mid-December to mid-January).

Fourth, intake of pulses as a food item touches an 'all time' low in the onth of Vaisakha and is higher in the months of Sravana, Agrahayana ıd Pausa.

Finally, the villagers consume a variety of off seasonal items of food thered from different sources depending on their availability. The deficit the principal elements of food consumption is made good (atleast rtially) by secondary food collected from the forests, common property sources, rivers and the ponds and sometimes even from the market. ost of these sources of food consumption cannot fully compensate for : fall in the 'quality' of food consumption level occasioned by fall in the ailability of rice. Hence there is a sharp fall in the quality food intake ecially around the months of Chaitra to Asvina which is aggravated ring Kartika and Agrahayana as per the food calendar. The women's oup pointed out in course of a semi-structured interview that with oletion of common property resources, forests and degradation of nds, the support received from them during 'critical periods' as sources food has declined considerably over time (3).

e 'Critical Periods' and Support by Wild Food

s significant from columns 2, 3 and 4, of the food calendar that there are 'critical periods', faced by the villagers. The first 'critical period' ur in the months of Chaitra, Vaisakha and Jyaistha, (mid-March to mid-e) taken together, when consumption of rice falls sharply, consumption otatoes come down to its lowest level and level of pulses consumed is k bottom, leading to entitlement failure. The second 'critical period' urs during the months of Asvina and Kartika, (mid-September to mid-ober) where again entitlement failure occurs by a fall in availability of and pulses, and hence by a decline in their consumption.

During the first 'critical period' the produce of the common property urces come to the rescue of the poor villagers. Reference is invited to mns 5, 6 and 7 in this regard. Fish, snails and water plants, collected ı the water bodies compensate, at least partially, the loss in protein in-caused by a fall in consumption of pulses. The reduction in calorie-ke caused by declining rice and potato intake is offset by the availability uits, like mangoes and jackfruits from village commons. Thus bounties ature help the rural poor to tide over the first critical period.

During the second 'critical period', The consumption of pulses fall (reaching 2 in Asvina) and then rises in Kartika but then the consumption of rice reaches the second low plateau (dropping down to 2 from 4 in Asvina). This is also the period when employment opportunities in the rural sector is limited as the harvesting season is yet to start and other economic activities are not enough to provide income to the poor to buy food from the market as well. Unlike the first 'critical period', the second 'critical period' has no safety net from the common property resources (CPRs) and micro-environment to help the rural poor to tide over their 'increased hunger'. Significantly enough this is the time when vegetables and leaves from the CPRs also reach the lowest level. And this incidentally is the period which roughly corresponds with the major festivities of the area, namely, Durga Puja, Bhatri Dwitiya and Kali Puja (Deepavali), which contributes towards increasing the distress of the poor households. Locally available wild food provide a safety net, howsoever, weak, to th poor households in the difficult months when both work and staple foo are at their rock bottom.

Commercialisation of Wild Food after 1993

Earlier, wild food was freely available from farmers' land and other commo property resources and provided food security to poor people in the lea seasons. Free access to wild food dwindled especially since 1994, leadin to increase in food insecurity, at higher levels than other years. As far a farmers' land was concerned, the wild food started getting sold in the lo market by the farmers, causing a phenomenon of 'marketisation' of wi food, to hedge against rising food prices for protecting their real incom The following were some items of such wild food and their market prices the time of visit to that area as indicated in Table 10.1.

TABLE 10.1: **Market Prices of Wild Foods**

Items	Local Price
susn sak	Rs. 6.00/kg
kaln.' sak	Rs. 1.00/3 small bundles
gima sak	Rs. 2.00/kg
thankuni sak	Rs. 10.00/kg (dried ones more expensive)
nate sak	Rs. 3.50/kg
snails were also sold.	

Apart from private lands, wild food also available from common property resources. Of late, with degradation of such resources, availability of wild food from CPRs shrank to a large extent and became negligible. Rural women who were the primary getherers of food were forced to walk long distances for the same. With shrinking supply of wild food their capacity to hedge against food insecurity of their households was enormously strained. Hence poor people in that area were either forced to reduce their consumption of wild food (which was earlier free) by going hungry or buying them (or their substitutes) from the market by generating additional income. However, livelihood opportunities also declined in that year and the food prices were one of the highest during that period. Hence, survival needs became of utmost importance and as an alternative to starvation, many found their way in contingency sale of local plantation (under joint forest management) to feed their stomachs and maintain their day to day existence.

Lessons from the Food Calendar

Some of the lessons to be learnt from the above exercise and the discussions which followed are as follows:

(a) Rural women, in general, are more proficient than rural men in depicting the variety of food which they generally collect from different sources.

(b) The variety of food available and the different sources of food are kept track of generally by the village women whether it is from ponds, river beds, forests, wild trees in the village and from nearby areas. It is they who are the main performers in terms of collection of raw food, fruits, leaves, snails and fishes for meeting food deficits in households (whether by eating less or supplementing from other sources).

(c) The village women try to hedge against low food availability, and tend to switch sources depending on the seasons. It is apparent as shown in the food calendar, that in some seasons more food is available in both quantity and variety such as in the month of Magha (mid-January to mid-February) as compared to the month of Asvina (mid-September to mid-October) when not much food is available from secondary sources.

(d) The concept of food security underlying the food calendar shows that availability of rice, potatoes and pulses provides the primary food security to the people, in the sense that these sources of food are grown by the people by the application of technology (in the economic sense). Columns 6, 7 and 8 of the seasonal food calendar indicate the secondary food security available to the people, in the sense that food available from these sources are bestowed by nature (through the commons, forests and wilderness) without any role for technology in production (again in the economic sense) at a time when primary food security is endangered. Significantly enough the second 'critical period' is the harshest period of the year when even nature does not come to the rescue of the poor.

Implications for Participatory Planning and Action by Panchayati Raj

Taking cue from the experience of village community of Arjuni mouza some lessons can be indicated for Panchayats, at local level, which can help the rural poor households to tackle their food-livelihood insecurity in a substantive manner.

1. It is important to realise for the sake of participatory planning and action by Panchayats, that one set of key informants regarding food security are rural women. They perform a host of activities which are mostly different from those of rural men. Such activities by tradition include collecting fuel and fodder, gathering food from forests and commons, fetching drinking water, cooking, child rearing, household activities and farm operations. Though many of such activities may not be directly visible and tangible in terms of economic gains, it is well accepted that the rural women play a crucial role in food gathering, cooking and distributing which make it important for them to participate in Panchayat planning and action. Hence, it would be a rewarding exercise for the Panchayats to solicit their pariticipation in order to learn about the knowledge gained through performing such activities.

2. Seasonal strategies for food-livelihood security are required to be intensified in consultation with the villagers especially during lean season with seasonal strategies to support livelihood, income and food of poor households of a community. Village community can be involved in raising nurseries for plantation of appropriate species. This would provide them with additional sources of revenues.

3. Participatory sessions with women villagers can be conducted to identify women-managed projects under self-employment programmes or plantation of trees and plants so as to increase food availability and decrease their hardship and uncertainty in collection of food. Practic

suggestions can be sought from the village women not only for planting of (wild) species but more so for their maintenance in order to ensure sustainability. The women can be empowered to collaborate in such projects in terms of their time and skills. Projects like way-side agro-forestry such as one referred earlier, can also be taken up by rural women and can be managed by them. Such agro-forestry projects can include seasonal plants whose flower, fruits, leaves, vegetables, roots and stems can be used to supplement the food intake of the villagers. The village women can suggest the plants which they would like to grow. The time that would be saved by rural women in collection of food can be gainfully utilised by them in looking after such projects and sharing the returns from such projects when available.

4. Immediate needs of individuals are important and may be different from the long-term community-based priorities. Long term gains hardly matter to people who are facing major problems of food-livelihood insecurity. The present Panchayat projects and schemes yielding long term gains, for example, from timber proceeds from social forestry models need to be re-modelled in terms of generating recurrent and short-term food-livelihood benefits to village community, which are immediate and supportive.

5. The fallow land and other selected areas can be planned jointly by the Panchayats with local villagers for eco-restoration. Species selection and plantation can be done by the village community for reforestation of degraded areas in the sanctuary. Such selection can be a mix of species, important to meet the immediate needs of the villagers. The local women groups can play a lead role in such selection.

6. Panchayati Raj institutions at all tiers can plan better supply and distribution through the public distribution system. The emphasis needs to be on the critical periods in the areas concerned when supply of cheap food can be augmented. The local Panchayat can arrange for 'off-season' employment opportunities by implementing vigorously wage-employment generation schemes so that the poor people have greater access to pulses and rice, especially during critical periods.

7. Again strategies are also needed by Panchayats to manage drought situations. As an illustration let us take the case of village community of Kushiara village at Mirzapur. As per the villagers, the local sanctuary (erstwhile forest) provides drought-proofing in terms of food security for survival under drought conditions. Some of the forest food taken by them during drought as described by the villagers are as follows:

— Wild borums fill the stomach and prevent getting hungary for 10 to 12 hours if consumption of such borums is followed by drinking of water after an hour.
— 'Amla'' fruits are combined with whatever little rice/wheat one takes during a drought period. They are boiled, meshed removing seeds and kneaded into wheat flour for making 'chappatis'. This increases the overall quantity of food intake during drought conditions.
— 'Kathmouli' fruits (long hanging black fruits) which resemble tamarind fruits are seen as drought food.
— Other selected wild fruits, leaves, stems, seeds, nuts, roots, etc. are also consumed as food during drought.

Hence, many Panchayats operating in drought-prone areas can plan for meeting drought conditions with the help of local resources and local knowledge. An inventory of action proposed by local villagers can help the Panchayat to do so.

8. There can be several poor groups within the same community and it is important to recognise their identities, needs and priorities regarding food-livelihood security for creating an enabling environment for their participation in Panchayat-meetings and decision-making.

9. Genuine efforts are necessary for the Panchayats for consulting the village community on planning for food-livelihood security and also involving them in such action plans. Such actions are likely to pay high dividends in the long run. The Panchayat leaders can use participatory tools for participating with village community in such planning and action.

10. The Panchayats can evolve some kind of a grain bank from which community members can borrow grains in times of deficit and repay them back when such situation improves. The other action by Panchayat can be in terms of encouraging formation of self-help groups amongst local community members.

11. The Panchayats can emphasize minor irrigation projects in local areas so as to increase opportunities for multiple cropping. This would lend its positive impact on locally available work opportunities.

12. Panchayati Raj does not operate in a vacuum. It is influenced by local needs and priorities in the area concerned. If such forces are not reckoned with then political participation for socio-economic development becomes naive and unrealistic and invariably, becomes unsustainable in the long run. The cross-currents of such variables can make or mar community participation and it is important to recognise the major forces so as to take steps to integrate them into Panchayati Raj or minimise their

distortionary influence over time. Again the communities concerned are the best judge of such factors and it is they who can be approached for evolving locally viable strategies in order to achieve and sustain food-livelihood security.

Survival needs of poor communities are to be recognised by Panchayati Raj institutions on a priority basis as pillars for strengthening community participation. In depressed areas with higher levels of poverty, day-to-day existence becomes uppermost on their agenda for living. The most urgent need of the poor community is that of alternative means of livelihood during lean seasons with agriculture being the mainstay in peak seasons or the poor villagers are left to themselves to cope with acute seasonal food insecurity due to livelihood problems. Options for supporting seasonal livelihood strategies planned by village Panchayat with support from the local State department or NGOs can strengthen the base for community participation. Unless survival needs of food and livelihood for the poor are met, community participation at the local level through Panchayati Raj institutions would run the risk of not being sustainable.

REFERENCES

Mukherjee, Neela (1993), *Participatory Rural Appraisal, Methodology and Applications*, Concept Publishing Co., Delhi.

Mukherjee, Neela (1995), *Participatory Rural Appraisal and Questionnaire Survey: Comparative Field Experience and Methodological Innovations*, Concept Publishing Co., Delhi.

Mukherjee, Neela, (1995), Forest Management and Survival Needs, *Economic and Political Weekly*, December 9.

Mukherjee, Neela, (1996), Resolving People-Sanctuary Conflict in Protected Areas, *Economic and Political Weekly*, January 27.

Mukherjee, Neela & Amitabha Mukherjee, (1994), Rural Women and Food Insecurity, What a Food Calendar Reveals, *Economic and Political Weekly*, Vol. XXIX, No. 11, March 12.

ELEVEN

FOOD SECURITY AND ROLE OF PANCHAYATI RAJ

KAMAL TAORI

Summary of Presentation

Panchayati Raj Institutions used to play a very active role in the holistic sustainable development including food security in India. With the advent of Bristishers, dependence on cities and industrial township increased and villages became supplier of only basic raw material. The value addition of rural raw material got included even after independence with the total scenario of total dependence of villages on cities.

With the effect of education, administration, economic, financial, transport and overall developmental package which were highly in favour of cities compelled the youth and entrepreneurs to leave the villages and migrate to cities for better postures.

This resulted in further aggravating the overall situation in the villages.

The ray of hope lies in Panchayati Raj enactment of the Government of India because of the following reasons:

(1) Constitutionally Panchayati Raj Institutions have been given certain duties, powers, and responsibilities.

(2) Mass aspiration of the villagers make it imperative that Panchayati Raj Institutions perform well.

(3) The development of technology, compulsion of self-employment, higher level of education make it compulsory that Panchayati Raj Institutions take up new and new challenges.

Food Security and Panchayati Raj Institutions

Panchayati Raj Institutions takes over various responsibility in terms of employment, health and they grow as self governing and powerful unit. The question of food security becomes first priority.

Reasons for Importance of Panchayati Raj in Food Security

(1) Panchayati Raj has been given various types of jobs to take infrastructural programmes by planning and implementing them.
(2) They have basic level of entrepreneurship and infrastructure.
(3) The rising expectation need some policy changes to make them more useful.

Policy Changes and Action Plan Required

(1) Our aim should be to develop model where integration of food security and good governance is achieved.
(2) Model is possible only with convergence of various on-going schemes/programmes of various departments of Government of India, State Government, Zila Parishad and the felt need of local Panchayat.
(3) Five basic spirits or forces of policy, effective technology, women and youth, economics and humanity must be integrated through effective marketing compulsions.
(4) The principle should be to do value addition on whatever raw material is available in the rural areas itself. This means *Swadeshi, Swabhiman, Swavalamban* and *Swarozgar.*
(5) The policy changes with reference to funding, technology, vocationalisation, monitoring, follow-up, reward and returns, transparency and viability have to be essential for replicable model.
(6) Value addition on rural raw material means entrepreneurship, risk taking, getting into market, entering into competitive field and constant watch for new development and new projects.
(7) The communication must become effective from the users point of view.
(8) Native ancient practices must be honoured for sustainable and effective food security.

The question of food security would also entail clubbing with biogas, organised maneuver, Neem based programmes and natural inclination to be with nature.

Globalisation and Self reliance concept have much greater role today. For this model have to be developed which bring out seemingly heterogeneity of this concept which became very powerful and unavoidable.

World Today and Need of Panchayati Raj for Food Security

We have various experiences of developmental planning of the last five decades. The developmental models of Communism or Capitalism well enough ensured long term sustainable for society. Whether it is greed or creed both are point to ensure suffering for the masses. It is only through decentralised system of practical self sufficiency which holds the key of sustainability. Both Panchayati Raj and decentralised methods of self-governance offers challenges. The food security is the basic security for the masses. By developing the following it is possible to achieve this in a shorter period.

1. Rural low cost guidance.
2. Rural based value addition technology.
3. Upgradation of traditional methods of storage, cultivation, seeds, insecticides and pesticides.
4. Communication in local language.
5. Dependence on outside production/markets be minimised.
6. Mind set of people of international forum be brought to local condition to understand the compulsions.
7. Low cost practical consultancy.
8. Continuous monitoring systems for further progress of manufacturing, servicing and business activities from the Panchayati Raj angle.

Before conclusion I would like to refer Father of Nation, Gandhiji who was strong advocate of self-governed villages, Panchayati Raj and overall self-sufficiency through self-help for all human beings.

TWELVE

ISSUES OF CONCERN FOR FOOD SECURITY AND NUTRITION (Experiences of Rajasthan State, India)

RAJ BALA

Prepared for National Conference on Panchayati Raj: The Key to Food Security and Nutrition

— New economic policy at State level translated by public representatives and top bureacrat as industrial development. Rajasthan State has declared new road (1995), mining (1994), industrial (1994) and loan policy to attract foreign investment in non-agricultural activities. Agriculture is now a days has taken back seat in the political agenda of the State.

— The land earlier used for agriculture is slowly converting into non-agriculture use. Rajasthan State has created 209 industrial areas. The fertile agriculture land around national highways and district headquarters is changed into industries. The impact of industrial pollution on adjoining agricultural land is not worked out.

— The expansion of large cities is another phenomenon which is pushing agricultural zone far away from core city. Forty-four villages around Jaipur city is taken away for future growth of the city. Rajasthan Housing Board has constructed more than 1.4 lakh houses on agriculture land which is adjacent to towns.

— The slow process of land acquisition for Public interest has made the farmers not to invest in the land where government is planning to acquire. The process takes more than 10 years.

For example in 1988, 11,000 bigha agriculture land is notified for developing urban project. Till today, no payment has been made. In such an uncertain situation, farmers are not investing on land to enhance productivity.

Around Jaipur, the establishment of Leisure city, New Jaipur, Prithvi Raj Nagar, Sirsi and Sitapur industrial area, Jaipur Sewerage treatment plant, Sanganer Rajasthan Housing Board Scheme, is under progress. For all these projects land is required.

— Rajasthan State has largest amount of Wasteland but the efforts made on the waste-land development is on papers only.

— The industries set up outside the municipal limit take up land which is not of immediate use. There is extensive use of land under industries. The land is acquired for future extension or for making profit at the time of industrial crisis.

— The agricultural issues are not tackled on top-priority. No perspective and time bound programme followed by government, e.g. from last five consecutive year Ghaggar River is playing havoc with the Kharif crops of Ganganagar district but no concrete action is taken up.

— There is continuous rise in the inputs of agriculture but the quality and quantity is not maintained e.g. the supply of electricity, quality of fertilizer, quantity of water.

— The land under agriculture is making a slow increase after 1990.

— The grass-root public representatives i.e. Sarpanch (village), Pradhan (block) and Zilla Pramukh (district) are mainly to carry out the social sector programmes for rural areas.

— The First State Finance Commission report (1995-2000) is silent on the role of Panchayat representatives as agriculture developer.

— The different Panchayat level representatives have no administrative and financial infrastructure provided to carry out agriculture related activities.

— The grass-root representative reflect the area characteristics. Therefore, there is a need to translate food security and nutrition concepts into laymen long usage and then make strategies to take this message to them.

THIRTEEN

WOMEN, FOOD SECURITY AND PANCHAYATI RAJ

AMBIKA MENON

Global Developments in Food and Agriculture

Hunger is a man-made problem. The world has enough to feed each man, woman and child. The seed of food deprivation was sown when humankind made the transition from a matriarchal society to a patriarchal one. With this transition, women lost their claim to land, to resources, to food itself. Progressively marginalised, their role in agriculture was seen as secondary and, finally, with the green revolution, almost non-existent. Rendered invisible, they continue to produce half of the world's food.[1]

The seed, though a long time dormant on account of Nature's bounty, has germinated. Natural resources are shrinking. Erosion has accelerated over the past 100 years. The allocation of resources, a decision controlled by men earlier and now by the rich and the powerful of the world, also primarily men, is grossly skewed and the powerless continue to remain bereft. It is no longer just women who have been distanced from productive resources but the food status of 800 million people is critical.[2] The poor starve or are underfed as they lack access to resources, natural or economic.

The annual income of the poorest two billion people is what the "developed" countries spend on military power in a year,[3] an expenditure which brings in its wake untold misery for millions, particularly women. Their bodies are violated and they are left to fend by themselves, with their men dead. The patriarchal world accords them little in terms of ownership or resources. Women own 1 per cent of the land despite being about 50 per cent of the population and doing 66 per cent of the work.[4]

An estimated 800 million people go hungry, largely on account of the North's policy to protect its access to and control over the natural resources of the South and due to the proliferation of wars and ethnic conflicts. At every one of the global conferences, including the recently concluded Habitat II, the North has tried to dilute its responsibility and to impose more encompassing conditionalities on the South. Women are doubly victimised on account of their fundamental dependence on natural resources and on account of gender. NGO forums at each of these conferences have tried to focus on women's particular distress.

Economic fundamentalism fosters and supports religious fundamentalism. The spread of fundamentalism, to some extent, rests on the hunger and deprivation of their constituencies. In terms of suffering and numbers, the worst victims are women. Regretably, there is insufficient gender disaggregated data but it is evident that women and children have been the worst victims of both economic exploitation and conflict.

Natural Resources

Natural Resources, to which the poor once had free access, is being passed off in the interests of the market. Water, fuel and fodder are getting increasingly difficult to access. Distancing women from natural resources on which they have a daily dependence has played a crucial role in the deteriorating quality of their lives and in their ability to provide for their families.

Measures to ameliorate the lot of the hungry and the dispossessed must recognise the special vulnerability of women in this hostile environment if sustainability of food security initiatives are to be ensured. With the pattern of local self-governance which is envisaged under Panchayati Raj, relevant action to resolve the most pressing problem of the people is entirely possible.

The Centre should expedite elections to Panchayats and ensure that the system is in place in every State. The first pre-planning step Panchayats should take is the collection of gender disaggregated data. Only on the basis of gender analysis of such data can development projects be planned with any degree of relevance. Tokenism in areas which we now term women's development, seen as a subset of development, will not lead to progress for all the people; nor will such development be sustainable. Women are the people directly responsible for food and this must be recognised in the fight against hunger.

Investment in Agriculture

Agriculture and Credit

The flow of credit to the rural sector is a serious concern of the new government and the focus is on the needs of small and marginal farmers; but are "small and marginal farmers" only men?

Experiments in extending credit flow to rural areas have failed on account of the inefficient delivery system, political pressure on banks and due to corruption, nepotism and populism. Women were not really in a position to access this credit; and, in the rare instances when they were, often had to contend with the additional oppression of sexual harassment.

Panchayats could play a significant role in ensuring a steady and adequate flow of credit, in monitoring and ensuring repayments and in supervising the delivery mechanism to pre-empt corruption, harassment and bottlenecks. In this connection, it is important to remember that women, because they have no collateral, have little or no access to institutional credit.

Drawing on the experience of the Grameen Bank, Panchayats could ensure an equal access to credit to women. Whatever a woman earns is spent on the family, primarily for food. Credit given to women will find its way more surely into the stomachs of the family than will that given to men. NGO experience with thrift groups and income generation activities substantiates this point.

Fiscal Discipline

Fiscal discipline is vital. Panchayats should monitor repayment schedules efficiently. Repayment, as NGOs have found, is not the central problem. Women are exceptionally disciplined in this respect as has been the experience of the Grameen Bank. Panchayats should soon have the power and the autonomy to militate against corruption and nepotism.

Water and Food Production

Access to Water

It is important, in the context of food security, to focus on water. Water access for agriculture will fall. Access to safe drinking water is diminising as mega projects upstream drastically impact on the availability of water downstream. The needs of rural settlements downstream are not considered in the planning process of large industrial projects. As the friends of the Doon proved in relation to limestone quarrying which had caused Sahasradhara—a thousand springs—to run dry, ecologically unsound development can be halted and, to a great extent, reversed. What is required is the will, the commitment and the endurance.

Lack of sewerage treatment plants and pollution control of effluents renders water downstream disease ridden and poisonous. It also destroys the soil as the villagers living on the banks of the Sone in Shahdol District of Madhya Pradesh discovered. They have organised themselves and protested the pollution of the river by the Orient Paper Mills. The State Government is now providing supportive evidence.

Indiscriminate use of fertilisers and pesticides poisons water in ponds and wells. Some development activities, such as the proliferation of tube wells insome regions, have led to interference with the water table and the drying up of traditional water sources.

Diversion of water is another prime example of unconcern. This pirating of water can and must be stopped. As Ashok Rathi and his small group, the Human Technology Forum, proved, if people stand up for their rights, even large industries have to bow to that pressure.

As pressure mounts to industrialise and to increase agricultural output, these factors will become more widespread. The peasants, powerless, will be deprived of water. Their yields will fall. Unsafe drinking water will prove as life threatening and harmful as insufficient food. Women's access to water is being increasingly restricted. This is adding to their drudgery as collecting and storing water is their responsibility.

Drinking Water

Panchayats could ensure that development projects give priority to the provision of drinking water. With federalism, States will have to follow suit and devolve power and resources to Panchayats. The reduced size of the new Kerala cabinet is seen as a precursor to this devolution. Panchayats will have a say in overall development planning and will be responsible for the implementation of development projects.

They should monitor water quality of the various water sources and take remedial action where quality is found to be deteriorating or unfit for human use. Pollution of water sources must be halted. They should interact with industry and ensure that water is not highjacked from the people or returned to the land as a poisonous effluent. There is no reason why the Panchayati Raj, with its recourse to political and executive power should not be as successful as private initiatives.

Irrigation and Watershed Development

The concept of Panchayat is based on the assumption of genuine dialogue with the people. If Panchayats can actively involve people in watershed development and give them a sense of ownership of the project as have NGOs in the field, the problem of local irrigation can be resolved. The accent of the Panchayat should be on conservation of water. It makes excellent sense to preserve and protect it.

The question of the involvement of farmers has been addressed in the policy document, 'A Common Approach to Major Policy Matters and a Minimum Programme' (CMP). It specifically points to co-ownership and farmer management of irrigation projects. Apart from being farmers, women's special relationship to water for constant domestic use and consumption needs to be considered in the planning of such projects. With sanitation, more water has to be fetched. Participation in planning and ownership rights ought to be ensured to women.

Food Marketing, Processing and Distribution

Cooperatives

Cooperatives are the vehicles for rural marketing; but only after a thorough revamping of the laws governing the system. SEWA, Ahmedabad has done commendable work in this area and their cooperatives are worthy of emulation. Equally, the recent troubles of the Khaira milk cooperatives with regard to government interference is indicative of the dangers inherent in the existing system.

Remodelled cooperatives could be an effective measure against food insecurity. Panchayats could unite and lobby for the necessary changes in cooperatives laws so as to make the system more people-friendly. Panchayats have an important function to ensure that the cooperative sector is a people's initiative and a vibrant rural marketing outlet.

It is important to note that both in thrift and cooperatives, it is women's groups which have been in the forefront despite the lack of an asset base. The benefit has been reaped by their families.

Agro-Based Industries

With the administrative focus on agriculture, allied activities take on new relevance. Further, the CMP makes a commitment to protect village and home based industries. Panchayats can initiate a participatory planning process with the people, all the people, to develop ancilliary industries based on a study of the inputs necessary for improving agricultural production like organic fertilisers and seed banks; and in value addition to the outputs such as food processing. The experience of Israel, a leader in agrotechnology and agroproduction, holds many lessons.

Public Distribution System

On account of domestic and social realities, rural women find it impossible to make repeated forays to the PDS outlet, necessitated by a poor supply system. Consequently, their families are worse off in terms of food access than others.

The United Front governments intention of instituting the system of special cards to families below the poverty line against which they can get essential items at half the PDS price and of excluding the more affluent from the system gives Panchayats a specific role. Panchayats have a responsibility in the meaningful restructuring of the PDS and in weeding out those availing of benefits without entitlement. By its monitoring of the PDS in rural areas, women's access to the national food stock could be ensured.

Lessons from the Green Revolution

The green revolution, inadvertently, led to an erosion in biodiversity as a result of traditional seeds being replaced by hybrids. It interfered with access to and self-sufficiency in seed. Women's most important role in agriculture was demolished. Panchayats, by starting local seed banks and emphasising the importance of variety, can help to reverse the process as have Navdanya in India and UBINIG in Bangladesh. The traditional role of women as seed preservers should facilitate this initiative.

Water sources, too, became polluted as run off from the fields flowed into ponds and tanks and seeped into wells. The proliferation and depth of tube wells had an adverse impact on the water table. Water sources dried up. Women's drudgery increased.

To a significant extent, the poors were displaced as will be evident from the statistics for urban migration. Small farmers, caught in a debt trap, sold their lands as in the command area of the Rajasthan Canal. Consequently, many rural families became female-headed and women faced a situation of responsibilities with no rights; or they became part of the urban poors.

Though the green revolution led to food sufficiency for the nation, it deprived the small and marginal farmers of self-sufficiency in food. Migrants were not in a position to buy their food as their skill was confined to agriculture, a skill which had no urban value. With the mechanisation of agriculture, many became migrant agricultural labourers in a buyer's market. Availability of food did not ensure ability to purchase. Food insecurity grew. The numbers of ill-nourished women multiplied.

Chemical farming ignored the importance of weeds to agriculture and to health. It was the knowledge of these small plants, oral knowledge handed down, primarily from mother to daughter, which had helped traditional agriculture and maintained the health of peasant families. Fortunately, once again, we are beginning to recognise the importance of these seasonal and seemingly insignificant plants.

Men travelled to towns to sell grain or to cities as migrants. Their life styles and needs changed. Often they formed liaisons and sometimes abandoned their families. The women, marginalised from agriculture, were further marginalised in the home.

The green revolution had a widespread impact on women's roles in agriculture. Though it has escaped attention, it took away from women their unofficial control over small kitchen gardens as the economics required that every bit of land go under hybrid seeds. Petty cash no longer came into their hands as they no longer traded at the local markets (*haats*) as bulk produce was sold at larger markets (*mundis*). Men controlled all the money. Women's access to markets and their ability to supplement the family's diet through trade/barter was seriously eroded. Their decision-making powers regarding household resource management diminished. Most significantly, their control over seed was lost.

The impact of the green revolution on women points to the importance of restoring to them their role in agriculture and of recognising and respecting their contribution towards the food sufficiency of their families. They would be a powerful force to combat seed monopolistic moves and for promoting more productive and sustainable practices.

Women need information and encouragement. The will is inherent in them. It would be a tremendous waste of potential if this strength is ignored by Panchayats. It is salutary to recall that when society was matriarchal, we worshipped the Earth and took from it only what we needed. We conserved and were fed. We need to reverse the process of exploitation.

Problems of Security and Ethics

Today, global policies and what nations see as compulsions are leading from biodiversity to chemical diversity. From self-sufficiency, we are moving towards dependency. The most cursory analysis of what has transpired since the Rio Conference will reveal the complete lack of ethics guiding policy and implementation. Is not ignoring gender a lack of ethics?

The Socio-Political and Economic Environment

In India, we have an opportunity, with the devolution of power to local bodies, to correct global policy at the local level. It need no longer be only a small, powerful coterie who decide policy. A surge of people's aspirations, men's and women's, for a life without hunger, can shape local policies.

Action for food security cannot succeed unless it creates a sustainable asset base for the poors, be it the ability to produce or to purchase. The government, starved for funds, cannot invest as much as it should in agriculture. It is necessary to mobilise people to invest in improving productivity, through savings and credit groups. Women's groups are remarkably successful; but if they must invest, women must own the land; not merely have access to it.

Panchayats and The United Front Government

Panchayats can play a very significant role in social mobilisation for action and in enlarging savings and credit activities; but it cannot succeed in doing this unless it recognises women's abilities. If promises are converted to action on the ground, government programmes can be strongly reinforced by this local action; and lead to food security.

From the United Front government's policy document, one fact seems clear: a move to decentralise. The CMP promises to "ensure devolution of administrative and financial powers to Panchayats and Nagarapalikas in all the States". Concern is evident regarding ownership of productive assets. The CMP recognises the need for land reforms and a more just and gender equitable distribution of all resources. In this exercise of redistributive justice, Panchayats can ensure that women, too, are equal beneficiaries.

Panchayats and Land Reforms

Land reforms are an important area of action for the new government. Land is the asset base of the peasant, the foundation of her/his food security. Panchayats can play a key role in distributive justice by ensuring that there is no caste or gender bias in the distribution of land.

Women's right to land has escaped attention. This anomaly has to be corrected, particularly in the context of the feminisation of poverty and the proliferating numbers of female-headed households. To an extent, food security for a third of the poors can be ensured by bringing these women into the ambit of land distribution. Women are much more likely to stay with the land, to put off migration as the very last resort, than are men. Land in their name is less likely to be sold.

Panchayats would be strengthening themselves if they strengthen the hands of women. If the United Front government is truly "representative, responsible and responsive", it will have to respond to the needs of women and play a responsible role in their upliftment. Genuine concern for the representation of women in decision making forums will have to be translated into providing them an enabling environment, a sense of belonging. Panchayats are the instruments to effect this change.

As long as women are condemned to a position where they have to leave when told to get out, there is no place for decision making in their lives. They must own an asset base from which they can act; and they will, as was proved in the Panchayat elections in Kerala. Education and awareness made the difference.

It is time that we realised that it is not reservations but empowerment which is the surest means to upward mobility. Panchayats can help to create the climate for such empowerment, a step which will make of women more efficient farmers and better providers of food to their families and themselves. With their knowledge of traditional farming and their new found understanding of transactions and the market, they will be the best agents for food security in the Panchayat area.

Panchayats and Education

The question of empowerment leads to the panchayat's role in education. With the commitment to the fundamental right to education declared in the CMP, primary education should become a Panchayat responsibility. An interesting NGO experience has been that mothers are excellent supervisers of schools though they themselves may be illiterate. It is they who have to take on the extra chores to free their children to attend school and it is they who are in a position to monitor truancy. Being illiterate themselves, they are constantly aware of their handicap and have a respect for empowering knowledge.

The importance of knowledge to them is its relevance to their lives. The present thoughtless uniform syllabus does not lead to this. The syllabus for rural primary schools should be altered to suit rural life styles. Panchayats could draw on the Mahatma's concept of Basic Education and introduce those activities which would empower the child to grow into a literate farmer. Not only mothers but the whole community will then be involved in education and the goal of such education would be an empowered and productive farmers, a vital step towards food security.

Education should be seen as the most efficient way to greater productivity and self-sufficiency and tailored to suit that objective. We are already using too much of the land. The demands on water are growing. Population pressure is increasing. Relevant education alone holds out hope for increasing food production.

Panchayati Raj and Development Programmes

The Panchayati Raj has an important role in development. The objective of introducing the system was to ensure grassroots involvement. Grassroots involvement does not mean dialogue only with the men of the community, as is usually the case. It should be mandatory to examine gender disaggregated data to decide who is to be consulted, whose needs require immediate response and whose opinion commands weightage in particular interventions. Who does what and for whom ought to be analysed.

The Panchayat should give thought to the question of how it is going to ensure the active participation of women in its planning and activities. It is not a matter of numbers but of whose voice is heard. Effort will find ample reward, for it is women who are most directly concerned with food security and who will cooperate willingly in efforts to ensure it. They have proved their capacity to build and to manage.

Food Security Assessment

In the assessment of food security, scant attention has been paid to women as producers or as victims. If we ignore the role of half the people involved in food production and consumption, how can we make a realistic assessment of the situation? It is only with complete data that we can make a correct assessment.

Women's Special Role in Agriculture

Apart from their role as food gatherers, women play a considerable role in agriculture. In India, in particular, women are not seen as farmers though they produce a major share of the family's food. The agricultural sector does not cater to any of their needs as farmers: not inland entitlements or access to productive resources or water. They are ignored in the designing of agricultural tools and implements and in the area of agricultural research. They do not figure in the reckoning of agro-based industries. Women, though they contribute over two-thirds of the labour, are not visible in agriculture.

It is important, in terms of food security, to note what the women would grow. Before the advent of the green revolution, women usually had a patch of land in which they grew more nutritious food than the bulk cereal. They practiced multicropping and rotation of crops, practices which point to better food and nutritional status.

Their most important role in agriculture was that of choosing and preserving the seed for the next sowing. Hybrid seeds ended this role but it would be a wise move to reinstate it by creating local seed banks. Voluntary agency efforts in this area, particularly that of Navdanya and Auroville, have shown that traditional local seeds are hardy and require the least external inputs. That quality of grain suits the dietary pattern of the people.

Panchayats can support and encourage the setting up of such seed banks by women. The traditional dietary pattern was more nutritious. The crops, more resistant to the vegaries of climate, should be reintroduced and healthy agricultural practices such as crop rotation, green manuring and multicropping should be promoted ana reinforced.

Women and Wage Labour

When they engage in wage labour, women are seldom paid the mandatory minimum wages. They face harassment and discrimination. They have not the time to organise and agitate for their rights or to protest against rampant sexual harassment on account of their triple roles. This lack of solidarity evident in the membership profile of trade unions, renders women fair game for exploitation.

Where there are development projects requiring wage labour, Panchayats should monitor payments to ensure that women are not discriminated against. There is adequate legislation to protect women but the will to enforce it has been deficient. In the matter of fair wages, the government is as culpable as the private sector, if not more so in that it is not implementing the very laws which it legislates.

Male Migration and Its Impact on Women

When rural families are dogged by food insecurity or an alarmingly deteriorating standard of living, the men tend to migrate to urban centres in search of job opportunities or wage labour. When men migrate, they leave the women and children behind. The latter wait for the monthly remittances to buy food. If remittances are not forthcoming, as is often the case, the women have to manage as best they can. Apart from availability and access, a disproportionately large number of women suffer from lack of means to buy food.

Rural women from female-headed households do not have the option of migrating in search of a job. They have to eke out a living in an unsupportive environment, both physical and patriarchal. Though sufficient gender disaggregated data is not available and impacts are still in the process of emerging, it is now being accepted that the new economic policy has had a more negative impact on women, particularly in the context of their already subaltern position in society. It is important, for ensuring food security, to take cognizance of women's special vulnerabilities and needs and of their abiding responsibility as victuallers.

Food Insecurity and Women

Food insecurity effects women the most. For them, opportunities and choices to tackle this problem are extremely limited. In poor families, it is women who have the least food, who eat last. Earlier women foraged in the nearby forests for leafy vegetables, berries, mushrooms, honey and fruits. The forests have all but disappeared. Where women do enjoy access to forests, they are often harassed by the forest department. This avenue for supplementing food and enhancing its nutritional value is fast disappearing. The condition of women is made worse by their powerlessness.

With the provisions under the Panchayati Raj, the possibility for reversing this condition is evident. As the persons directly responsible for household resource management, women, empowered, can be easily motivated to take action towards food security.

Women's Status

The Panchayati Raj Department can open the doors to power and decision making forums to women. Further, by recognising women's important role in agriculture, the Panchayats can identify and focus on the specific needs of women for access to productive resources; and to the enhancement of their skills. Panchayats could ensure a more significant role for women in the Panchayat and in the forums under its supervision such as Joint Forest Management. By recognising that women do almost two-thirds of the work and need the knowledge and the tools to upgrade production, they could influence agricultural research initiatives and tool design—and, in the process, production.

Success Stories

The experience of Pani Panchayats in Maharashtra in water, of SEWA—Ahmedabad in organising the unorganised sector, in banking and cooperatives and of Annapurna Mahila Mandal and SEWA—Lucknow in income generation have some visibility but there are many smaller initiatives, involving women, that could provide guidelines. These need to be identified and studied and replicated with necessary modifications. Panchayats should try to create data banks so that information is available to all who seek it. Women are particularly starved of information and dialogue, especially in the *purdah* regions of the country.

Grain Banks

There are several voluntary agency initiatives which have been successful in ensuring a measure of food security, many of them, a reintroduction of older practices. One of the most significant has been the concept of grain banks. Latterly in disuse, it is a familiar concept. There is no dependence on outside agencies such as banks. It is run and controlled by the people themselves and it deals in a currency they are familiar with, which they can evaluate and directly used. In villages where grain banks have been established, and sometimes in the surrounding villages, people have not had to face hunger.

Women, left to tend the home farm or as heads of households, are equal partners and have equal access to the benefits. It has been found that women are good managers of grain banks. Both Agragamee in Kashipur and Gram Vikas in Kalahandi have had rewarding experiences with this initiative. Many NGOs, all over the country, have embarked on this intervention.

Prior indebtedness would make contributions to the grain bank an unbearable hardship for the poor unless measures to increase productivity are instituted simultaneously.

Rural Banks

Agricultural credit need not wait on the government. Initiatives such as the SEWA Bank and the Grameen Bank, both intended to be women-oriented, have shown the way. Women have excellent fiscal discipline. Timely and sufficient credit will be a great incentive to greater production. Panchayats could sow the seed by promoting and supporting self-help groups.

Rural banks may grow out of a federation of self-help group as is evident from SPARC's study of women's access to credit. The Creditwatch Consultations of Swayam Shikshan Prayog, facilitated by SPARC, have indicated the wealth of successful and innovative initiatives in the area of savings and credit, which could serve as a resource pool for Panchayats. Women, all over the country, have created a space for themselves and for their empowerment.

Food Aid

Food aid is vital in times of natural and manmade calamities; but, prolonged, it can vitiate the capacity of the people to produce their own food. If a country has had to resort to food aid, it is inevitable that there will be more women that men in the surviving adult population though sufficient gender disaggregated data is not available to support this contention. It is important that remedial interventions target women so that they may be enabled to produce enough food for themselves and their children.

Food Production and Population Growth

Though food production has registered enormous bouyancy over the past 50 years, the time has come when the population growth will outstrip t, particularly in the food insecure countries of the world. The only solution is to increase productivity and take measures to minimise population growth.

The demographic profile, too, is changing. As the world gets richer the numbers of those who are haunted by hunger increase. In these increasing numbers, women occupy a particularly vulnerable position. The feminisation of poverty is an accepted fact but poor women labour under a double burden, pauperisation and gender.

Productivity will rest on the introduction of sustainable farming practices. Productive land has actually diminished and we cannot fell forests if we want to protect an already fragile Earth. Water is an increasingly scarce resource and there is a real fear that we are already tapping fossil water sources. High external inputs of chemical fertilisers, apart from its undesirability, require irrigation. Irrigation at such levels is no longer feasible. There is only one option: sustainable agriculture. Women, as the experience of NGOs in Africa has proved, are willing to put in the extra labour and are able participants.

With the increasing emphasis on education, there is hope that the population growth will stabilise or even reverse. Kerala is evidence of the correlation between women's education and population growth. If advocates of population control continue to address only women, they are either ignorant of social conditions or wilfully hypocritical. In a society where women have no control over their bodies and religion plays a crucial role in family size, men have to be educated.

Health affects population growth. The promised health centre for every 5000 persons, if it is properly staffed and supplied, may help. Primarily, ill-conceived schemes like Norplant should not be introduced as it erodes the credibility of the family planning exercise. It is recognised that a women's access to health care is severely limited and practices which put her health in additional danger ought not to be promoted.

Impact of Food Production on the Environment

The increasing demands of agriculture and industry have had a disastrous impact on the environment. We are faced with depleting natural resources and an ever widening ecological imbalance. Women as food, fuel and fodder gatherers, are particularly distressed by this development.

Women and Natural Resources

Women are the first victims of ecological imbalances. Lack of access to resources impinges directly on their time to engage in wage labour. This reduces their earning capacity and, by extension, their buying capacity. The hardship caused directly to women by limestone quarrying activity in the Doon Valley and resultant distancing of water, fuel and fodder is typical of the particular deprivations women have to face as a consequence of ill-conceived industrial activity and environmental destruction.

Slash and Burn Practices

The practitioners of *jhum* or *bogoda* are the very people who, are the most food insecure. Women enjoy greater control over these lands and its precipitate erosion affects them directly. Yet they are compelled to persist because they have been driven to the most marginal and hostile lands; pushed back, inexhorably, from the more fertile tracts and the plains. It is a desperate effort to produce food to keep starvation at arm's length.

To halt the practice, women should be given more viable land, with titles. It is not that the people do not know sustainable practices for they are its authors. It is that they have no alternative. Since we created their distress, it is for us to find the remedy.

Where their foreparents have domesticated every one of the foods we eat and the animals which serve us, we with all our science and technology, have not domesticated a single additional strain.[5] All we have done is that we have taken their achievements and their lands. The least we can do is to ensure their achievements and their lands; and the least we can do is to ensure their food security for it is they who have given it to us.

Food Production and Nutrition

It is not enough that sufficient food is produced. There must be assured availability, access and the power to purchase it. In the process of the green revolution, a subtle change has been effected in the eating habits of the rural people. From the more nutritious millets and tubers, they have moved to hybrid rice. This change has affected nutrition adversely. Women's health has been the most affected. Malnutrition has made inroads into productive capacity.

Panchayats can play a role in promoting those traditional crops which had more nutritional value. Further, where it is no longer possible to supplement the diet by gathering from the forests, the concept of a nutrition garden and the promotion of fruit trees and berry plants in agroforestry would improve the nutritional status of the people. It is possible to incorporate food production and attention to nutritional value by an informed mix of planting activity.

Agricultural Research

The experience of Israel where the *kibbutz* served as an agricultural research station should be a pointer to Panchayats when they liaise with agricultural institutions. Research should serve the farmer. Research stations should identify the needs in the field and seek solutions which are relevant to field conditions. Too often they prescribe a general panacea without taking into consideration the local ecological and environmental balance and fuel and fodder requirements. This factor has a direct impact on women and yet, few if any agroforestry or crop rotation patterns are planned on the basis of their compulsions to collect these items.

Traditional practices ought to find wider promotion, acceptance and application. In the area of agriculture, one of our greatest follies has been the devaluation of traditional knowledge and practices, both outcomes of centuries of experiment and experience. The greater illiteracy in women and their lack of access to information has helped them to preserve this knowledge. The oral tradition has persisted from mother to daughter. Agricultural research needs to take cognizance of traditional practices and women's knowledge.

The worst victims of value-neutral research have been women who, through illiteracy and the social practice of marginalising women, are starved of all information. They are not in a position to make an informed choice and are debarred from even the village discussions where new interventions are analysed. Yet, women farmers are the best conservationists, the last to give up traditional practices and in the forefront to reinstate them as has been UBINIG's experience in Tangail, Bangladesh.

Women play a central role in food production and food management. Panchayats would do well to harness their power for development in its efforts to ensure food security. While planning interventions to counter food insecurity, panchayats should bear in mind that women are not only producers but also reproducers. What they reproduce, they protect and nourish. Food security, for them, is a central concern. This unique culture of women has to be recognised if strategies to combat hunger are to prove effective.

Though the original concept of Panchayati Raj has been diluted, there is still enough teeth in it to make a sizeable dent in the problem of hunger. Today, with the government accent on social justice and agriculture, the Panchayats are happily placed to play a central role in assuring food security.

With the government's stated concern for women's representation in all facets of national life, there is no reason why the rural women should continue to be ignored. With the projected devolution of power and funds to local bodies and the emphasis on grassroots planning, Panchayats must empower themselves to discharge this role with efficiency, with understanding of the needs of all the people and with a sense of commitment and responsibility.

Panchayats have to motivate themselves to rise out of the quagmire of *laissez faire* and gender blindness which have been the hallmark of governance in this country over the recent past. They should judiciously exercise the powers for change vested in them, by the people and the government. If they fail, history will judge them severely for they would have failed despite an enabling environment. If they succeed, as they ought, the country will be on its way to food security for all.

REFERENCES

1. UN Statistics.
2. FAO, World Food Summit Secretariat
3. "Social Integration", 1995... World Summit for Social Development
4. UN Statistics
5. Bernard Declercq's synopsis of Le Sol, La Terre et les Champs by Claude Bourguignon.

FOURTEEN

PANCHAYATI RAJ—THE KEY TO FOOD SECURITY AND NUTRITION

SHASHI PRABHA GUPTA

Nutrition and national development have been recognised as two sides of the same coin. Without adequate nutrition the development of the human resources of a country cannot be at its best. The nutritional status of a community particularly of its vulnerable groups comprising children, expectant and nursing mothers has been recognised as an important indicator of national development and the measurement of national development is by social development indices. The varying degrees of malnutrition among children and women determine the morbidity and mortality rates in the country such as Infant Mortality Rate, Mortality Under 5 years, Maternal Mortality Rate, Crude Death Rate and Life Expectancy at Birth—the indicators which reflect the development of a country. Thus, "nutrition" emerges as one of the most important pre-requisites for national development.

Nutrition has always been a priority for India. The Constitution of India in Article 47 recognises the responsibility of raising the level of nutrition of the people among its primary duties. Nutrition was considered as an important outcome of various developmental plans and nutrition as a separate chapter started appearing since VI Five-Year Plan highlighting its importance in the national development. The Minimum Needs Programme started in the V Five-Year Plan also included Nutrition as its important component. The adoption of the National Nutrition Policy in 1993 by the Government reflects the vision and abiding interest of the planners and the policy makers as well as nutrition scientists in nutritional welfare of the country. The Nutrition Policy recognises nutrition as a multisectoral issue and also that nutrition affects development as well as development affects nutrition. The multi-sectoral strategy advocated by the Nutrition Policy highlights the importance of direct nutrition interventions for specially vulnerable groups as well as through various development policy instruments which will create conditions for improved nutrition. The policy has identified key areas for action in various spheres like food production, food supply, education, information, health care, rural development, women and child development, people with special needs, and monitoring and surveillance.

In order to translate the Nutrition Policy into forceful, viable sectoral programmes, a National Plan of Action on Nutrition has been developed and released in April 1995. This comprehensive document encompasses the role of 14 concerned sectors of the Government like Agriculture, Food, Education, Civil Supplies, Health and Family Welfare, Information and Broadcasting, Food Processing Industries, Environment and Forest, Labour, Welfare, Rural and Urban Development and Women and Child Development in achieving the goal of optimum nutrition for the people. The programmatic thrust on nutrition requires a strong interface between all these sectors.

The implementation of National Nutrition Policy envisages emphasis on issues like creation of National and State Nutrition Councils, Inter-Departmental Coordination Committees at Central, State and District levels, Special Working Groups in the concerned sectors, Mobilisation of resources for nutrition components and monitoring and nutrition surveillance of the population. The Department of Women and Child Development being the nodal Department for coordinating the implementation of Nutrition Policy through the concerned sectors of the Government proposes to set up a National Nutrition Policy Cell, headec by an Additional Secretary, to be devoted exclusively for the purpose o nutrition promotion. A major task for the Nutrition Policy Cell will be tc ensure that nutritional objectives are not only articulated in variou developmental/sectoral plans and policies, but are also matched by plan of actions and there is close coordination between these sectors t achieve the goals set in the National Nutrition Policy.

Expanding the Nutrition Intervention Net through ICDS so as t cover all vulnerable children in age group of 0-6 years and the expectan and nursing mothers, has been the mandate of the Nutrition Policy. Th ICDS which aim to improve the nutritional and health status of vulnerabl groups including infants, pre-school children, pregnant and lactatin mothers through providing a package of services that include supplementary nutrition, pre-school education, immunization, health chec up, referral services and nutrition and health education, is now increasingl being recognised as the most viable vehicle for achieving the National Nutrition Goals by the year 2000 A.D. The Nutrition Goals can be summed up as under:

— Ensuring household food security.
— Reduction in prevalence of Protein Energy Malnutrition, chronic undernutrition and stunted growth among pre-school children particularly among 0-2 years old.
— Reduction in incidence of low birth weight to less than 10 per cent.
— Elimination of blindness due to vitamin 'A' deficiency and reduction of Bitot's Spots in pre-school children to less than 0.5 per cent.
— Reduction in iron deficiency anaemia among pregnant women to 25 per cent.
— Reduction in prevalence of IDD to less than 10 per cent.
— Communicating basic nutrition information to all.
— Ensuring nutrition and health care of adolescent girls.
— Upliftment of quality of life of rural women.
— Taking care of the elderly—particularly the women.

The achievement of these goals would also help in achieving the goals of reduction of Infant Mortality Rate (IMR) to less than 60 per 1000, reduction in Child Mortality Rate (CMR) to less than 10 per 1000, and reduction in Maternal Mortality Rate (MMR) by at least 50 per cent by 2000 A.D.

The ICDS Scheme which started in1975-76 in just 33 blocks in the country has now been universalised during 1995-96 and all the 5,291 Community Development Blocks and 310 Major Urban Slums have been sanctioned ICDS projects in the country. Thus, by the end of the VIII Plan (from March 1997), the ICDS scheme will provide vital services to about 5.4 crores beneficiaries including pre-school children, pregnant women and nursing mothers. The National Evaluation of ICDS carried out in 1992 has identified various striking aspects of the ICDS scheme. The maximum impact of the scheme is clearly reflected insignificant decline in the severely and moderately malnourished children in the country as also in significant decline in Infant Mortality Rate (IMR). Thus, bridging the nutritional needs of the vulnerable groups namely infants, pre-school children, school children, adolescent, expectant and lactating women by way of supplementary feeding should be viewed as an emergency food requirement since malnutrition is a silent emergency and neglect of the same could push the vulnerable groups into a stage of no return.

Utilising ICDS scheme for achieving the National Nutritional Goals would require focussed attention on specific areas like reaching the adolescent girls, sharing the cost on account of supplementary nutrition, streamlining the flow of funds, setting up of District Women and Child Development Cells (DWCDs) in the DRDAs, providing chreche service at the Anganwadies, revitalising the training of ICDS functionaries, increasing the number of ICDS supervisors for effective supervision and involving the community in the monitoring through IMY groups. The IX Plan proposals give due emphasis to these issues in the implementation of ICDS.

The Adolescent girls will be included within the ambit of ICDS so that they are made ready for safe motherhood, their nutritional status is improved and they are given some skill upgradation training with special emphasis on nutrition and health awareness. The adolescent girls also constitute an important resource in the community which need to be utilised for improving the outreach of services. As per the schematic norms, while operational costs of an ICDS project are met by the Central Government, the State Governments are required to make provisions for supplementary nutrition. Due to financial constraints, the sanction and operationalisation of ICDS projects have been invariably delayed by the States, thus affecting the delivery of vital services under the programme. The Central Government, therefore, proposes to share the 50 per cent of the cost of supplementary nutrition component with the State Government.

The setting up of District Women and Child Development Cells (DWCDs) in the existing DRDAs in all the 515 districts in the country is envisaged to streamline the flow of funds to the ICDS projects directly.

The involvement of community and the Panchayats in monitoring the services under the ICDS is envisaged through Indira Mahila Yojana (IMY) Scheme. The Scheme aims at organising women at the grass-root level to facilitate their participation in the existing interventions of the Government. The IMY launched in 200 blocks in August 1995 aims at convergence of services of different departments of the Government, awareness generation among women and economic empowerment of the women. There will be representation from the local Panchayats in the IMY groups. The women groups created under IMY would also have a role in formulation of the district level plan reflecting women's priorities.

The training activities at different levels would be revitalised and women Panchayat members would be involved in various training programmes.

The concept of 'Grain Banks' at the community level involving the active role of Gram Panchayats is also under consideration to ensure household food security for the people.

The consumer awareness/nutrition education of the people for improving household food security and intra-familial food security deserves a multipronged programme for ensuring nutritional security of the individuals. A due place to this important aspect needs to be given in the efforts towards ensuring Household Food Security.

Role of Concerned Sectors in Achieving Household Food Security

The achievement of household food security requires commitment and inputs from a variety of sectors, particularly, the Agriculture, Food, Civil Supplies, Food Processing Industries, Rural Development, Women and Child Development and the Media. The role of all the players is equally important in achieving household food security. In the first instance there must be adequate production of various foods with special emphasis on pulses, coarse grains, oil seeds, milk and milk products, fruits and vegetables rich in B-carotene (vitamin 'A'), iron, vitamin 'C' etc. These foods must be made available to the people at affordable prices and in remote areas through PDS infrastructure. Further, the people must have the purchasing power to procure the available food. Awareness about right type of foods for meeting the nutritional requirements of different age groups is also essential to enable them to make right choices from the available food. Once the food is procured in the family, the intra-familial distribution among various members belonging to different physiological age groups according to their nutritional needs is also important.

Post harvest technology, building infrastructure to reach perishables to the market are also important issues to take care of the horticultural products. Thus, various sectors like Industries, Rural Development, Women and Child Development etc. are involved in increasing the production, the availability, the purchasing power, the utilisation and consumption by the most needs age groups. Some of the main issues that needs tc be taken up by the concerned sectors are as under:

(i) Agriculture

To augment the production of pulses, millets and oil seeds, milk and milk products etc., besides sustaining foodgrain production through measures like multi-crop management, transfer of technology etc.

To increase the production of fruits and vegetables rich in B-carotene, iron and vitamin 'C' through nutrition oriented horticultural activities including home gardening and agricultural extension and to control prices so that these are available at affordable prices.

(ii) Food

To ban the export of pulses, provide foodgrains to common people at affordable prices and build adequate grain storage infrastructures.

(iii) Civil Supplies

To ensure effective and speedy implementation of Revamped Public Distribution System and provide a better package as per the nutritional requirements.

(iv) Food Processing Industries

To promote production of low cost processed nutritious foods.

(v) Rural Development

To make concerted efforts to improve the purchasing power of the people.

(vi) Women and Child Development

To care for the Nutritionally Vulnerable Groups and to create Nutritional Awareness among the people through inter-personal as well as mass media approach so as to enable them to make right choices from the available food.

FIFTEEN

DEVELOPING A SYSTEM FOR MANAGING FOOD SECURITY THROUGH PANCHAYATI RAJ

RANJAN MOHAPATRA

Problem of Food Security: An Analysis

The problem of Food Security is rooted in,

(a) food production in and around the centres for consumption,
(b) income generation for the poor to have purchasing power to buy food.

Food production is dependent upon, land holding, cropping practices, climatic conditions, technical and market support available etc.

Income generation is dependent upon the availability of economic activities in or around the Panchayat, which again depends upon the natural resources, processing skills and the marketing support available.

The responsibility of addressing these issues lies with the Government (both Central and State) and the Panchayats.

But the centre of Action is the Village Panchayat.

Panchayati Raj after the 73rd Constitutional Amendment, is the local Self-Government with authorities and responsibilities to look after the needs of the population living in a Panchayat. Food being the primary need of the people, providing adequate to the people the year round, it can be made the primary focus of the Panchayat Management. All other developmental programmes and activities can revolve around Food Security.

The process of planning, implementation and control of a system for organising food production and income generation (preferably from food production and processing and marketing) can best be organised in the micro-level at the Panchayats, the primary grass-root level organisation, with the support from the higher-ups.

The Strategy Proposed

To make the Panchayat Management, achieve food production to meet the total demand of all the families in a Panchayat based on the natural resources available or provide income needed to purchase necessary food.

The Issues Relevant for Implementing this Strategy

(a) Capacity of the Panchayats to plan and implement the food production and income generation.
(b) Market Intelligence System to support the planning and implementation of development and food security programmes.
(c) Integrating the planning process of the Panchayats with the National level planning.
(d) Work culture in the Panchayats and the level of trust and confidence of the Government officials in the Panchayat Management.
(e) Technical inputs for food production enhancement.
(f) Marketing of food products.
(g) Political will.

Action Plan Recommended

1. Make each Panchayat assess the food required and income needed to purchase required food for each family per year, assess the expected annual food available per family.
2. Calculate the surplus or deficit and plan for the food production in deficit Panchayat and marketing of the surplus food of the surplus Panchayat.
3. The Panchayat-wise demand, supply of food, surplus or deficit to be fed in a National level data bank through NICNET, to be used for a micro level planning for

   (i) food production, and
   (ii) marketing.

Food production plan to be supported by Technical experts from the Government.

In addition to the above,

(a) develop market intelligence through NICNET for all food products and make it available to all Panchayats.

(b) develop data on Panchayat-wise climatic conditions, which can be used by agriculture scientists for assessing the potential food production like, cereal, grams, fruits/nuts, vegetables etc.

4. The data from above will provide a clear picture of the region-wise surplus/deficit position for each product category, which can be a base for formulating strategies for,

   (a) movement of foodgrains,

   (b) processing of food items, branding and marketing them through appropriate channels to provide best returns to the producers, employment to the labour involved in food processing and marketing.

   (c) Developing new cultivation of food products based on climatic conditions and R & D to meet the local food needs.

5. Provide technical inputs for food production enhancement.
6. Provide management training to the Panchayat officials for managing the whole process of planning, implementing and control. (*Capacity building*).

Organisation Needed to Manage the Programme

The organisation needed to implement this programme should have specialists and divisions in agriculturists, marketing experts and the structure can be;

National Co-ordinator (All Co-ordinators to be professional with accountability)

—NICNET (info. planning, implementation and control)

—Agricultural Scientists

—Management Experts

—Marketing Experts

State Co-ordinators State Co-ordinators State Co-ordinators

District Co-ordinators District Co-ordinators District Co-ordinators District Co-ordinators

Panchayat Panchayat Panchayat Panchayat Panchayat Panchayat

(Entire structure connected through NICNET)

Activity Flow

Panchayat	*DC*	*SC*	*NC*
Planning, for food production and income generation	—Marketing support —Storage support —Market Intelligence support	Policy support Financial support	Policy support Fin. support
—Implementation	—Training support —Techical support for food production		

NGOs can effectively contribute in the process of planning and implementation by adopting a Panchayat, even Corporate Houses can contribute by adopting a Panchayat or a District.

Note:

DC: District Coordinator

SC: State Coordinator

NC: National Coordinator

SIXTEEN

INTEGRATING DISASTER MITIGATION WITH FOOD SECURITY AT PANCHAYAT LEVEL

MIHIR R. BHATT

Though supply of food remains on the top of the relief list after natural or manmade disasters, integration of food security with disaster mitigation remains a rare idea, even in the provisional version of the draft declaration of World Food Summit (scheduled 13 to 17 November, 1996, Rome) titled "Towards Universal Food Security: Draft of a Policy Statement and Plan of Action". This is a matter of concern. Even more so at local level. The ANGOC-FAO organised consultation of more than 100 NGOs from the Asia and the Pacific in Bangkok, Thailand, 29-30 April, 1996, discussed the said draft declaration around five themes: (1) Role of Civil Society People's Participation and Gender Equality; (2) Empowerment through Access to Resources; (3) Sustainable Paths to Food Security; (4) Trade and Investments; and (5) Food Emergencies and Preparedness. The Deliberations, drafted into a declaration is now available from FAO. Shift in the orientation of the document and more emphasis on the ownership role of primary stakeholders, the poor, over the food security at household and settlement level was demanded. In other words food security at village level is more important than at national level in disaster situations.

The group working on Food Emergencies and Preparedness, consisting of wide Asia-Pacific regional representation, including that from India, Laos, Philippines, Vietnam, Thailand, Malaysia, Australia, and others, suggested alternative perspective to the draft commitment to endeavour to meet transitory and emergency food requirements in ways that encourage recovery, development, and a local capacity building to satisfy future needs. In India, where Panchayati Raj, that is local governance, is enacted through the Parliament, such integration of disaster mitigation with food security should be done at local level. Local access and local ownership of food security is possible through Panchayats.

The treatment of emergency food needs as an aberration of natural food sector development has come under sustained criticism. Food emergencies, natural or manmade, are not isolated "events" that require top-down emergency responses. The group also pointed out the increasing percentage of national budgets and non-government aid spent on emergency response to need for food after a disaster or conflict. Same types of disasters affect same population in same villages almost every year. Same quantities of food is supplied by same donors bought from same businesses to the same victims. The governments, donors, and some non-government organisations respond by providing the same relief and rehabilitation food assistance each time.

I wish to suggest an alternative perspective to look at the food needs in disasters and conflicts as unresolved problems of food security development—as part of the 'normal' development of food secure Panchayats in India.

There is a direct link between supply of food after disasters or conflicts and food conditions in society during what is called 'normal' times. This link is more evident and crucial at village level and Panchayats face it all the times. But policies on Panchayats or Food Supply or Disaster Mitigation do not adequately look at Panchayat level linkages. Therefore, policies remain sectoral. It is important to understand this link to identify the social causes and effects of disasters—and how to deal with them especially where access and ownership of food is concerned. To understand and give emphasis to the link between disasters and food conditions in villages during such 'normal' times there is greater room for the strategy of food intervention to focus on mitigation rather than on *post hoc* responses or supply of relief food from the State or Central agencies.

All food security development activities, at national and Panchayat level, should pay more attention to mitigation and preventing impacts of disasters. Disasters and conflicts should have a bearing on identifying priorities for food sector development, determining how these are carried out, and assessing their results. The other important implication of this perspective is the need to know more about hungry people who are victims of disaster. We must look at their position in social, political and economic structures during 'normal times' to understand how a disaster affects their domestic and Panchayat food security I wish to suggest. There is ample evidence of local communities taking local actions, without the government or sometimes each NGOs to, to create their own food relief supply, buffer stocks, and access systems. These experiences do not come out policy level.

Relationships of food sector structures within society determine why certain communities are more vulnerable to disasters than others. These forces and factors dictate who has access to power political and economic of distribution of food and food resources of various types, and thereby who has more access to food benefits, and who has more control over what they eat. Also, food relief, often perpetuate the unequal power relationships between community groups, landless and farmers, men and women, etc. While, it is possible to use food relief as a tool to change such relationships, directly or indirectly.

These food sector relationships and structures are often consolidated and maintained by social institutions. These institutions take various forms-national food corporations, public distribution systems, agriculture pricing commissions, State market boards, agriculture finance companies, consumer societies, or marketing yards. All these are centralised distant, and owned by those who are not the primary users of the system. These institutions formalize relationships between individuals at family level; within households and families; between classes and groups; and between individuals and the State and other social organizations, such as private food or fertilizer companies, agriculture banks, and foodgrain traders. Inequalities between classes, ethnic groups, and gender categories are often a result of, and reinforced by, these institutions that support existing food distribution and ownership systems. And such concentration of power over the most basic human need, especially in the times of crisis, is not recognised by most food sector policies.

I wish to argue that it is important to analyse these food sector relationships of society in normal conditions to understand the degree of famine vulnerability of different sections of the population. For effective disaster mitigation, we must develop strategies to change those institutional structures which increase people's insecurity during and after a disaster. The most direct and important way to do so is through giving more power and matching resources—human and financial—to Panchayats. There are such models—in Gujarat there is Shakti Packet Scheme in Banaskantha district and in Andhra Pradesh the Centre for Environmental Concerns has its own food security—which need to be used supported with venture funds to expand and experiment.

Reforming food security relationships in favour of local communities lies at the root of strengthening the community's capacity to cope with the impact of disasters that cause food emergencies.

According to the alternative perspective, Food Security should be made the focus of any food or relief intervention and should form the essence of the 'community-based approach' to disaster mitigation. Participatory methods are a crucial strategy. Participation should seek to secure the involvement of different social categories at every stage of implementation of food relief to food security. The most direct way to do so is to let the Panchayats develop their own designs or models. More focus should be given to special groups such as widows, child-labour, informal sector workers, disabled, tribals or minorities.

Accountability and transparency are also integral elements of the alternative perspective. Centralised food security system does not always assure this. Food relief is charity. And charity can get away with anything. Waste or misallocation or leakage of food supplies assigned for relief is a common news item after all most all disasters. A greater degree of accountability on the part of various actors involved in food relief is called for. These actors could be State institutions at different levels and NGOs working at the field level. They should be primarily accountable to the hungry victims. They should be able to rate the efficiency and effectiveness of the relief supplies. This is possible only when the Panchayats are directly and effectively involved in developing such local food securities that integrate development and disaster needs.

Most disasters, due to their disruptive character, provide an opportunity to transforming existing relationships, and making a fundamental change in society. Disasters and conflicts are an opportunity to change existing food security relationships and develop new institutional structures that will allow disadvantaged groups to reduce their vulnerability to hunger or starvation. The following framework for integrating food security with disaster mitigation is recommended.

Integrating Food Security with Disaster Mitigation at Panchayat Level

Food Relief	Food Security
Need for food during disasters or conflicts viewed as an event for charity to Panchayats.	Need for food during disasters or conflict is part and parcel of the normal process of development of food security by Panchayats.
Linkages of food security with conditions in Panchayat during normal times less analysed.	Analysing linkages of food security with Panchayats during normal times is fundamental for integrating disasters or conflicts with Food Security.
Technical and legal solutions and focus on production or supply of food is main focus of the central food agencies and policies.	Emphasis on local access to food solutions that change relationship and structures in Panchayats. The objective is to reduce Panchayat's vulnerability and strengthen their capacity to access and own Food Security System.
Centralised government owned or market driven food production institutions dominate in the intervention strategies. Less participation of Panchayat as food user or hungry victims of disasters.	Participation of Panchayat representing victims of disasters paramount in intervention strategies.
Implementing foods or relief agencies less accountable to victims or food users and their process less transparent to Panchayats.	Ensuring accountability to victims and food users and transparency in implementation process emphasized.
Interventions for relief are made after the event occurs.	Mitigation of disasters or conflict the fundamental aim of building local food security by Panchayats.
The objective of food intervention is to return to situation before the disaster.	Disasters or conflicts viewed as opportunities for social transformation and creation of local Food Security System by Panchayats.

Thanks are due to ANGOC in Philippines, FAO office in Thailand, Richard Forsyth of ACFOA in Australia, PRIA in New Delhi, and Duryog Nivaran: South Asian Initiative in Disaster Mitigation.

AGRICULTURAL GROWTH AND POVERTY ALLEVIATION

SEVENTEEN

INTERVENTIONS FOR NUTRITIONAL SECURITY

ARUNA SHARMA

Review of nutritional status in the country on the basis of nutrition surveys conducted by the National Nutrition Monitoring Bureau (NNMB) of ICMR suggests more than 50 per cent of children in rural India are malnourished or undernourished. Inspite of interventions through externally aided programmes, efforts by State and the centre more than 15 per cent of children suffer from severe degree of under nutrition. The significance of "moderate" and severely undernourished children is that the mortality rates due to common childhood infections, like measles, diarrhoea, and respiratory infections are several fold higher in them as compared to children who are "normal" and "mildly" malnourished.

All these years the problem has been tackled either as a medical problem or of social welfare by providing either ready to eat food or mid-day meals. Results of repeat surveys (NNMB) indicate that there has been little improvement in nutritional status of rural population. The fact that the average measurements of heights and weights of males and females alleges, remained almost unchanged, speaks of lack of expected secular increase in growth during last 15 years. Comparison of weight for age profile of children in Madhya Pradesh has shown 0.2 per cent reduction in prevalence of "severe" mal-nutrition Orissa 4 per cent, Andhra Pradesh 6 per cent and Maharashtra as high as 15 per cent.

Nutritional status of people is as much as a function of their food consumption and distribution pattern as it is of their purchasing power, social status and environmental condition in which they live. Its assessment therefore, involves not only the analysis of data on dietary and nutrient intake, anthropometry and nutritional morbidities but also calls for an understanding of the socio-economic and cultural correlates of nutrition.

Physical measurements like height, weight, body circumference and skin folds and indices based on these anthropometric measurements reflecting physical growth, are now considered to be the objective and quantifiable indicates of nutritional status.

Horticulture Interventions for Improved Food Security

The vital parameters reflect as adverse situation of the overall health and nutritional status certain micro nutrients cannot be synthesized by the body and, therefore, have to be provided in diet. Ready to eat food or mid-day meals may answer the need for calorie intake but tend to overlook of providing these essential micro-nutrients in the diet. The intervention should focus more on:

(a) Working out daily menu within the purchasing capacity.
(b) Encouraging kitchen gardens (aganwadis) so as to get micro-nutrients from vegetables and fruits grown in them. The calendar should be worked out so as to get micro nutrients all around the year in rural areas.
e.g. Agro Climatic Zone—time table for all the month and days of the year (annexure).
(c) Making efforts to specially train households for post-harvest handling. Much of vital nutrients are lost because of improper handling.

— Vitamin A, Vitamin C, folate and iron are in green leafy vegetables and yellow or orange fruits such as Mango, Papaya and citrus fruits.

The landless urban poor is the other most adversely affected group in terms of the consumption of micro-nutrients as most of their food has to be purchased. The prevalence of Vitamin A deficiency and anemia is therefore, greatest in the urban slum areas. The rural poor are in a somewhat better position if they have access to land and can grow their own foods. From a nutritional viewpoint, forests play a critical role in the life of the tribal people where the availability of protective foods is greater.

The role of horticulture is, therefore, very vital in providing these micro-nutrients to poor people and thereby raising their nutritional status.

Unfortunately, asserted earlier the problem has been dealt either as a health or welfare issue—the need is to focus on encouraging poor people to consume the fruits and vegetables in their daily diet. Unfortunately, the recent meticulously drafted State policy on nutrition of Tamil Nadu also overlooks the above focus. The coordinated approach talks about agriculture as it is in the restricted sense of increasing the overall productivity and production. There is a need to focus on nutrition policy in making these micro-nutrients available through daily intake of balanced diet.

Tribhawandas Foundation at Anand has tried to encourage housewives to cook nutritious diet by focusing more on methods of cooking i.e. post harvest handling, a concentrated effort on these lines is necessary.

A viable method whereby families can meet their daily, requirements for micronutrient is by growing their own fruits and vegetables in backyard food gardens in rural areas. The Integrated Child Development Service (ICDS), under the Department of Women and Child Development, has the potential to develop such food gardens with assistance of Directorate of Horticulture through the activities of its aganwadi centres (AWCs).

The increased production of fruits and vegetables will not by itself improve nutritional status. Horticulture should specially focus in working out nutritional kits in terms of vegetables seeds and fruit tree saplings to be grown in the kitchen garden so as to get regular supply of micro-nutrients in their daily diet all round the year. These kits should be suitably worked out for different agro-climatic zones. These nutritional kits should also be worked out for different size of backyard gardens.

High rates of post harvest losses prevent these foods to assist to improve the nutritional status. Preservation is, therefore, needed to maintain the nutritional level and eating quality food during times of shortage. Hence in combination with the establishment of backyard food gardens, the programme will therefore, strengthen post harvest storage and preservation of horticulture crops from backyard gardens. There are many low cost techniques available to preserve foods from spoilage while retaining a large proportion of essential nutrients.

CARE— India has recently completed a successful six year project on backyard food gardening in the Indian State of Karnataka.

For urban-slums seasonal menu should be worked out within different limits of their purchasing capacity with cheap fruits and vegetables including egg so as to ensure their regular intake of nutrients. Simple practices like mixing 1 kg of Soyabean in 10 kg of wheat takes care of protein deficiencies. Similarly, special efforts be taken to bring out awareness in post-harvest handling and methods of cooking to retain valuable nutrients.

Hence Department of Horticulture to initiate backyard food gardens and post harvest handling for nutritional security to improve nutrition intake of segments of the rural and urban poor. It is necessary to focus on having a plan of action on nutritional security. Food Security which the country has attained unfortunately does not guarantee improving nutritional status. A programme like this will enhance the impact of ICDS by reinforcing the nutritional messages to mothers and it will ensure the increase in availability of appropriate foods at home. Gardens can make a very significant contribution with regards the availability of vitamin A, C, foliate and iron, also to a lesser extent calorie intake the strategy should be supplemented with the available of suitable planting material, water and land in backyards.

The strategy to emphasize to increase processing and preservation capabilities along with post-harvest handling.

The specific objectives are to:

- enhance the capability of Anganwadi Workers (AWWs) to carry out the nutrition education component of ICDS effectively in order to improve the intake of fruits and vegetables in the community generally but particularly of pregnant and lactating women and preschool children;
- promote production and therefore, availability of such foods at the household and community level by developing the capacity of families to establish backyard food gardens;
- develop system for the technical and support to participating mothers for sustainability of the gardens;
- create an awareness about nutritional aspects of the diet and the benefits of fruits and vegetables with specific reference to dietary source of vitamin A;
- to train family members in simple, low cost methods of food preservation that will extend the shelf-life of backyard garden products and produce attractive processed foods for later consumption or sale;
- to assist families to supplement the income of the household by the sale of surplus processed food where appropriate;
- implement a series of pilot intervention in selected areas in order to build up a State level strategy and methodology for nutrition garden development.

Outputs and Activities Output

A policy and comprehensive implementation strategy for promoting integrated home garden development and nutrition education to combat micro-nutrient deficiencies in needy areas.

Activities

The information of a State Level Coordination Committee led by the (Department of Horticulture DOH) and with representatives from the Department of Women and Child Development (DWCD) and NGOs, such as CARE etc.

This committee will determine the programme direction and ensure the overall coordination of planned activities.

- The formation of State and Block Level Implementation Committees with representation from the DOH, ICDS Supervisors, NGO field staff and Panchayati Raj.
  These committees will formulate and plan the detailed activities to implement the programme and assume over all responsibility for management and evaluation in their particular block.
- In each block that participate in the programme, a base-line survey will be undertaken by an NGO (using PRA techniques) to determine the facilities for creating backyard food gardens, including availability of water; any previous practice of rearing home gardens and, if so, the crops grown; awareness of micro-nutrient deficiencies and foods that are rich in their sources; information regarding consumption, nutritional status and health; current post harvest preservation practices.
- Develop extension messages and educational packages for nutrition, household horticulture and post-harvest preservation improvement and field test the adaptability of these packages.
- Identify the range of micro-nutrient rich foods suitable for cultivation in the various agro-climatic zones of Madhya Pradesh.
- The training of AWWs in nutrition education (by FNB), backyard food gardening (by Rural Horticulture Extension Officers) and post-harvest preservation (by Home Science Extension Officers).
- The training of all interested ICDS beneficiaries initially in nutrition education and also creating an awareness of the programme being

implemented. The nutrition education will emphasize the importance of fruit and vegetables, particularly in the diets of children and pregnant and lactating women. Nutrition education should be given to the mothers prior to the information on establishment of backyard food gardens as it is expected that improved awareness of the importance of fruit and vegetables will motivate mothers to establish home gardens.

— The selection of crop mixes and suitable garden layout design, followed by the establishment and maintenance of "model" gardens in an actual backyard context at AWCs or some other appropriate location.

— The DOH will provide a specified number of good quality seeds and seedlings of selected crops to all participating ICDS mothers, at an appropriate time and suitable to the agro-climatic zone that are also rich in the required micro-nutrient. Funding for this could be tapped from the assistance given by the National Horticulture Board for establishment of nutritional gardens in rural areas.

— The DOH or NGO will adapt simple systems of household water harvesting for irrigating gardens and establish demonstration of these systems in villages. It will also incorporate simple non-chemical methods of pest-control for home gardens and develop an illustrated home garden pest-control manual.

— The establishment of backyard food gardens at all interested ICDS mothers, households and community gardens where appropriate.

— The Panchayati Raj to ensure support for the backyard food gardens by appropriately involving family and community members in various programme activities as they are developed.

— The Panchayati Raj, in collaboration with the RHEO, will establish seed banks at AWCs. The mothers will be instructed on how to harvest seeds that will form the basis of these seed banks and ensure the low costs of input and sustainability of the programme.

— Staff at Home Science Colleges will train AWWs, representatives of Panchayati Raj and field staff from NGOs such as CARE in the basic technologies of home preservation of fruits and vegetables. There will be particular emphasis placed on safe food processing to avoid food poisoning, low cost, appropriate technologies for processing, packaging and storage and maintaining food quality.

— Where a large number of gardens are successfully established over a number of years and excess processed food is available for sale, selected, AWWs will be trained in packaging, display and selling techniques, together with basic quality assurance techniques, to assist those families that wish to increase their income by sales of excess produce.

— RHEO will assist the ICDS Supervisors in monitoring and supervising the programme activities in the villages.

— To assess the impact of the intervention programme on the health, knowledge and dietary practices of households.

EIGHTEEN

RECONSTRUCTING INDIAN AGRICULTURE

DEVINDER SHARMA

Indian agriculture is once again at the crossroads. Twenty-five years after the seeds of green revolution were sown, Indian agriculture is faced with a crisis of sustainability. It is the sustainability of the production momentum achieved immediately after the green revolution had set in that is emerging as the biggest issue confronting Indian agriculture.

With declining productivity in the frontline agricultural States of Punjab, Haryana and western Uttar Pradesh, and with little hope a quantum jump in foodgrain production from the drylands, constituting nearly 70 per cent of the country's land under plough, the threat to India's food security was never so great. Complacency emerging from the unmanageable stocks of 'surplus' foodgrains, following normal monsoons for eight years in a row, has relegated agriculture to the bottom of the national agenda. Such is the growing indifference to anything related with agriculture and food that the policy makers as well as the enlightened media does not find it any more to be news worthy.

Paradigm Shift

The days of the green revolution as the only saviour for the hungry millions are over. From the time of a top-heavy model of agricultural growth, wherein technology along with essential inputs, were disseminated among farmers in the better endowed regions of the country, the 21st century will see a marked shift in agricultural growth—a growth that should possibly come from low-input agriculture based on location specific needs and appropriate technology drawing inspiration from the traditional farming practices.

In 1930, crop yields in India, Pakistan, Egypt, Britain, Mexico and the United States were of the same level. It was the transformation brought about through the process of industrial agriculture in the next forty years that pushed Indian agriculture in the category of "underproductive and inefficient farming practices". In the aftermath of the green revolution, the focus is once again on restoring the pride in traditional agriculture—a truly sustainable system nurtured through the ages.

The development focus, therefore, has to shift to the grassroots. The paradigm shift in technology transfer comes at a time when India has already decided to reactivate the *Gram Panchayats*, a massive network of democratically—elected grassroot forces. The new agricultural revolution, that is beginning to take roots, will follow the bottoms-up approach. After all, agricultural practices evolved by the rural communities have stood the test of time.

The *Gram Panchayats*, though not adequately equipped to transfer sustainable farm technologies, can certainly be the partners in the monumental task of agricultural reconstruction. The democratically-elected *Gram Panchayats*, after the landmark 73rd Amendment to the Indian Constitution, do provide a ray of hope. Adequate training can help bridge the technology gap. To create more awareness of the improved farming practices a beginning can be made by providing extensive training to the members of the *Gram Panchayats*.

Panchayat Training

The Mumbai-based Dr. P.V. Mandlik Trust has been organising training camps, appropriately called "Awakening Camps" for *Gram Panchayats* for nearly two years now. The Trust feels that while the need for conducting such camps was great and the participation was unexpectedly high, a new methodology had to be developed based on the literacy level and the social consciousness of the members. Overcoming these initial hurdles and learning by experience, the Trust was able to conduct 34 such camps in 1993-94 in which more than a thousand *Gram Panchayats* members participated, a majority of them being women.

In the second phase, ending in March 1996, the Trust organised 41 camps for 1,600 participants. A few of these camps were exclusively for village *Sarpanches*. Among the various activities associated with the training programmes is a mandatory visit to the famous development model of Ralegaon Siddhi in Maharashtra. This aspect of training, the experiment in social transformation as demonstrated by Annasaheb Hazare, proved to be an eye-opener for the participants.

Ralegaon Siddhi is not the only village to have emerged free from the chains of poverty and malnutrition that engulfs much of rural India. Hundreds of miles away, a ray of light has dawned on the dark existence of hapless families in the famine-stricken belt of Palamau district in Bihar. It is not what is generally referred to as the 'trickle down' effect that has transformed the lives of people in at least 300 villages of Palamau but the determination to make judicious use of natural resources for the benefit of the community. The common link between Ralegaon Siddhi and Palamau, as I understand, is the emphasis on self-reliance.

Chakriya Vikas Pranali

Among some of the successful models of agricultural growth through judicious use of naturally available resources, which can form an integral part of *Gram Panchayat* training, is the *Chakriya Vikas Pranali* (Cyclic Mode of Development) in the perennially drought-stricken belt of Palamau in Bihar.

It is difficult to perceive the transformation through the CVP system unless one realises that these 300 villages are like an oasis in the degraded region. When hundreds of villagers and animals had moved out of these areas for want of food, the CVP areas had remained unaffected. I believe that any system that survives the worst of biotic and abiotic stress conditions, what to talk of severe natural calamities like drought and floods, has the inherent capacity to sustain itself. And that is what CVP has shown.

The system is called cyclic as the benefits from one investment cycle becomes capital input for the next one, and thus goes on providing employment and income to make the village self-reliant. Breaking away from the text-book model of sustainable development, P.R. Mishra, who earlier had transformed the Sukho-majri village in Haryana, tried a new approach: first of all, the entire uncultivated barren land belonging to people or the government was pooled together so as to make an economically viable unit of 8-10 hectares. Individual's share of land is recorded in a land pass book so as to reduce the possibility of future disputes.

Every hutment in the village plants ten or more types of fruits, vegetables, fodder trees etc. the income so generated is shared under a mutually agreed system of 3:3:3:1.

10 per cent income for the welfare fund (Kalyan Kosh)
30 per cent income to land owners
30 per cent income for CVP workers, and the remaining
30 per cent income becomes capital for village infrastructures.

The system is operative under an open accounting scheme being run by the Society of Hill Management School (SHRMS), which in turn is managed by an elected body. All decisions relating to planning and implementation are taken by members themselves. All the workers in the CVP are called as 'students' who learn by doing and also teach by doing.

Like in Sukho-majra, various soil conservation and moisture-retention techniques have been put into practice by the 'students'. Small check dams, water-harvesting structures and vegetation barriers have been erected. Ridges raised along the slopes have helped conserve every drop of rain water and also help in checking erosion. To maximise the gains from the available piece of land, CVP is following a three-tier system of plantings.

It has been computed that as many as 32 lakh trees of different species were planted on about 650 hectares of land between 1987 and 1991. While the trees have a long growth period, villagers have already begun to derive incomes by selling vegetables, millets and grasses that they grow under the trees. Not satisfied with the gains achieved so far, the CVP began working on a system that educates the villagers and their children. After all, it is well known that illiteracy aids perpetuation of poverty. The establishment of 'land financed schools' than took roots.

Already twenty such schools are running and many more are proposed, it all began when nine land owners agreed to pool 60 acres of land at village Chhecha in Barwadhih block of Palamau. Under the revised system of sharing for schools, 60 per cent of surplus income arising after treatment of the 60 acres goes for running the school. Each student plants and maintains some trees for which receives a stipend.

The Society has plans to further strengthen the concept of land financed schools and extend it further to include land financed hospitals and community centres for care of widows and orphans. And if made available a large chunk of land lying barren in Dorami, the Society plans to even set up a University of CVP.

The Society is the only one in the country to have paid back the financial support received from the government. The Society believes that if it cannot itself become self-sustaining it has not business to speak and work in the name of sustainable development. And herein lies an important message for the *Gram Panchayats*.

NINETEEN

POST-HARVEST TECHNOLOGY AT FARM LEVEL

Important for Food Security

G.K. GIRISH

Introduction

The basic philosophy in the evolution of the system of Food Security is to ensure "Foodgrains for all". Food Security, self-sufficiency and self-reliance have been the recurring theme in the evolution of the food economy in India. Previously following four components of National Food Security have been identified.[1]

(i) Improvement of production and productivity of irrigated as well as rainfed areas;
(ii) Imparting greater stability to production;
(iii) Building up of sufficient grain reserves i.e. buffer stocks; and,
(iv) Organization of an efficient distribution system.

Food Security is also significant for lower income group, old people, expectant mothers and growing children. It is, therefore, imperative for any Government to bring in such policies and schemes that could ensure food and nutritional requirements for all the people particularly the less privileged one.

In the context of nutrition, all food items, pertaining to product of livestocks and food crops, foodgrains are important. As per 38th round (1983) of National Samples Survey, about 44 per cent of the total consumer expenditure in rural India was on foodgrain.

Despite the same Ministerial working group set up in the Ministry of Agriculture recently has observed that on the basis of average net production of cereal for consumptions during the last 3 years, 1991-93, 1501 K Cal/energy per capita per day, is provided by creals alone. Taking average energy requirement of 2,200 K Cal per day, cereals are alone providing about 68 per cent of the total energy requirements.[2] Hence this Chapter is limited to post Harvest Technology of Foodgrains.

To cope with current and future, foodgrains demands, various Governments have traditionally emphasized two lines of action:

(a) reducing future demand by slowing population growth; and
(b) augmenting food supplies by expanding production. A third vital complementary measure, however, reducing the loss of food during and after harvest has not been adequately emphasized. Minimizing food losses is also known as "hidden harvest" which increases the availability of foodgrains.

In India, approximately 65 per cent of foodgrains are retained at farm level for food, feed and seed. Quantitative and qualitative losses occur due to Physical (temperature and moisture), Biological (micro-organisms, insects rodents, birds and mite), Chemical (breakdown of the produce, pesticides etc.), Engineering (structural and mechanical, handling) and Transport and Marketing factors.

A series of efforts have been made to initiate the work on PHT in India since 1985. Girish reviewed the subject and two detailed reviews have been published.[3,4]

Magnitude of the Problem

Keeping the production of foodgrain 182 million tonnes in view, the minimum retention pattern at farm level (65%) and the magnitude of loss at farmers levels (to the tune of 10%), the total loss suffered by the farmers per annum can be assumed as nearly 11 million tonnes of foodgrains. Valued at more than Rs. 3300 crores. An effort is being made by R&D and extension organizations in the country to minimize losses.

Research on PHT at Farm Level

The first step towards establishing an Institute in India was in the year 1950 when Central Food Technological Research Institute was established at Mysore with a mandate to train personnel and evolve technology relating to food processing and preservation.

In 1958, the Department of Food started a centre at Hapur known as Grain Storage Research & Training Centre with the main objective to train the personnel of State Governments engaged in food procurement/storage and distribution. This centre was upgraded during 1968-1973 with the technical and financial assistance of UNDP and GSRTC was redesignated as Indian Grain Storage Institute. Two field stations at Ludhiana and Bapatla (later shifted to Hyderabad in March 1979) were established in 1968-69. Subsequently, three stations of IGSI at Jabalpur (October 1980), Udaipur (February 1981) and Jorhat (may 1981) were also established. The objectives were:

> The overall objective was to minimise the losses of foodgrains by development of modernised grain storage practices for the farmers, traders, cooperatives and large scale storage to foodgrains in the country and also evolve the methodology to be adopted by the Save Grain Campaign which has its headquarters in the Department of Food. The specific objectives were:

(1) To develop code of practices for proper grain storage and handling by recommending economically effective techniques for control of insects, rodents birds, besides checking effectively the micro-organisms.
(2) To investigate the nature, extent and degree of losses due to these factors, different agro-climatic conditions.
(3) To develop improved type of storage structures, grain dryers, grain handling cleaning and grading equipments besides improvement in the traditional storage structures/equipment, using locally available materials.
(4) To evaluate the developed and recommended methods before releasing for population throughout the country by development of suitable extension material and semi-technical literature on grain storage and quality control in foodgrains.
(5) To train personnel from various organisations in proper grain storage and handling practices.

The Council of Scientific and Industrial Research's Regional Research Laboratories at Trivandrum, Hyderabad, Jorhat, Bhubneshwar and Jammu contributed on food and feed post-harvest technology.

The Ministry of Agriculture established the State Agricultural University (SAU) under ICAR umbrella results in establishment of

Department/Sections, agricultural processing/processing and food engineering/agricultural structures and process engineering in agricultural engineering, Department of Entomology, Food Science, Food Technology in the Faculty of Agriculture.

ICAR launched All-India coordinated Project on post-harvest technology, processing and storage of jaggery, oilseeds processing etc., ICAR's latest initiative is on establishment of Central Institute of Post-Harvest Engineering and Technology (CITHET).

Pilot-Projects on Post-Harvest Technology of Foodgrains

A pilot project, improvement of rural family storage and processing of foodgrains in some selected blocks of Tamil Nadu has been implemented between 1979 and 1982 with the support of FAO's Special Action Programmes for Prevention of Food Losses and was implemented by Avinashalingam Home Science College (Avinashalingam Deemed University, Coimbatore). The objective of the project was to contribute to the reduction of Post-Harvest Food Losses at the level of small scale and medium scale farmers in Tamil Nadu.

The immediate objective of the project was: (i) To improve the farmers capability to reduce post harvest food losses in 100 villages in Tamil Nadu through the introduction of improved processing and storage techniques. (ii) To continue the programme of reducing post harvest losses by incorporating post-harvest technology into the work assignment of female village level workers. The project activities took place in three districts of Tamil Nadu i.e. Coimbatore, Periyar and Salem. Some of the important post-harvest practices adopted in the villages were as follows:

- — Rat Proofing by using various techniques in the villages.
- — Improving indigenous storage structures by salicoat painting.
- — Using various insecticides for insect pest control and rodenticides for rat control.
- — Curative treatment by using ethylene dibromide.
- — Popularising metal bins and pucca *kothies*.

On-Going R&D Programmes

Various on-going R&D programmes are as under:

(i) Introduction of newer prophylactic chemicals in place of existing ones which have developed resistance against stored grain insect pests;

(ii) Introduction of fumigants which have better toxicity and penetration power;

(iii) Development of lighter fumigation covers;

(iv) Replacement of timber as dunnage with plastic/RCC;

(v) Effective bird and psocid control techniques;

(vi) Evaluation of non-chemical insecticides for grain storage;

(vii) Introduction of single dose anti-coagulant/rodenticides;

(viii) Study on resistance among stored grain insects against insecticides;

(ix) Storage problems of other agricultural commodities of durable nature;

(x) Introduction of bulk storage and transportation techniques;

(xi) Development of grader and dryer;

(xii) Assessment of storage losses at farmers, traders, cooperative and corporate levels;

(xiii) Study on the safe moisture limits of various commodities under different agricultural Climatic zones;

(xiv) Problems associated with high moisture paddy in early harvested crop;

(xv) Estimation of driage losses in paddy, rice and wheat in commercial warehouses;

(xvi) Self life of milled products and their fumigation techniques;

(xvii) Efficacy of new packaging of fumigants;

(xviii) Development of metallic structures, their fabrication and evaluation in the entire country;

(xix) Improvement of indigenous grain storage structures and non-metallic bins;

(xx) Surveys of mycotoxin contamination in foodgrains;

(xxi) Study on pesticidal contamination in foodgrains.

Extension Technology of Scientific Storage of Foodgrain in India

Nearly two-third of the total foodgrains produced in the country are retained at farm level where considerable losses take place both in quantity and quality due to insects, rodents and other factors as the storage conditions at farm level are not proper. For minimising the losses, the Ministry of Food have been implementing rural-based scheme of Save Grain Campagin. At present 17 save grain teams situated in different parts of the country are operating in selected areas in close collaboration of State Governments (Annexure I). The major planks of the campaign are Training, Demonstration and Publicity.

(A) Training Programmes

In discharging its primary responsibility of management of the country's food economy, the Ministry of Food undertakes several complex tasks such as procurement of foodgrains, building up and maintenance of requisite buffer stocks, providing for their storage, their timely movement to various parts of the country and deliver to the distribution agencies. To fulfil this objective, several types of training programmes are organised to create a band of workers who in turn render technical services in fulfilment of the above mentioned tasks.

(a) Training Programmes at Apex Level

Long-term training programmes are organised in the country. The courses are for a duration of eight weeks.

(b) Short-term Courses

36 such courses are organised for the benefit of in-service personnel.

(c) Special Courses

Special courses are offered for the benefit of pest's control operators, extension workers, flour millers and rice millers etc. and the duration of these courses vary from 2 to 4 weeks. The syllabus is modified according to the individual needs.

(d) Training Programmes at Farmers Level

(i) Stipendiary Training Courses

These are of 15 days duration for the benefit of farmers, traders and representatives of cooperatives storing foodgrains. These are arranged at village or Panchayat level. 186 such courses are conducted in a year in the entire country and in each course 50 participants are included. The training is imparted in local language and supplemented by various audio visual media and field demonstration.

(ii) Motivators Courses

These courses are of five days duration and in each course 50 farmers are included. 186 such courses are organised during a year.

(e) Courses organised by Central Warehousing Corporation

(i) Central Warehousing Corporation organises one month's training programme in management concepts and techniques of warehousing, for middle level executives of Central and State Warehousing Corporations.

(ii) Special Training Programmes on Personnel Management Rules and Practices of Office and Records Management. This is of one month duration course.

(iii) All India Warehousing Training Courses for field officers.
This is for one week duration.

(f) The Food Corporation of India is imparting training programmes for four weeks duration for in-service candidates. Besides the above courses, special programmes are tailored for the people who are working in the movement of grain and financial rule management etc.
Some new programmes have launched. They are as under:

(g) Organisation of Training Courses for Rural Artisans

The stipendiary training courses for rural artisans have been introduced by Science and Technology Advisory Committee (STAC) (Food) at IGSI and its five field stations. The aim of organising these training courses is to create a band of trained artisans, who can undertake the construction of modern storage structures and improvement of existing traditional storage structures based on the technology developed by IGSI as per the need of farmers to minimise post-harvest losses in foodgrains. This will also help in generating self employment for the trained artisans. The first such training course was conducted at the main institute at Hapur for two weeks and 25 candidates were trained in the course. However, 12 such courses have been organised till date. Theory classes as well as practical demonstrations were arranged to the trainees on fabrication of metallic bins, components of pucca *kothi* and mud bin etc. Thereafter, the trainees were allowed to fabricate the same item themselves under the supervision of technical staff.

On the successful completion of the training courses each trainee was awarded a certificate and stipend of Rs. 500.

(B) Demonstration Programmes

Demonstration programmes on insect pest control, rodent control in houses and fields, improvement in indigenous grain storage structures are organised in the villages during training courses so that farmers may use these techniques of scientific storage of foodgrains themselves. All the inputs like insecticides, fumigants, rodenticides, polythene sheets, salicoat, outlets and inlets are being provided free of cost by Government of India during the demonstration programmes. To safeguard the foodgrains from moisture damage, moisture proofing of indigenous mud bins as well as modern pucca *kothi* is also being arranged for the benefit of farmers during the training courses.

(C) Publicity Programmes

In oder to make the farmers increasingly aware about the importance of saving grains during storage, multi-media publicity is arranged with emphasis on audio visual aids.

The publicity programmes are conducted by distributing leaflets and handbills, arranging film, slide and puppet shows, delivering talks on radio and television and by organising exhibitions in the villages. Special demonstration kits, education kits and exhibition kits have been designed so that within 15 minutes small exhibitions are organised in the village on the subject. The main objective of publicity programmes is that more and more farmers including farm women in the villages may learn about the importance of scientific storage of foodgrains.

Some features and video films on scientific storage of foodgrains in Hindi and regional languages have been designed to educate the target groups regarding the scientific storage of foodgrains and these films are shown in the villages during training, demonstration and publicity programmes.

The farmers are also well informed about the source from where they can get the pesticides and metallic storage bins and other inputs for their use. For continuation of this programme, band of volunteers is also trained so that after the withdrawal of Central and state teams, the volunteers may continue these programmes and may keep liaison with our offices periodically in case of any need.

One of the main projects under Save Grain Campaign is development of nucleus villages as demonstration units. A nucleus village would be one in which atleast 30 per cent storage structures are improved upon and atleast 10 per cent of the total storage structures available in the villages are modern storage structures such as metal bins, pusa bins and pucca *kothies*. Financial assistance to the tune of Rs. 2 crores during Eighth Plan has been provided for metal bin programme. Besides this, Rs. 2 crores have also been provided for non-metallic storage structures and development of nucleus villages.

Main Achievements

Modern Storage Structures

The use of modern/improved storage structures at farm level, if adopted will provide answers to many of the storage problems. This will minimise the losses, external moisture, cross infestation, bird and rodent trouble. Grain can be fumigated easily. Girish *et al.* (1971)[5], Narasimhan and Girish[6] (1977), Ramam and Girish (1977)[7], Berewar and Girish (1983)[8] evaluated in various indoor, outdoor, underground, above ground, metallic, non-metallic structures under various eco-climatic zones for paddy and wheat.

A. Metallic Structures

Some of the viable designs were multiplied. An amount of Rs. 357 lakhs was advanced to 20 State Government/Union Territories as a revolving fund. The State Governments got the bins fabricated through Agro-Industries Corporations, Government workshops and cooperative organizations. More than 7 lakhs metallic structures were purchased by farmers. This programme has generated very good demand for metallic bins and as a result private enterpreneurs have come forward to fabricate and supply metallic bins to the farmers.

B. Non-metallic Structures

There is a growing demand at farm level to construct cement concrete structures within their premises. Besides this, efforts have been made to improve the traditional storage structures which are not only economical but are very suitable for different agro-climatic conditions. So far more than 1.5 lakhs non-metallic structures have been erected. More than 1.5 lakhs traditional storage structures have been improved and made storage worthy.

Foodgrain Storage Organisations in the Country

Following organisations are dealing with the foodgrains:

(1) Food Corporation of India (FCI)
(2) Central Warehousing Corporation (CWC) and State Warehousing Corporations (SWC)
(3) National Cooperative Development Corporation (NCDC)
(4) Rural Godowns
(5) State Governments and their Agencies

The total scientific storage capacity is about 42 million tonnes.

Public Distribution System in India

The PDS has been functioning for more than four decades now leaving aside the old rationing system. Of course, it remains one of the weaker components of food policy. However, this system played a great role by making available rice and wheat at fixed prices to consumers in all nooks and corners of the country, thereby preventing the spectre of families in any part of the country. The distribution network also supplied grain for the "Food for Work" type of programmes taken up on a large scale to fight the drought. The main weakness in PDS is that it is not reaching effectively to the real poor. There is an urgent need for proper monitoring. The following suggestions are made for improvement in the functioning of PDS.

(i) Delivery of Stocks to FPSs should be on actual and not on sample weighment.

(ii) Retail price at FPSs should be uniform throughout the State/area after weight-averaging the transport cost for the FPS.

(iii) Regular supply of good quality grains has to be ensured.

(iv) Entitlement card's easy availability and improvement in its design and durability.

(v) FPS doorstep delivery of PDS commodities instead of delivery to FPS owners at FCI godowns.

(vi) Improvement in the viability of FPSs.

(vii) Enlarging the basket of PDS commodities to enhance its utility as also to improve economic viability of FPSs.

(viii) Streamlining of the supply chain by construction of small intermediary godowns between FCI's base godown and FPSs in the interior.

(ix) Introduction of a more effective Management Information System.

Scenario of PFL in India

UNDP/FAO project IND/67/585 On-farm Community and Storage (1968-73) in India based at the Indian Grain Storage Institute at Hapur in the Ministry of Food, developed spectrum of designs of storage facilities and code of practices for controlling insects, rats, moisture etc. and are being disseminated throughout the country.

The pilot project PFL/IND/001 improvement on rural family storage and processing of foodgrains in Tamil Nadu was implemented during 1979-82 with the support of the FAO special action programme for the prevention of food losses and implemented by Shri Avinashalingam Home Science College in close collaboration with Ministry of Food.

PFL/IND/002 project on improvement of rural family storage and processing of food started in February 1988 in selected blocks in Tamil Nadu and terminated in February 1991 and PFL/IND/003 commenced from

1st September 1992 to October, 1995.

The above mentioned two projects are being implemented under the advice of Ministry of Food with an immediate objectives of (i) introduction of Post Harvest activities in the framework of current agricultural and rural development activities of regular extension workers in Tamil Nadu and (ii) One self sustaining cost effective food preservation unit operating in each selected pilot district block by the end of the project.

Scenario of PHT in Asia-Pacific Region

World conference on Agrarian Reforms and Rural Development (1979) called for policies and strategies aimed at increased self-reliance, improved nutrition and eradication of poverty. Women contribute to achieve those goals through their involvement in various agricultural operations. Of these, collection and storage of foodgrains is considered an important activities in most of the Member countries of the Centre on Integrated Rural Development for Asia and Pacific (CIRDAP), in which women folk plays dominant role in agriculture.

A regional Workshop on Training of Rural Women in post-harvest loss prevention was held at national institute of Rural Development, Hyderabad, India in collaboration with CIRDAP from 8th-14th August, 1988 on the subject which was attended by me as a representative of India.

In 1974, the FAO Food Security Programme was launched, under which Multi-disciplinary missions visited countries to formulate policies and plan action programme to improve security. In 1977, the PFL Programme were launched and became operational in January 1978.

The three major constraints on post-harvest loss in the developing world were as under:

(a) Lack of information concerning magnitude of the losses, their nature, causes and most effective techniques for reducing or preventing them.
(b) Lack of infrastructure for the implementation of loss prevention measures.
(c) Lack of investment in food loss prevention.

The PFL programme carried out activities as under in the five main areas.

(a) Food loss assessment surveys, which are conducted as the basis for action programme for food losses reduction.

(b) Provision of practical assistance to Governments to combat losses at various stages in PFL system.

(c) Training and building up national capabilities.

(d) National focal point for food loss reduction programme.

(e) Strengthening research and development and information programmes.

The establishment of regional network on PHT (RNPT) at Bangkok started 1984-87 (Phase I) and 1987-90 (Phase II). Various workshops/seminars/training programmes were organised on PHT for various countries of Asia and Pacific (13 infrastructure, inflow of technologies from the advanced REGNET countries to minimise post-harvest losses at farm level.

Export Orientation Strategy

At present India is marginally surplus of the foodgrains. Strategy should be to export this marginally surplus grain in the international market at reasonable prices. It is essential that national specifications should be modified at par with the international grain standards for this purpose.

It is essential that the procurement of foodgrains for export purposes should be according to international grain standards and there should be separate storage of such grain so that it is available for export. A National Grain Inspection Agency should be set up which can monitor the quality of the foodgrains for export purposes and issue the certificate.

A national policy should encourage the farmers to produce the better qualities of foodgrains so that they can get a remunerative prices for their produce. The Government should start the export enhancement programmes so that farmers and exporters can compete with the major foreign exporters of the foodgrains in international market.

There is a need to develop facilities for man-power training at national level for such specialised job besides setting up a division in the Ministry of Food for studying the international market, quality parameters, shipping and grain requirement of the different importing countries.

Recommendations

To minimise the food losses, the following recommendations are made:

1. Replacement of traditional storage structures by modern ones with reasonable prices.
2. Improvement of the traditional storage structures to make them storage worthy.
3. Use of newer insecticides replacing old chemicals against which insects have developed resistance.
4. Propagation of safer insecticides, rodenticides and fumigants at farm level where technical expertise is not available.
5. Development of code or practices for godown hygiene and sanitation and control of psocids.
6. Development and evaluation of cheaper portable dryers for high moistured grains.
7. Introduction of cheaper combine harvester.
8. Development of suitable cleaner and grader for foodgrains.
9. Introduction of bulk transport, storage and handling system of foodgrains.
10. Introduction of staggered procurement system to avoid rush at the same movement.
11. Introduction of grades in the specifications based on chemical quality parameters.
12. Development of wooden crates by plastic one in commercial storage.
13. Replacement of wooden crates by plastic one in commercial storage.
14. Strengthening of the national infrastructures with particular reference to rural Save Grain Scheme and R&D with Ministry of Food.
15. Establishment of National Storage Advisory Committee on the pattern of Science and Technology Advisory Committee to boost the Research, Development and Extension Activities in post-harvest fields.
16. Publishing of post-harvest technology news letter at national level.
17. Setting up of Coordination Committee for monitoring the functions of R&D, training and extension on PHT and another Committee for transferring technology to the farmers.
18. Strengthening of pesticide residue and mycotoxin monitoring labs at national level.

NOTES

1. Annonymous, (1976-77), Report of the Department Food, Ministry of Agriculture and Irrigation, Government of India. p. 2.
2. Mishra, V.N. (1992), A.P.O. Training Course on Improving PHT, APO Manual.
3. Girish, G.K. (1974), Training Manual, Post Harvest Prevention of Waste and Losses of Food Grains. APO: 143-60.
4. Girish, G.K. (1990), Post Harvest Technology in India Warehousing Management of Stored Food Grain (Regional Workshop). Proceedings published by GOI and FAO. p. 145-60.
5. Girish, G.K., B.R. Berewar, R.K. Goyal, R.P.S. Tomar and K. Krishnamurthy (1971), *Evaluation of Some Modern Rural Storage Bins for Storage of Wheat*. p. 84.
6. Narasimhan, K.S., G.K. Girish (1977), *Evaluation of Storage Structure for Storage of Paddy*. p. 75.
7. Ramam, C.P., G.K. Girish *et al.* (1977), Improvements of Existing Rural Grain Storage Structures with Special Reference to Andhra Pradesh. p. 14.
8. Berewar, B.R., Girish, G.K. *et al.*, *Farm Level Modern Storage Structures*. p. 61.

ANNEXURE - I

Location of Save Grain Campaign Teams and Areas Covered by Them

S. No.	Location of full-fledged teams	Area Covered: State	Area Covered: U.Ts.	S. No.	Location of skeleton teams	Area Covered: States	Area Covered: U.Ts.
1	2	3	4	5	6	7	8
1.	Ahmedabad	Gujarat	Dadra & Nagar Haveli, Daman & Diu				
2.	Bangalore	Karnataka	—	1.	Trivandrum	Kerala	Lakshadweep
3.	Bhopal	Madhya Pradesh	—	2.	Raipur	Madhya Pradesh	—
4.	Bhubaneswar	Orissa	—				
5.	Calcutta	West Bengal, Tripura & Sikkim	Andaman & Nicobar				
6.	Chandigarh	Punjab, Himachal Pradesh and J&K	Chandigarh				
7.	Guwahati	Assam, Manipur, Nagaland & Meghalaya	Arunachal Pradesh & Mizoram				
8.	Ghaziabad	U.P. and Haryana	Delhi				
9.	Hyderabad	Andhra Pradesh	—				
10.	Jaipur	Rajasthan	—				
11.	Lucknow	Uttar Pradesh	—	3.	Varanasi	Uttar Pradesh	—
12.	Madras	Tamil Nadu	Pondicherry				
13.	Patna	Bihar	—				
14.	Pune	Maharashtra	Goa				

Note: Total 14 full fledged teams and 3 Skeleton teams.

TWENTY

SOYBEAN FOR FOOD SECURITY AND NUTRITION

P.S. BHATNAGAR

Race between food increase and population increase continues unabated. Notwithstanding the boost in world food production, one out of five persons in the developing countries is chronically under-nourished. Around 200 million children are suffering from protein-energy malnutrition and over 2000 million experience micro-nutrient deficiencies. The main cause for this had been non-accessibility to the food, particularly of people below the poverty line. This is more pertinent in the context of India, where on one hand the food reserves are in the tune of over 36 million tons and on the other, there is silent crisis of protein and calorie deficiency depriving millions of human beings from exploitation of their physiological and intellectual potential.

In India with predominantly vegetarian society, following considerations are needed to be addressed for food security and nutrition.

(i) Declining production of pulses resulting drop in pulse-protein availability to the masses demanding appropriate cost effective substitutes of vegetable origin.
(ii) Enhancement and stability of food availability as well as accessibility.
(iii) Augmentation of per capita income.
(iv) Availability of cash in lean period when other sources for cash earnings of an individual in the critical group are dry.
(v) Increase in employment opportunities.
(vi) Enrichment of food quality in the period when conventional sources of vegetable protein are meagre or exhausted.
(vii) More efficient use of land for protein and oil.

(viii) Overall development, particularly of rural areas.

Role of soybean with reference to above inter-related factors in the present context have been notable.

Impact of Soybean

Soybean is being utilized as nutritious high protein food since 3000 B.C. (Hymowitz, 1970). Different adjectives widely used to designate it as miracle bean, golden bean, cow of the field, meat of the field, gold from the soil, pearl of the orient, cindrella crop etc. indicate the high value ascribed to soybean from early times. Occupying 62.44 million hectares and producing 123.76 million tons (1995-96 forecast), soybean tops in world production of oilseeds and edible oil. In addition, it is the lowest priced source of high quality protein for man either directly as food or indirectly through animal products.

Nutritive Value

In terms of biological value and Net Protein Utilization (NPU), soybean protein is superior to maize, wheat and rice (Table 20.1). Considering the world average of soybean yield to be around 1.98 tons/ha with approximately 38 per cent protein, the per hectare production of high quality protein would thus be 0.72 tons/ha. The corresponding figures for wheat and maize are estimated to be 0.27 and 0.46 tons/ha respectively (Table 20.2) (Selleck, 1983). Thus, protein productivity of soybean has been reported to be as high as 6.8 kg/ha per day, which is second only to Limabean among the important legume and cereal crops (Table 20.3) (Pimental *et al.*, 1975). In accordance with the FAO standards, soybean protein is well balanced for essential amino-acids (Table 20.4). It is rich in lysine—an essential amino-acid which is low in cereals. Also, soybean protein maintains high level of both energy and protein (Table 20.5). Further, soya-oil with as high as 85 per cent polyunsaturated fatty acids of total lipids with 60 per cent of which being essential fatty acids (Nwar, 1985), is known to be of high food quality for human consumption. This establishes unequivocally that soybean could be as best substitute of ever declaring pulse-protein for overcoming malnutrition in human beings. Expectation of improving the protein availability for food for masses through animal source would be only a fallacy.

TABLE 20.1: Biological Value of Protein from Selected Commodities

Source	Biological value	Protein score	Net Protein utilization
Egg	96	100	100
Soybean	72	70	56
Corn	54	45	55
Wheat flour	53	50	52
Rice (milled)	61	—	59

Source: Kaldy, M.S. 1972.

TABLE 20.2: Per Hectare Protein Yield of Some Crops

Crop	Crop yield t/ha	Crop yield in protein
Soybean	1.9	0.72
Corn	5.1	0.46
Wheat	2.3	0.27

Source: Kaldy, M.S. 1972 and Ma, Rhu-hwa and Zhang Kan, 1983.

Overall Development and Accessibility to Enhanced Nutritious Food

In India, increase in soybean hectarage and production have been spectacular (750% and 1554% respectively during 1979-80 to 1993-94). This has been mainly due to its more remunerative cultivation. Today, soybean is being cultivated on about 5 million hectares in the country. It has attained third place next only to Groundnut and Mustard in national production of oilseeds and edible oil. Besides, it has enabled export earnings of over Rs. 15,000 million per year. Soybean has revolutionized rural economy and has resulted overall development with conspicuous socio-economic upliftment of Indian farmers. Thus, augmenting income and increasing employment opportunities effecting accessibility to the available food as well as enhancing total protein availability in the country, soybean has provided perceptible household food security and nutrition.

Soybean is being more efficient user of land for protein and oil production, and has largely occupied farm stretch, otherwise lying fallow.

TABLE 20.3: **Protein Productivity of Major Cereals and Grain Legumes**

Crop	Estimated yield t/ha	Crop yield in food energy 10^6 K Cal	Protein content %	Crop duration days	Protein productivity kg/ha/day
	(1)	(2)	(3)		(4)*a
Legumes					
Soybean	1.7*c	6.9	38	95	6.8
Lima bean	3.2	-*b	25	115	7.0
Cowpea	1.8	—	25	80	5.6
Peanut	1.6	—	26	120	3.5
Winged bean	1.4	—	31	112	3.9
Chickpea	2.5	2.3	20	125	4.0
Mungbean	0.9	2.9	24	75	2.9
Cereals					
Rice	5.0	18.1	7.5	140	2.7
Wheat	2.3	7.6	11.9	100	2.7
Maize	4.0	14.0	9.5	120	3.2
Sorghum	3.5	11.7	10.1	110	3.2

$*a = \frac{1 \times 2}{3} = 4$; *b = Not available; *c = World average for 1979.

Source: Pimental *et al*., 1975.

TABLE 20.4: Essential Amino Acids in Soybean Seed, Flour, Concentrates and Isolates Compared with FAO Standard Requirements (g 16g—1 N)

Amino acid	FAO standard	Soybean			
		Seed	Flour	Concentrate	Isolate
Cystine	4.2	1.3	1.6	1.6	1.3
Isoleucine	4.2	4.5	4.7	4.8	4.9
Leucine	4.8	7.8	7.9	7.8	7.8
Lysine	4.2	6.4	6.3	6.3	6.4
Methionine	2.2	1.3	1.4	1.4	1.3
Phenylalanine	2.8	4.9	5.3	5.2	5.4
Threonine	2.8	3.9	3.9	4.2	3.6
Tryptophan	1.4	1.3	1.3	1.5	1.4
Tyrosine	2.8	3.1	3.8	3.9	4.3
Valine	4.2	4.8	5.1	4.9	4.7

Source: Weingartner, 1987.

The crop is providing raw material to agro-industry consisting of over 150 soybean processing plants. Consequently, fabulous employment opportunities both at farm as well as in the industry is provided. Thus, soybean can play key role in providing food security and nutrition by way of overcoming high priced pulse-protein inadequacy with low priced soya-based high quality protein food. Importance of soybean as low priced source of high quality protein, particularly for lactating mothers and children of weaker section of society dominating in the developing countries can possibly be no more ignored.

The Fallacy

Often, exaggerated anti-nutritional factors in soybean are oligosaccharides, stachyose and trypsin inhibitor. These are not uncommon in other legumes too. Trypsin inhibitor can be completely destroyed by moist heat of about 100°C or boiling soybean for 10-20 minutes. Processing, cooking in water, germination or fermentation can substantially reduce flatulence factors of soybean.

The beany flavour, is a major factor soybean as food in India is caused by oxidation of fatty acids (linolenic acid, etc.) due to enzymatic complex (lipoxygenases). During this process, chemical compounds

TABLE 20.5: Chemical Composition of Uncooked Soybean and Other Raw Foods

Food (100 g)	Calories	Carbohydrates (g)	Proteins (g)	Lipids (g)	Minerals (mg)		
					Ca	P	Fe
Polished rice	364.0	79.70	7.20	0.60	9	104	1.3
Whole wheat	353.7	70.10	12.70	2.50	37	386	4.3
Maize	363.3	70.70	11.80	4.50	11	290	2.5
Black beans	343.6	62.37	20.74	1.27	145	471	4.3
Soybean seed	395.0	30.00	36.10	71.70	226	546	8.8
Beef	111.0	—	21.00	3.00	12	224	3.2
Beef liver	130.3	—	20.20	5.50	8	373	12.1
Eggs	150.9	—	12.30	11.30	73	224	3.1
Cow milk	63.0	5.00	3.10	3.50	114	102	0.1

Source: Franco, 1986.

responsible for this disagreeable beany flavour are produced. Broken seeds providing exposed substrate (fatty acids) to lipoxygenase enzyme in the presence of water aggravates the problem (Nelson, Wei and Steinberg, 1980). Both processing strategy and genetic architecture of soybean has resulted overcoming the problem of beany flavour.

Food Uses of Soybean

Food uses of soybean can be broadly grouped as (i) Whole soybean, (ii) Defatted soyaflour, (iii) Soya-oil (Table 20.6).

(i) Whole Soybean

Boiled or sprouted soybean is highly nutritious food. Further, soya-milk and Tofu (soya-paneer) made from whole soybean are highly nutritious and cost effective substitute/supplement of cow's milk and milk-paneer.

(a) Tofu (Soya-paneer)

Tofu is coagulated and pressed soya-paneer. It is very much similar to milk-paneer in texture, appearance as well as taste and can be highly efficient low priced substitute of milk paneer (Table 20.7). Organoleptic studies conducted in the country have established good acceptability of soya-paneer (Tofu) as a substitute of milk-paneer (Bhatnagar, 1986). During the period of milk shortage in the country when in cosmopolitan cities, milk products are banned, soya-paneer would be in high demand. Milk-paneer is considered prestigious and priced dish, particularly in northern India. From the view point of nutrition, soya-paneer is a good egg substitute with low Sodium, low Cholesterol, low calorie and is gluten free. Nutritionally, soya-paneer ranks very high and is prescribed for lowering the blood cholesterol.

(b) Soya-milk

Beverages based on soybean either whole or in blend could be of high commercial and nutrition value. With proper formulation and product mix as well as restricting the price, its potential in substituting/supplementing cow's milk at low price is bright

TABLE 20.6: Important Food Uses of Soybean
(Low priced high protein food products significantly low in fat, calories and cholesterol)

WHOLE SOYBEAN	DEFATTED SOYFLOUR	SOY-PROTEIN ISOLATE SOY-PROTEIN CONCENTRATES	SOY-OIL
— Beverages	— Fortification of	— High protein food biscuits,	— Salad dressing
Whole, blends	cereal and legume flour	granules etc.	
milk extender			
— Coagulated products	— Fortified foods	— Fortified/fabricated	— Cooking oil &
Tofu/Paneer	Bread, biscuits and cake	Meat extender	shortening
	Chapati (Indian pan-cake)	Meat analogues	— Hydrogenated oil
	Baris and papad	Textured vegetable products	
	Dosa, Idli, Wada		
— Flour	Sweet meats	— Substitute/Replacement	— Margarine
Full fat		foods	
Low fat	— Substitute product-	— Restructured meat products	— Mayonnaise
	'besan' etc.	Patty products	
		Frozen desserts	
— Fermented products			
Tempeh	— Coagulated products	Cheese like products	
Soy-sauce	Tofu/Paneer etc.		
Miso			
Yogurt	— Fermented products	— Infant food	

(Contd.)

TABLE 20.6: (Contd.)

WHOLE SOYBEAN	DEFATTED SOYFLOUR	SOY-PROTEIN ISOLATE SOY-PROTEIN CONCENTRATES	SOY-OIL
Cheese analogues	Tempeh		
	Miso	— High energy food	
— Sprouted/cooked beans	Soy-sauce	beverages	
	Yogurt		
— Fried/roasted nuts	Cheese analogues	— Soy protein fibre	
	— Beverages	— Soy protein gel	
	— Breakfast & snack foods		
	— Textured soy products		
	— Meal extender		
	— Soy-milk powder		

TABLE 20.7: Composition of Nutrients in 100 gms of Tofu

	Tofu	Chinese style Tofu (Doufu)	Silken Tofu (Kinu-goshi)	Soy-milk	Wine ferm-ented Tofu (Doufuru)	Grilled Tofu	Dry Soy-bean	Defatted soybeans	Kinako & Roasted soybeans
Food energy calories	72.00	87.00	53.00	42.00	175.00	82.00	392.00	322.00	426.00
Moisture per cent	84.9	79.3	88.4	90.8	52.0	83.0	12.0	8.0	5.0
Protein per cent	7.8	10.6	5.5	3.6	13.5	8.8	34.3	49.0	38.4
Fat per cent	4.3	5.3	3.2	2.0	8.4	5.1	17.5	0.4	19.2
Sugars per cent	2.3	2.9	1.7	2.9	13.6	2.1	26.7	33.6	29.5
Fibre per cent	0	0	0	0.02	1.2	0	4.5	3.0	2.9
Ash per cent	0.7	0.9	1.2	0.5	11.6	1.0	5.0	6.0	5.0
Calcium Mg	146.0	159.0	94.0	15.0	165.0	180.0	190.0	220.0	190.0
Sodium Mg	6.0	7.0	23.0	2.0	458.0	15.0	3.0	4.0	4.0
Phosphorus Mg	105.0	109.0	71.0	49.0	182.0	120.0	470.0	550.0	500.0
Iron Mg	1.7	2.5	1.2	1.2	5.7	1.9	7.0	8.4	9.0
Vit. B Mg (Thiamine)	0.02	0.02	0.02	0.03	0.04	0.02	0.50	0.45	0.40

(Contd.)

TABLE 20.7: (Contd.)

	Tofu	Chinese style Tofu (Doufu)	Silken Tofu (Kinu-goshi)	Soy-milk	Wine ferm-ented Tofu (Doufuru)	Grilled Tofu	Dry Soy-beans	Defatted soybeans	Kinako & Roasted soybeans
Vit. B2 Mg (Riboflavin)	0.02	0.02	0.02	0.02	0.18	0.02	0.20	0.15	0.15
Vit. B3 Mg (Niacin)	0.5	0.6	0.3	0.5	0.6	0.4	2.0	2.0	2.0

Note: Regular Japanese tofu varies in protein content from 6 to 8.4, and in water content from 87.9 to 83.9 per cent, the mineral data above refer to Tofu (and Kinugoshi) solidified with Calcium sulphate Kinugoshi and the rich soymilk prepared at tofu shops vary protein from 4.9 to 6.3, and in water content for 89.7 to 87 per cent. Commercially-distributed soymilk varies in protein from 3.6 to 5.8, and in water content from 90.8 to 88.2 per cent. Thick age prepared with nigari often contains upto 17.7 per cent protein and only 58.7 per cent water. Differences in composition depends primarily on the method of preparation, the type of solidifier, and the grade and protein content of the soybean used.

Source: Standard Tables of Food Composition (Japan), FAO Food Composition Tables, and USDA Composition of Foods (Wasn, D.C.).

(Table 20.8). In the past, quite a few entrepreneurs launched production and marketing of soya-milk under different names in India. However, due to high packaging cost and overhead expenses, encouraging results were not obtained. Nevertheless, with needed precautions and overcoming the flaws, commercial and nutritional advantage of the product can be taken in the context of food security and nutrition.

TABLE 20.8: Composition of Whole Milk and Soya-beverage

(Per cent dry weight basis)

	Whole milk	Unflavoured	Flavoured	Soy fortified milk	50/50 soymilk blend
Milk solids Not fat	9.00	—	—	9.00	4.50
Butterfat	3.25	—	—	—	1.63
Vegetable fat	—	2.00	2.00	2.00	1.63
Soy protein isolate	—	3.62	3.62	3.62	1.81
42% HFCS*	—	—	8.00	8.00	—
42 D.E** Corn Syrup	—	6.00	—	—	3.00
Sodium Citrate	—	0.20	0.20	—	—
Salt	—	0.05	0.05	—	—
Stabilizer/ Emulsifier	—	0.10	0.10	—	—
Total solids	12.25	11.97	13.97	33.62	12.57
Protein	3.24	3.26	3.26	6.49	3.26
Fat	3.25	2.00	2.00	2.00	3.25

* High fructose corn sweetener.

** Dextrose equivalent.

(ii) Defatted Soyaflour

Soya-meal or defatted soyaflour—a by-product of soya-oil industry is being exported to the extent of 98 per cent of its production in the country. Nutritionally, defatted soyaflour with over 55 per cent high quality protein is precious. Its export resulting protein drain from a country, when several hundred millions of its populace are facing protein calorie malnutrition is paradoxical. Under the present context of shortage and high price of pulses soaring beyond the purchasing power of common Indian, soya-protein in the form of defatted soyaflour or in any other form is the only solution.

Defatted soyaflour can be utilized in various ways for direct and indirect use to the human populace such as:

1. Food

(i) Fortification of wheat flour— fortification with soyaflour at the rate of 5-10 per cent without any effect on organoleptic or physical properties of wheat flour can result utilization of atleast 8-16 lakh tons of defatted soyaflour in the country. This will result higher protein content in wheat flour and its additional availability for the masses to take care of nutrition and calorie malnutrition. Convincing benefits in terms of financial gains are evidenced in Table 20.9 (Sulebele, 1988).

(ii) Supplementation/substitution of *besan* (horsegram flour)— after minor processing of soyameal, it could be used as *besan* with significant financial and nutritional advantages. 'Soya-besan' will be about half the price of conventional *besan* of horsegram needed in millions of tons in the country.

(iii) Substitution/supplementation of blackgram—for production of conventional *baries, papad* and south Indian preparations like *vada* and *dosa* etc. substitution of blackgram will be of economic and nutritional advantage. Due to very high price of blackgram, an essential component in these cuisines, its substitution/supplementation by defatted soya-flour will bring down the food price considerably and make their increased availability at affordable price to ensure food security.

(iv) Texturised Soya Products (TSP)—as low priced substitute of protein food, TSP will provide cost effective nutritive gains.

(v) Energy food like *Sattu*—use of soybean in *sattu*—poor man's energy food could make available high protein food.

(vi) Bakery products—soya-meal could be used in variety of ways in bakery by mixing it with wheat flour for making bread, cakes, pastries, biscuits etc. with improved texture and crumb quality.

TABLE 20.9: Cost of Supplementation of Wheat Flour with Soy Flour

Assumptions:

Cost of wheat flour (whole)	Rs. 7.50/kg
Cost of soy flour	Rs. 10.00/kg
Yield of chapatis/kg flour	40
Av. weight of one chapati	25 g

Sample	Cost/kg (Rs.)	Cost/ chapati (Paise)	Protein (%)	Total Protein/ chapati	Total dietary protein inta (200 g flour basis) (gms)	Cost of per gram (paise)
1. Whole wheat flour	7.50	18.75	12.10	3.025	24.2	6.20
2. 5% soy-flour in wheat flour	7.63	19.08	13.99	3.497	28.98	5.46
3. 10% " " " "	7.75	19.38	15.89	3.972	31.78	4.87
4. 15% " " " "	7.88	19.70	17.78	4.445	35.56	4.43
5. 20% " " " "	8.01	20.03	19.68	4.920	39.36	4.07
6. 25% " " " "	8.14	20.35	21.57	5.392	43.14	3.77
7. Soy-flour 10.00 25.00	50.00	12.500	100.00	2.00		

Source: Sulebele, G.A. 1988. SOPA Digest, Issue 12. p.7. (Price of wheat flour and soy-flour have been revised).

(vii) Coffee whitener—use of defatted soyaflour in coffee whitener would be financially and nutritionally advantageous.

(viii) Substitution of milk and milk protein in high energy food products—this will result bring down the price of such exorbitantly priced products.

(ix) Production of protein hydrolysates, soya-concentrates and soya-isolates would be highly remunerative and cost effective in high protein food industry.

2. Feed

Importance of soya-meal as protein source in feed for livestock, piggery and poultry is undisputed. It is for this reason, Indian soya-meal has good international market.

3. Aqua-Feed

Soyameal is known to be frugal source of protein substituting costly protein source in aqua-feed.

Suggested Strategy

For harnessing benefits of soybean in national perspective, its use in augmenting availability of edible oil should continue unabated. Further, in the context of food security and nutrition, efforts to popularise use of soya-meal or defatted soyaflour—a lowest priced high quality source of protein in food and feed industry should be efficiently and effectively made. Some of the action points could be:

(i) fixing up realistic PFA standards for defatted soyaflour/DOC at par with other similar food products like *maida, sooji, besan*, etc.;

(ii) incentives like relaxation in excise duty, provision of soft loans, priority in providing electricity, preference in allotting premises etc. to encourage setting up soyameal based food/feed industry;

(iii) enacting and prescribing fortification of wheat flour with soyameal/ defatted soyaflour to the extent of 5-10 per cent and making them available through fair price shops;

(iv) legislating fortification of bread mix and other bakery products with soyameal/defatted soyaflour to the extent of 2 per cent.

responsible for this disagreeable beany flavour are produced. Broken seeds providing exposed substrate (fatty acids) to lipoxygenase enzyme Now is perhaps the high time, when effective steps, as suggested be taken so that this lowest priced source of high quality protein could be used in India to enable:

(a) plugging of the protein drain from the country and making available lowest priced high quality source of protein to provide food security and nutrition particularly to masses, who cannot afford high price of other protein foods;
(b) delinking of foreign dependence of soya-industry for sustainable household security achieved through soybean farming and industry.

Panchayati Raj to be the Key for Harnessing Benefits of Soybean

One of the major factor for having not been able to so far harness benefits of soybean in the context of food security and nutrition in Inida had been lack of awareness, particularly in the target groups. Panchayats can play dramatic role in creation of awareness about the financial and nutritional benefits of foods based on whole soybean or defatted soyaflour. At Panchayat level, the accruable gains from soybean to the society in general and malnourished poor in particular can be convincingly documented through various AV-aids. Also small scale food industries based on defatted soyaflour or whole soybean can be launched in cooperatives. Thus, Panchayati Raj can in real sense be key to plug the protein drain for food security and nutrition in India and other developing countries.

REFERENCES

Bhatnagar, P.S. 1986. Soybean—Its Food Uses and Modern Food Industries, in Modernisation of Food Industry, 'AHARA'—An International Food Exhibition (Jan. 25-Feb. 7, 1986). Trade Fair Authority of India.

Franco, G. 1986. Table de composicao quimica de alimentos, 7 ed. Rio de Janerio, RJ, Brasil, Athenen.

Hymowitz, T. 1970. On the Domestication of Soybean. *Econ. Bot.* 24: 408-21.

Kaldy, M.S. 1972. Protein Yield of Various Crops as Related to Protein Value. *Econ. Bot.* 26: 142-44.

Ma, Rhu-Hwa and Zhang-Khan. 1983. Historical Development of Soybean Production in China. Proceedings of the first China/USA Soybean Symposium and Working Group Meeting, Urbana, Illinois, USA, 16-18.

Nelson, A.I., Wei, L.S. and Steinberg, M.P. 1980. Foods from Whole Soybeans, in F.T. Corbin, ed. Proc. 2nd World Soybean Res. Conf., Raleigh, 26-29 Mar. 1979, pp. 745-62. Boulder, CO, USA, Westview Press.

Nwar, W.W. 1985. Lipids. In C.R. Fennema, ed. *Food Chemistry*, 2nd ed. pp. 139-244. New York, NY, USA, M. Dekker.

Pimental, D., Dritschilo, W, Krummel, J and Kutzman, J. 1975. Energy and Land Constraints in Food Protein Production. Science, 190: 754-61.

Selleck, G.W. 1983. Soybean for Tropics and Sub-tropics. Proc. Itl. Sympo. on Soybean in Tropics and Sub-Tropics TARC, Japan, Sept. 26-Oct. 1, 1983: iii-iv.

Sulebele, G.A. 1988. SOPA Digest, Issue 12, p. 7.

Weingarter, K.E. 1987. Processing, Nutrition and Utilization of Soybeans, in S.R. Singh, K.O. Rachie and K.E. Dashiel, eds. Soybeans for the Tropics: Research, Production and Utilization, pp. 149-78. Chichester, UK, Wiley-Interscience Publications.

TWENTY-ONE

AGRO-INPUT SUPPLY: Cooperative's Experience

VIRENDRA KUMAR and B.P. GOVIL

India's population is very close to one billion mark. It has grown up three fold since independence. It is with God's grace and scientific achievements in the field of agriculture, that India is today, by and large self-sufficient in the field of foodgrain production.

India has made a spectacular progress in foodgrains production from 50.82 mt in 1950 to 192 mt in 1995-96 (Table 21.1). The wheat production which was 6.46 mt in 1950-51 has gone up to a record level of 63 mt. Likewise rice production has increased four fold from about 20 mt to 81 mt in 1994-95. The gross production of foodgrains may have to reach around 220 mt by the end of ninth five year plan from out of the available 147

TABLE 21.1: Area Production and Productivity of Foodgrains in India

Plan/Year	Area (million ha)	Production (million tonnes)	Productivity (kg/ha)
I Plan	110.6	66.85	605
II Plan	115.6	82.0	710
III Plan	115.1	72.4	629
IV Plan	126.5	104.7	827
V Plan	129.0	131.9	1022
VI Plan	126.7	145.5	1149
VII Plan	127.8	176.4	1380
1991-92	121.9	168.4	1382
1992-93	123.2	179.5	1457
1993-94	122.8	184.3	1501
1994-95	123.5	191.0	1547.0

m/ha of arable land operated by 90 million operational holdings. Not only food, the demand for fuel, fibre and fodder has also to be met to sustain the growing population from the same piece of arable land.

Important Agro-Inputs

From among various components responsible for productivity and overall agricultural production the Agro-Input supply and management is the most important. Seeds, fertiliser, irrigation, credit pest control measures, are the principal Agro-Inputs for farming. Their timely supply, effective and efficient utilisation is crucial from productivity point of view. This is more important in a subsistence agricultural economy like ours which is peasant oriented.

India has made appreciable progress on the front of Agro-Input production and supply. Some details of Agro-Inputs are given below:

Seeds

Seed is the basic input in agriculture and has direct bearing on per unit production. Presently about 60 per cent of the home grown seeds are used by farmers. The experience has shown that their yield potential is quite limited in comparison to seed grown by following proper seed growing techniques. Various private and public sector organisations are engaged in the production of high yielding and hybrid varieties of seeds of various crops. Important ones being National Seeds Corporation, State Seed Corporation, State Farm Corporation of India and various private organisations. In the Cooperative sector, IFFCO and Kribhco are also producing quality seeds.

As a result of sustained efforts in the direction of production of HYV of seeds the supply position has increased from 0.18 million quintals in 1953-54 to 6.15 million quintals in 1994-95. Table 21.2 and 21.3 show production of Foundation and Certified seeds during 1992-93 to 1994-95.

Fertiliser

Fertilisers have played a very significant role in India's self sufficiency in food production. This is the reason that fertilisers figure prominently in all agricultural development plans of the Government of India. It is estimated that fertilisers alone account for 40 to 50 per cent of the foodgrain output in India. As a result, the consumption of fertiliser nutrients has gone up

TABLE 21.2: Distribution of Foundation Seed

(Lakh/Quintal)

Crop	1992-93	1993-94	1994-95*
Cereals	2.5	2.1	2.1
Pulses	0.4	0.2	0.3
Oilseeds	0.7	0.9	1.1
Fibres	0.1	0.1	0.1
Total	3.6	3.2	3.5

*Estimated

TABLE 21.3: Distribution of Certified Seed

(Lakh/Quintal)

Crop	1992-93	1993-94	1994-95*
Cereals	36.7	38.1	47.1
Pulses	3.4	3.4	3.7
Oilseeds	10.8	11.4	8.0
Fibres	2.1	2.1	2.7
Total	53.0	54.9	61.5

from a mere 69 thousand tonnes in 1950-51 to 13.86 mt in 1995-96. On per hectare basis, the comsumption has increased from 5 kg/ha in 1950-51 to 76 kg/ha in 1995-96. Table 21.4 gives progressive increase in fertiliser nutrient consumption commencing from first Five Year Plan till 1995-96. It is noted that the pace of fertiliser consumption and foodgrain production has been almost identical.

Pest Control

Increase in crop productivity and cropping intensity has also resulted in an increase in the incidence of crop pests and diseases. As a result, the consumption of pesticides (technical grade material) has increased from only 2.35 thousand tonnes in 1950-51 to more than 72 thousand tonnes. Presently, however, there is a growing realisation in favour of Integrated Pest Management (IPM) utilising the best combination of available control techniques to pest problems. IPM is ecologically sound, economically

TABLE 21.4: Fertilizer Consumption

('000 tonnes)

Plan/Year	Nitrogen	Phosphorus	Potassium	Total
I Plan	107.5	13.0	10.3	130.8
II Plan	211.7	53.1	20.0	284.8
III Plan	574.8	132.5	77.3	784.6
IV Plan	1829.0	649.7	359.8	2838.5
V Plan	3419.5	1106.9	591.5	5117.9
VI Plan	5486.0	1886.4	838.5	8210.9
VII Plan	7797.2	3221.0	1328.0	12346.2
1991-92	8046.2	3321.2	1360.6	12728.0
1992-93	8427.0	2844.0	884.0	12155.0
1993-94	8789.0	2669.0	908.0	12366.0
1994-95	9511.0	2945.0	1064.0	13520.0
1995-96	9875.0	2837.2	1154.3	13866.7

*Provisional.
Source: FAI, New Delhi.

viable and socially acceptable.

Cooperatives in the Service of Farmers

The cooperatives originated as an institutional agency for delivering crop loans in a small way. Now there are more than 3,53,000 cooperative societies having a membership of 175 million and employing a working capital of more than Rs. 76,000 million. During 1993-94, a sum of 85,000 million was provided to the farmers as short, medium and long term credit by the Cooperatives constituting 56 per cent of the total institutional credit. Cooperatives with service as their main motto have tried to integrate credit into supplies of inputs and marketing of agricultural produce. Whenever wanted, they have helped in the Government efforts such as special development programmes like the oilseeds and pulses.

The agricultural marketing cooperatives numbering more than six thousand deal with special commodities and with agricultural produce. They are affiliated to Cooperative Marketing Federations at the State level or with their respective commodity federations. These cooperatives deal with a wide range of agricultural commodities like cereals, pulses, oilseeds, plantation crops, fruits, vegetables, fibres etc. They also provide various pre- and post-harvest services. A number of agricultural processing units have also been set up by marketing cooperatives. They are afiliated to NAFED at National level. These cooperatives handle substantial quantity of agricultural produce and have large storage capacity in rural areas.

Agro-Input Distribution through Cooperatives

Among various agro-inputs, fertilizer and credit is the main input in which the cooperatives are dealing, though some of the State Marketing Federations also procure and supply other inputs like Agro-chemicals, seed and implements etc. These are the main canalising agency for the distribution of Agro-inputs to farmers on behalf of the Government.

Prior to 1966, Cooperatives were given priority in fertilizer distribution. With the introduction of HYV of wheat and several hybrids of other crops, the demand for fertiliser increased many fold and the business became lucrative for private trade. Government agreed to Sivaraman Committee recommendation and allowed private trade to deal in fertilisers alongwith cooperatives. Today, Cooperatives distribute about 33 per cent of the total fertiliser distributed in the country. They supply fertilisers and other inputs in the nook and corner of the country. During 1994-95, IFFCO alone contributed 12.7% N and 15.1 % P_2O_5 to the National Nutrient production by producing 13.84 lakh tonnes of nutrients of nitrogen and phosphorus. Total sales which comprised urea, DAP and high analysis NPK complex fertilisers amounted to 32.16 lakh tonnes with total turnover of Rs. 1932.89 crores. Likewise during 1994-95 Kribhco, a sister IFFCO concern in the cooperative sector produced 14.66 lakh tonnes and sold 15.45 lakh tonnes of urea. The Service Centres numbering 65 owned by Kribhco supplied fertilisers namely, Urea, DAP and Zinc Sulphate and seeds and agro-chemicals worth Rs. 1637 lakhs to farmers directly in the States of Punjab, Haryana and Uttar Pradesh.

IFFCO Experience of Supplying Agro-Inputs Under One Roof

IFFCO introduced the concept of providing essential agro-inputs like fertilisers, seed and agro-chemicals alongwith agricultural advice under one roof by opening its first Farmers Service Centre (FSC) in 1976 at Karnal in Haryana with the following objectives:

— To supply timely and adequate quantity of inputs at reasonable price. Also a supply simple farm equipment free of cost for community use.

— To provide technical know-how to farmers.

— To educate farmers by intensively working in villages adjacent to Farmers Service Centres.

A Field Officer, who is Graduate/Post Graduate in agriculture is the incharge of FSC. Sales proceeds of the FSC is maintained by the salesman. Salesman also acquires sufficient knowledge on agro-inputs and advises farmers on their proper use. A helper is responsible for upkeep of the centre and also attends to the customer and the visitors. Literature on crop production is available on the centre and regular liaison is maintained with the farmers.

During 1994-95, IFFCO supplied agro-inputs worth Rs. 88 crore through its 175 Farmers Service Centres located in 12 States.

IFFCO-NCDC Farmers Service Centres

The National Cooperative Development Corporation (NCDC) requested IFFCO to come forward and collaborate in developing certain primary agricultural societies on the lines of IFFCO FSCs. The main objective of adopting some societies under IFFCO-NCDC scheme was to increase the viability of selected societies which are already dealing in supply of farm inputs. The margin money of Rs. 30,000 was provided by NCDC as a loan to each society and IFFCO extended its cooperation by providing a sum of Rs. 12000 to each society which comprised Rs. 6,000 as subsidy for supply of farm implements and equipment and another Rs. 6,000 towards furniture and upkeep of the showroom of the society. Rs. 4,000 was also to be contributed by each society towards furniture and upkeep of the show room. In addition, IFFCO Field Officer provided technical know-how.

This scheme was subsequently modified during 1987-88 as under:

— Besides IFFCO, Kribhco and States or commodity Federations also to act as lead agencies.

— Selection of cooperative retail outlets to be done on a cluster basis i.e. group of 30-40 retail outlets run by primary agricultural credit societies including primary marketing societies in a compact area.

— Margin money increased from Rs. 30,000 upto Rs. 1 lakh per society depending on the type and size of society. Assistance to be routed through State Government

— A State Level Coordination Committee may be set up to implement and monitor the scheme.

One of the important objective is to generate cash sales of inputs. All inputs are arranged by the nodal agency. Promotional programmes are organised around the societies to promote balanced fertiliser application and also to generate sales for the society.

Presently 1,450 such societies are adopted under this scheme in 13 States. During 1993-94, 1.12 lakh tonnes of fertilisers were sold through these societies.

EXPERIENCES OF NGOs AND OTHER AGENCIES WORKING WITH PRIs

TWENTY-TWO

FOOD SECURITY AND NUTRITION RELATED ACTIVITIES LINKED TO THE PANCHAYAT

INDIRA CHAKRAVARTY

Introduction

In the State of West Bengal, the Panchayati Raj system is firmly rooted and strongly as well as effectively functional for over 20 years in the entire rural area. The Panchayat has a three-tier system: Village Panchayat, Panchayat Samity (Block) and Zilla Parishad (District).

Each Panchayat has at least ten different permanent committees to take up and look after activities in agriculture, irrigation, use of waste land, transport, road, domestic water supply, cottage industry, health etc. through mid-level planning which is integrated with macro level (block and district) trainings, equipments, etc. In fact the Government of West Bengal, is now directing about 40 per cent of rural development funds directly to the Panchayat, which is an unique case. However, they also raise or arrange for local funds for recycling and generating economic support.

In fact, most of the developmental and welfare activities in the villages are under the purview of village Panchayat, managed by the elected leaders. The Panchayat in the State has an infrastructure and experience of handling matters related to socio-economic development, and above all has the support of the communities as well as the government. In West Bengal, Panchayat is using and utilising waste land, setting up small scale irrigation, distributing fertilizers, providing storage facilities even to small and marginal farmers and also has set up village markets.

As an outcome of the highly monitorised Panchayat system, the food production, mainly in terms of cereal, potato and fish production, have increased several folds, in quantity and varieties. This has given a sense of security in terms of food availability, mandays of work, income-generation and equitability in distribution, as a result of which migration of poor villagers in the lean seasons from villages to the towns and industrial areas has significantly decreased. Although there is long way to go to establish "Food Security", but there is an unanimous feeling that the interventions need to be based on localised food production, market availability, rational pricing and equitable access to the food produced. A clear trend is visible in West Bengal that if the Panchayat system is further strengthened by the end of the IX Planning period, the poor and the weaker sections and selected groups (such as women) in rural areas may get the maximum benefit as far as the Food Security is concerned. This will, undoubtedly, be the prime factor for reduction of overall poverty and malnutrition and enhancement of the human resource utilisation. However, to achieve Food Security, the Panchayat has to inculcate scientific knowledge, attitude and practices of the mass through informal or formal mass education, specially involving the women.

In West Bengal, production of cereals e.g. rice, wheat, barley, maize and other cereals increased from 8,043.2 thousand tonnes in 1980-81 to 12,190.2 thousand tonnes in 1992-93. The pulse production fluctuated having an output of 238.8 thousand tonnes in 1980-81, 175.0 thousand tonnes in 1991-92 and 198.9 tonnes in 1992-93. An increased production was also achieved in oil seeds (150.4 thousand tonnes in 1980-81 to 410.8 thousand tonnes in 1992-93). Potato production showed an increased trend of 1,971.8 thousand tonnes in 1980-81 to 4,779.1 thousand tonnes in 1992-93.

With regard to protective foods, which are essential for keeping the nutritional balance, the production of vegetables at the National level inclusive of a wide variety of fruits, vegetables, nuts and spices has increased from 34 to 53.8 billion tonnes during the period of 1985 to 1990; production of milk by about 60 per cent viz. from 21 million tonnes in 1971 to 53.7 million tonnes in 1990; egg production by 350 per cent, viz. from 6 billion in 1971 to 21 billion in 1990. However, due to huge population growth from about 55 million to 85 million during this period, the per capita availability has not improved significantly.

To establish a proper food security, for all the people particularly for the underprivileged poor living in the villages, local micro level planning has to be carefully evolved for enhancement of the food production through the help of the local Panchayat. This will ensure not only the production and intake of cereals but also of the protective foods like vegetables, fruits etc. However, this has to be linked to enhancement of literacy, scientific awareness like storage, preservation, processing, cooking practices etc. of locally available foods so that the community can get the maximum benefit out of what is produced.

Programmes Taken up by the All India Institute of Hygiene and Public Health in Coordination with the Panchayats in West Bengal

Over the past 60 and odd years the Institute has been associated with rural health, nutrition and sanitation cares through its network of rural units in the state of West Bengal. A large number of studies, surveys, researches, pilot projects and intervention measures were taken up by the institute in village areas of various districts of West Bengal, as well in the North Eastern belt of the country, with the support from various international as well as national agencies like FAO of United Nations; UNDP, World Bank; UNICEF, WHO, IDRC, Hunger Project; ICMR, CSIR, ICAR, the Planning Commission, the State Public Health Engineering Department, The Rajiv Gandhi National Drinking Water Mission and various other Ministries and Departments of the national and State level. The main objective of these surveys or projects was to improve the health, nutrition and sanitation status as well as consciousness of the rural mass, including the role of women suitable for various activities based on the local conditions. Many of these activities were conducted with the cooperation and collaboration of the local Panchayat Samitis, along with the help and support from the Department of Rural Development and Panchayat, Government of West Bengal. Most of the time, committees were formed at the state, district and village level to ensure flow of information and proper intersectoral coordination among all concerned Departments at all levels.

The impact of these activities have also been specially assessed by using various indicators. The results obtained were shared with the administrators, local leaders and communities, through the Panchayats, to help to develop suitable strategic plans of action.

The following is the summary of some of the recent programmes carried out in the rural areas of West Bengal with the active support and involvement of the Panchayat by the All India Institute of Hygiene and Public Health which are linked to food security and poverty alleviation.

1. *Development of Training Material for the Elected Leaders of the Panchayat*: In West Bengal there are about 68,000 elected members of Gram Panchayats out of which about 28,000 are women. These members were trained with the help of a training module manual along with audio-visual aides (video cassettes, pamphlets etc.) developed for this purpose with the support of the Hunger Project. The training was imparted in cooperation with the department of Rural Development and Panchayat, Government of West Bengal. Training materials used were two video cassettes, (one on the general responsibilities of the Panchayat and the other on issues related to public health) and one training manual covering all general issues on Public Health and nutrition—highlighting the role of the Panchayat.

   The material was used to train the key trainers, the Panchayat Pradhans, the Karmadhakshas, the women office bearers and all the elected members of the Panchayat. Presently evaluation workshops are being carried out to assess the post training KAP of the elected leaders in some selected districts of the State.

2. *Horticultural Interventions and Homegardening linked to Nutrition Education, for Combating Vitamin A Deficiency in the Rural People*: The project was supported by FAO of United Nations and introduced in three blocks of the most drought prone district of Purulia in West Bengal, covering about 40,000 of the population. The Panchayat workers, local volunteers, NGO workers along with Panchayat leaders, upto the Zilla Parishad level were sensitised and trained on primary concept of food security, nutrition and health care along with their role in the upgradation of the health and nutritional status of the people.

   The basic component of this programme was to make green leafy vegetables (GLV), other vegetables and fruits rich in carotene to be made available to each and every individual out of the production in his/her own homegarden or nearby fields. The villagers were trained and three central nurseries were developed one for each of the three blocks with the help and support of the local Panchayats. The output included preservation of high yielding varieties of seeds, homegardening of various vegetables and fruits rich in carotene, improving cooking practices that favour minimum loss of vitamins and minerals, preservation of excess produces; using local fortification methods, maintenance of personal hygiene, consumption of safe water to prevent diarrhoeal diseases which drain out available nutrients and so on.

The programme was a success in terms of increasing the level of production as well as of consumption of carotene rich fruits, significant reduction in the prevalence of Vitamin A deficiency signs and symptoms, increase in awareness of the villagers and improvement in general KAP on nutrition. 100 per cent of the families had greens grown in the backyard throughout the year. Consumption levels of greens in all groups rose by 30-70 per cent, thereby increasing vitamin A equivalent consumption by the same extent. Eye and other signs of vitamin A deficiency reduced markedly specially among the young children. About 10-20 per cent or more of the mothers were found to have acquired some knowledge on role of carotene rich foods in preventing diseases and ailments for maintaining good health and including GLV in the daily diets of the children. Moreover, on an average each family generated an income of about Rs. 3-5 per day (mainly by the women of the house) by selling the extra greens produced.

Various types of visual and audio-visual materials (audio and video cassettes), books, pamphlets, posters, rural plays and dramas etc. were developed for the purpose. The highlights of the project and its achievement were presented to the Hon'ble members of the Assembly of Government of West Bengal at the Assembly house to get their reaction. Hon'ble members of Assembly strongly spoke for the replication of such a project in other districts and the chairman of the Planning Board, Government of West Bengal assured that the project module would be considered during the State planning process.

3. *Fishing Project for Poor Villagers for Food Support and Income Generation*: This project was introduced for the villagers to make themselves self-reliant economically by catching fish, using it locally and selling the excess. The Money Back system was introduced so that the beneficiaries could return the capital with a small interest which could be reinvested for a new group of beneficiaries. The grant was utilised in buying equipments like net, boat, fish-feed, etc. This was done through a local NGO network at North 24-Parganas through the Panchayat.
4. *Small Scale Animal Husbandry (Goat Rearing):* As per advice and guidance of the local Panchayat at Jaipur in Bankura district some of the rural tribal clans were supported in their age old occupation of goat rearing that would give them good economic return and food support. A plan of developing a cooperative is

presently being supported.

5. *Development of Curriculum and Training of School Girls on Health, Nutrition and Environment:* A curriculum has been developed and tried at a rural secondary school for girls, to make them aware about the various aspects of Food and Nutrition like Home Gardening, health and hygiene and particularly environmental sanitation. Certain specific health issues which are of special relevance to girls was also added on. This was done in a school run by the Howrah Panchayat. This programme is not only improving the KAP of the girls but also of the family as a whole.
6. *Development of a Panchayat Support and Revolving Fund for a Cooperative Health Care System in Rural Areas:* This project aimed at setting up health clinic facilities by a NGO called the Vivekananda Rural Health Clinic which was started in August 1994. The objective was to give Health Care and Nutrition linked education and food support for the poorest of the poor.
7. *Role of Panchayat in MCH Services in the Rural Areas:* This study was supported by WHO. The findings indicate that the women who were aware of the MCH services given from ICDS or Primary Health Centres, had better haemoglobin status, higher birth weight of babies, better personal hygiene, etc.

   The study clearly revealed that Mahila Mandal and Panchayat Samitis played a great role to influence the illiterate, semi-literate and other village women to gain access to health facilities at MCH clinics. Misconception about folifer tablets consumption was minimum with those who had participated in the meetings conducted by Panchayat and Mahila Samitis. Giving greens to pregnant women and young children was also practised regularly by families who had attended the community education camps. These families took initiatives to produce greens and fruits throughout the year in the home gardens. It was concluded that focus group discussions, Mahila Samity meetings and the Panchayat can play a key role to improve the health of women by motivating them to use the existing MCH services and by enhancing food consciousness. This was conducted through a NGO, under Mandra Unnayan Samsad, Panchayat and the Urban Health Training Centre of the All India Institute of Hygiene and Public Health, Singur, Hooghly district.
8. *Health and Nutritional Status of Tribal Groups in Chronically Drought Prone Areas of West Bengal to Suggest Suitable Intervention Strategies:* The study conducted in Balarampur and

Barabazar Block of Purulia district with support of the local Panchayat clearly indicated that in areas with higher irrigation coverage (i.e. 28%) by small scale irrigation had more production of food as compared to the lessor irrigated areas (around 2.5%). Remarkably, however, the health and nutrition indicators showed no remarkable difference when compared between the two. This clearly indicated that food production has to be linked to other strategic intervention like pricing, availability, distribution and other supportive inputs like health care, education, environmental protection etc.

9. *Impact of Sanitation and Clean Water Supply on the Nutritional and Health Status of Tribal Groups:* In a study supported by WHO, and coordinated by the District, Panchayat, Midnapore, Socio-behavioural aspects of tribal people of Midnapore district, towards personal hygiene, domestic sanitation, use of latrine and food taboos were studied.

   The study, indicated that factors like ignorance, traditional food taboos, lack of safe drinking water, non-availability of sanitary facilities, high incidence of parasitic infestation needed special attention and incentive by the Panchayat.

Conclusion

The Department of Biochemistry and Nutrition of the Institute has been playing a key role in coordination with other Departments viz. Sanitary Engineering and Environmental Sanitation, Occupational Health, Epidemiology, Health Education, Microbiology, Preventive and Social Medicine, Public Health Administration, Public Health Nursing and Health Statistics, not only to train but also to evaluate several new strategies to ensure food security and food availability along with the help and support of the Department of Rural Development and Panchayat, Government of West Bengal.

The studies conclusively indicate that sustainable food security in the rural areas has to be achieved through small scale localised planning and the success of that would depend mainly on participation of the Panchayat. Issues that need special attention are horticultural interventions (Home gardening), food distribution and availability at family level, food preservation and fortification, safe water supply, environmental sanitation, etc. All these activities cannot be ensured without the active support and coordination from the Panchayat.

TWENTY-THREE

CASE STUDY OF UTTRAKHAND HIMALAYAS

M.L. DEWAN

Panchayati Raj

Historically self-governance at village level was not unknown to communities in the Indian subcontinent. Historians have recorded that even a thousand years ago, there was enviable democratic decentralization wherein the village was vested with the power to govern itself through elected village councils. One finds such examples over a wide geographical area throughout the pre-colonial period.

After the emergence of the national movement, especially after Gandhiji's appearance, the idea of local self-governance at the village level gained prominence. In 1946, Gandhiji said, "Independence must begin at the bottom. Thus, every village will be a republic or Panchayat having full powers. It follows, therefore, that every village has to be self-sustained and capable of managing its affairs. Unfortunately after independence, the leadership wanted the Indian State to retain its centralized character thus undermining local self-governance.

Of late, the political leadership has been prevailed upon to accord constitutional mandate to the local self-governance system in the form of Panchayati Raj. Under the new Act it is compulsory for the States to hold elections to Panchayats; its provisions provide an opportunity to the weaker sections including women to participate in Panchayat institutions at all levels.

The Indian society is pluralistic, characterized by the multiplicity of ethnic, linguistic and religious groups. This socio-cultural pluralism in society also displays a variety of local self-governance systems.

As indicated, the 73rd Constitution Amendment has considerably widened the area of operation of the Panchayati Raj institutions (PRIs). As grassroot local organisations. The PRIs are expected to identity the felt needs and aspirations of the people and as such they can give a fillip to all kinds of activities in rural areas with the sole aim of bringing about rural transformation in real sense of the term.

As defined in the Constitution, "Panchayat" means an institution (by whatever name called) of self-government constituted under article 243B for the rural areas. Panchayat area means the territorial area of a Panchayat.

Here, it is pertinent to point out that the Panchayati Raj system is not new to India. However, with the amendment of Panchayat Act, Panchayats have been accorded recognition as harbingers of effecting change in rural scene. What is to be noted is that all the 29 items added to the Eleventh Schedule of Constitution are directed towards economic uplift, the true implementation of which will elevate the economic status of villagers. Following are the 29 items of activities as enunciated in the Constitution.

1. Agriculture including agricultural extension.
2. Land improvement, implementation of land reforms, land consolidation and soil conservation.
3. Minor irrigation, water management and watershed development.
4. Animal husbandry, dairying and poultry.
5. Fisheries.
6. Social forestry and farm forestry.
7. Minor forest produce or non timber forest produce (NTFP).
8. Small-scale industries, including food processing industries.
9. Khadi, village and cottage industries.
10. Rural housing.
11. Drinking water.
12. Fuel and fodder.
13. Roads, culverts, bridges, ferries, waterways and other means of communication.
14. Rural electrification, including distribution of electricity.
15. Non-conventional (Renewable) energy sources.
16. Poverty alleviation programmes.
17. Education, including primary and secondary schools.
18. Technical training and vocational education.
19. Adult and non-formal education.
20. Libraries.
21. Cultural activities.

22. Markets and fairs.
23. Health and sanitation, including hospitals, primary health centres and dispensaries.
24. Family welfare.
25. Women and child development.
26. Social welfare including welfare of the handicapped and mentally retarded.
27. Welfare of the weaker section, and in particular, of the Scheduled Castes and Scheduled Tribes.
28. Public distribution system.
29. Maintenance of community assets.

Rural enterprise development is a must to achieve the result expected of PRIs. Pooling of resources is essential for the success of any venture, particularly related to rural areas. However, it has been seen that pooling of existing available resources of both manpower, infrastructure and expertise have been lacking in the past. What is now necessary is a new orientation in the entire gamut of economic activities so that the rural sector is endowed with plentiful resources to feed a variety of activities, including the aforesaid 29 items.

To concretise rural enterprise development there is a need to work together by all concerned. The concept of Planning, Research, Action, Codification Extension and Loaning (PARCEL) must also be practised. This concept also ensures fuller utilisation of investment through organiser-entrepreneurs with a view to facilitating sustainable self-employment enterprises.

Panchayati Raj and Poverty Alleviation Action Plan

According to Indian Economic Information Year Book 1988-89. The Poverty-stricken Population in India is given in Table 23.1 below.

TABLE 23.1: Poverty-Stricken Population in India

Category	Annual income Slab (Rs.)	No. of families (million)	Percentage
Destitute	0 - 2,265	0.99	2.33
Very very poor	2,266 - 5,000	6.13	13.83
Very poor	3,501 - 5,000	16.93	21.50
Poor	5,000 - 6,400	20.25	45.71

The estimate of Poverty Ratio in Rural and Urban sector shows that in 1991-92, 272.8 million rural and 58.9 million urban are below poverty line. According to the statistics of Labour Bureau the number of unemployed both educated and uneducated is on the rise and heading towards explosion and is about 120 million.

Poverty is a direct offspring of exploitative policy and can only be removed through development of a participative system. This participative system has to encompass all aspects of life bearing on various issues influencing the policy planning. The removal of poverty visualises a certain amount of co-ordination, linkages, monitoring, funding and internal resource generation through marketing.

Himalayan Region Especially Central Himalayas—Uttrakhand (Hill Area of UP)

This region is highly vulnerable to the natural processes of weathering and erosion. Nature's regulatory mechanism to control the rate of the erosion is the vegetation cover which has been reduced or even removed by human use and MISUSE including deforestation leading to degradation of vast fragile lands, steep upper slopes and sensitive middle slopes and Shivalik range. This has resulted in increasing subsidence, land slides, exhausted soils, rapid soil loss due to water runoff, heavy siltation, frequent floods and droughts in the region and adjoining Indo-Gangetic Plains. Poverty of land and people has resulted in Migration of People from several pockets where soil does not yield enough crops and is a matter of great concern. The people migrate into cities also because no income generating activities are in the hills thus overcrowding and resulting in slums where quality of life and human dignity are almost absent.

The time is ripe, rather overdue to analyse various aspects of Rural Industrialization, linkages between agriculture, rural development, and rural industrialization for attacking the high levels of poverty through efficient Resource Utilization and Sustainable Development including Financing, Marketing and Entrepreneurship training and Action Programmes leading to income generation and increasing prosperity.

A strategy for the Himalayan Conservation and Development

1. Establishment of nurseries, transplanting and protection including various types of fencing;
2. Reduction of the dependence on fuel wood through promotion

renewable energy and other associated measures;

3. Imparting special corrective treatment to severely damaged areas as well as those affected by land-slide;
4. Regeneration of springs, water harvesting and management;
5. Integrated land and water use and water-shed management;
6. Promotion of income generation activities;
7. Participation of the Himalayan communities;
8. Government participation and promotion of above strategies.

Systems of Agriculture Production

Broadly there are two systems based on irrigation facilities but according to different agro-ecological factors these further can be divided into six farming situations (NARP, Hill Campus, 1989) given in Table 23.2.

New Dimension of Food Security and Nutrition in Mountain Systems of Uttrakhand

Contracted to Agricultural System *per se* Food Security necessitates New Dimension involving Tree Crops and other Nutrition and health giving or income generating horticultural crops description below:

1. *Horticulture*

As the land capability of crop production is usually lower for field crops production, and as

(A) Trees are able to utilize land water and climatic resources in the mountain system. Horticulture (fruits and nuts) are an efficient system of land and water management. Uttrakhand's capability is reflected in "Uttrakhand Horticulture Dairy and Guide" in the find stages of preparation by TFL/HIMCON. Jointly with well known Horticulturist Dr. Harbans Singh. Fruits are usually divided to:

(a) Perishable fruits such as plum, pear, peches, berries of varying types.

(b) Semi-perishable fruits such as: apples, apricots including "chulu" hard pear etc.

TABLE 23.2: Farming Situations of Central Himalayas and their Vegetations is summarized below

Farming situation	Altitude (m)	Appropriate area (Ha)	Appropriate area (%)	Soil	Dominant forest flora	Principal crops & fruits
I. Irrigated lower hills	600 - 1200	6.14	12%	Alluvial sandy loam	Shorea robusta Pinus roxburghii	Rice, Wheat, Onion, Potato Radish, Cauli-flower, Citrus, Mango
II. Rainfed lower hills	600 - 1200	4.09	8%	Residual sandy loam	Shorea robusta, P. roxburghii	Ragi, rice, wheat, citrus mango
III. Mid hills South	1200 - 1700	18.41	36%	Sandy loam	P. roxburghii, Grewia optiva, Celtis australis	Rice, ragi, wheat, potato, tomato, peach, plum
IV. Mid Hill north aspect	1200 - 1700	12.27	24%	Brown forest soils	Quercus leucotri chophora, Rhodo-dendron sp.	Ragi, rice, wheat, tomato, potato, peas, cole crops, peach, plum, apri-cot apple

(Contd.)

TABLE 23.2: *(Contd.)*

	Farming situation	Altitude (m)	Appropriate area (Ha)	Appropriate area (%)	Soil	Dominant forest flora	Principal crops & fruits
V.	High hills	1700 - 2500	6.14	12%	Red to dark black loam	Q. leucotri-cho-phora, Q. floribunda, Rhododendron arbo-reum, Cornus capitata	Amarnath, ragi, french bean, peas, cole crops potato, apple, apricot pear, walnut
VI.	Very high	2500 - 3500	2.04	4%	Red to dark black clay loam, meadow type soils	Q. semicarpifolia, Abies pindrow Picea smithiana, Cedrus deodara	Amarnath, buck-wheat, peas, cole-crops, potato apple, almond, apricot
VII.	Alpine Pastures	> 3500	2.04	4%	Heavy textured meadow soils	Denthonia cachym-meriana, Juniperus sp., R. compenulatum	No crops and trees

(c) Non-perishable nut fruits such as walnuts, almonds, pecannuts, sweet chestnuts etc.

(B) *Vegetables*

(a) Seasonal include vegetables for local use like tomatoes, beans, peppers, brinjals, okra,
(b) Creeper vegetables like squash, cucumbers, kadoo, torai,
(c) Cash crop vegetables like peas, potatoes, onions, garlic, ginger and turmeric.

(C) *Floriculture*

A New aspect of horticulture is gaining prominence in Uttrakhand includes roses, gladiola, and other exportable flowers

(D) Medicinal and herbal plants are also gaining ground including Geranium, Rosemarry, Bulgarian Roses, Lavender, Pyrethrum, Kala Jeera, Salvia, Wild Roses etc.
Also a number of Medicinal Plants such Saussia Lappa, Picoliza Scrophalus, Paeonia Emovi, Polygonal Vertic Illahum Aconitu Atrox, Aconitu Hetrophyte Selinum Lauichion. Angelia Archenyica including many·others such as Texus Baccata (cure for cancer) and others required by many drug firms.

2. *Water Harvesting*

Promotion of above Horticulture crops is efficient when assured water for irrigation is available — hence water harvesting is a must in Uttrakhand.

Water Harvesting Measures include

(1) *Polythene Lined Tanks*

We are using multi-layered prefabricated Polythene tanks which are fitted into dug pits with mud plastered walls. Each tank is of 10,000 litres capacity.

2) *Spring Water Rejuvenation*

Springs are being rejuvenated by vegetal treatment of the catchment area and minor engineering works like digging of trenches and water retention/storage chambers which store all the spring flow without any loss. Normal capacity is of 3000-5000 litres.

(3) *Chals*

Traditional water storage ponds are being made with mud-plastered walls. However, in a few cases use of cement is permitted. A series of chals (about 10,000 litres capacity) are being made preferably in the higher reaches of a village. These chals due to slow percolation of water also provide a regular source of seepage water to rejuvenate springs. These chals have various uses like irrigation, drinking water for animals and birds, water pond for buffaloes, flood control device etc. These are usually stored at an average cost of Rs. 0.20 per litre cap. 2,000 for 10,000 litre capacity.

(4) Ferro Cement tanks are Roof Water Harvesting—Although costly their use in getting prevelant as these are multi purpose use including drinking. Household use, nursery irrigation etc. These cost about Rs. 9,000 for 3000 litres capacity, fairly permanent but cost Rs. 3 per litre.

(5) Soil and Water Conservation: As the action is being taken on the watershed management basis. Soil and Water Conservation measures like gully plugs, retention walls or vegetative conservation are adopted.

3. *Income Generating Activities*

These include:

(i) Apiculture
(ii) Sericulture
(iii) Mushroom culture
(iv) Processing of Local Produce for Local Conservation such as bread, biscuits, dairy products etc.,

(v) Wool, Cotton and Silk Weaving and other operation for marketing.

4. Animal Husbandry and Fisheries

— Grasses and Legumes
— Fodder and Trees
— Improving Breeds, Nutrition and Managment and Training Programme in Animal Husbandry.
— Aquaculture— Including Fresh Water fisheries in streams, lakes and open water harvesting structure.

5. People First— Principles and Practices of People Participation

These are given in my Book Chapter V "People's Participation in Himalayan Eco-system Development."
Concept Publishers, 1991, and are summarized below:

1. Development of Local Institution
2. Need for Bureaucratic Reorientation
3. Internal Values in Bureaucracy
4. Promoting People's Participation.

Steps Needed by development promoted for large-scale people's participation are:

(i) Go to the people
(ii) Live with them
(iii) Learn from them
(iv) Serve them
(v) Love them
(vi) Plan with them
(vii) Start with what they know
(viii) Build on what they have

5. Raising people's potential
6. Inspiration and social energy through:

— Ideas
— Ideals

— Friendship.

7. Training can help a lot.

Conclusions and Recommendations

1. The physical systems of the Himalayas, being relatively young, are highly vulnerable to the natural process of weathering and erosion. Nature's regulatory mechanism to control the rate of this erosion is the vegetation cover. The rate of change brought about by these processes is altered by human use and misuse of the system.
2. Trees for life are harbinger of tree and fruit revolution in Indian Himalayas.
3. A strategy for Himalayan conservation and development has been developed and should be implemented.
4. Partners in development:
   (a) Mahila mandals, youth groups, schools and colleges of respective regions;
   (b) Collaboration with partner agencies in voluntary sector;
   (c) Promotion of self-reliance amongst Himalayan communities.
5. Panchayati Raj is a great boost to People First and their participation in their own future development. A care has to be taken that Panchayati Raj Institute at the village level does not get politicalized and is there to serve the people and represent their genuine interest. There is unfortunately a trend of urbanized self interest seeping into Panchayati Raj System in the Rural areas and a great caution is to be exercised. This requires Promotion of selfless and common interests rather than individual benefit of these in power.
6. Resource Utilization and Wealth from Waste whether it involves Land, Water, Forest, Plant or Crop Resources are the Heart of Recommendation.
7. Training in Technologies, Entrepreneurship, Marketing and Working together for common interest are the key Recommendations and these will lead to Panchayati Raj being harbingers of Food Security and Nutrition for the Rural Masses of Uttrakhand as has been shown by some case studies in selected villages where NGO's Peoples and even Government agencies are working together in harmony and holistically for the benefit of Himalayan communities.

NOTES

1. Katyal Taori, (1994), *Rural Industrialization.*
2. Katyal Taori, (1996), *Panchayati Raj and Corporate Sector.*
3. M.C. Dewan and Katyal Taori, (June 1996), *Entrepreneur Development and Rural Industrialization for Himalayan Communities in Uttrakhand.*
4. M.L. Dewan, (1991), *People's Participation in Himalaya Eco System Development*, Concept Publishers.
5. PRIA, (1996), *Participation and Governance*, March.
6. V.K. Kediyal, (March 1996), *Issues and Possible Interventions from Drought Prone and Rainfed Agriculture of Central Himalaya*, G.B. Pant Univ. of Agr. and Technology, Hill Campus.

TWENTY-FOUR

FOOD SECURITY IN PANCHAYATI RAJ INSTITUTIONS THROUGH AGRO FORESTRY BASED PROGRAMMES: A Cooperative Experience

O.P. GAUR

Importance

The Panchayati Raj Institutions at Village Level are Gram Panchayat, Cooperative Society and Village School. These three institutions being nearer to the village people, play a very important role in the programmes related to food security.

The cooperative societies are primarily organised to provide economic and social benefits. A Cooperative society by its concepts comprises of the members, work for members and is managed by the members. In our country the cooperative societies are providing agricultural inputs like seeds, fertilisers and pesticides to the farmers to increase the food production. Similarly, a vast resource in the form of wasteland is available in each village of our country. Through appropriate soil conservation measures and Agro-forestry programmes the soils can become most important resource to increase the income of the farmers by providing fruits, milk, meat and other edible products which form the part of food and livelihood for the rural people.

The forests are also necessary to provide fodder for cattle and other animals. Fuel wood is available from the forests and as economic activity poorer section, particularly women depend on their income by selling the fuel wood in nearby towns in the villages. Presently millions of rural women spend considerable time and efforts in collecting fuel wood and fodder and water since the forests got depleted. The deterioration in forest resources thus have a direct impact in terms of food security on rural masses, particularly on women and children. The forest cover is, therefore, beneficial for the environment as well as for the economic status of the people. The forests also serve as a sink for polutants like carbon dioxide and are beneficial to maintain the atmospheric temperature at proper level.

The National Forest Policy finalised in 1988 primarily focusses attention on preservation, conservation, maintenance and sustainable use of forest resources enhancing the industrial environment. It highlights that the "National goal should be to have a minimum of one-third of the total land area of the country under forest tree cover". The most important objective of the National Forest Policy is to increase sustainability in the forest cover in the country through massive afforestation and social forestry programmes especially on all degraded and waste lands through the people's participation. In the recent past, wasteland development through afforestation has attracted wide support and interest among NGOs and other institutions. The community involvement has been found to be of great significance in the implementation and monitoring of the forest activities particularly on non-forest revenue lands, village pastures and other degraded lands.

Forestry and Food Security

Food security is the physical access to food, of all people, at all time. Food security depends on the reliability of production and on people's access to supplies. In rural areas forest and farm trees provide major support to agricultural production through improving soil conditions and maintaining ground water. Forest also provide food fodder and fuel and means of earning income thereby have direct or indirect impact on people's food security. Forestry contribute to food security in many ways through following linkages between forestry and household which can be broadly divided into three main groups:

Environmental

Trees influence surrounding environment, both at micro and macro level which help in providing stable environmental conditions for sustainable food production. Forest also provide for restoring soil productivity and genetic diversity. The effect of forest can play an important role in improving micro climate, reducing soil erosion and can reduce sedimentation in watershed areas. All the above factors helps in increasing food production.

Production

The direct impact of forestry and food security is food produced by forest trees such as fruits, nuts, gums, roots and leaves. Forest also provide habitat for many animals and birds and other wild life. Trees and shrubs provide an essential source of livestock fodder.

Socio-Economic

Socio-economic links between forestry and food security are those that links produce and service of forest to the people who depends on them. Food obtained from trees and forest make direct contribution to family diet which provide supplementary nutrition. Millions of rural poor earn money from processing and selling of major and minor forest products.

IFFCO Pilot Project

IFFCO's involvement in agriculture and rural development for the last two decades prompted it to launch a pilot project on farm forestry in 1986-87. The objective was to provide fuel and fodder to the village farmers and farm women. The fodder is meant for cattle who in turn are linked in providing animal waste which can be utilised for bio-gas plants. This can further help in the improvement in the health of women who suffer greatly while cooking on ordinary *chullahs*. This project also emphasizes on the social and economic aspects of the forest management by empowering farmers, particularly women and ensuring that the species of such trees are grown which benefit to the local community at large.

Location

The programme was initiated in the districts of Sultanpur, Rae Bareli, Pratapgarh and Allahabad in U.P., Sagar in Madhya Pradesh and Udaipur in Rajasthan. Total 4040 ha. of land has already been put under plantation by organising 32 Primary Farm Forestry Cooperative Societies (PFFCS) of which 17 are in U.P., 10 in Rajasthan and 5 in M.P. The societies now own capital items consisting of tractors, land and building etc. They have created irrigation facilities by installing tubewells and pumpsets. Centralised nurseries have also been established for the common use of all members.

Major Activities

The project work under the Primary Farm Forestry Cooperative Societies comprises three major activities viz. afforestation, soil and water conservation and associated activities like pisciculture, bee-keeping, dairy, *dona pattal* making, durry-weaving and garments stitching.

Role of PFFCS

In order to bring all the facilities within the reach of members, the farmers are motivated to form the Village Level Primary Farm Forestry Cooperative Societies. This society takes up the activity as a nodal agency for securing various funds and implement the entire forestry project work. IFFCO renders all technical guidance and training facilities to the members and cooperative personnel to make the society a functional and viable unit. Each PFFCS is having 175 to 250 ha. of land and membership of 200 to 300 ha. Elected Board of Directors and a full time paid secretary manage the society. The societies are functioning with their offices in the villages and are also undertaking various associated activities which generate regular employment to the members and sustain income to the societies.

Role of Women

Women are most important members so far as the Farm Forestry activities are concerned since they are responsible for arranging fuel, fodder etc. They have contributed significantly in executing the programme and actively participated in the decision making, nursery raising, planting trees and other works including soil conservation. Due to gainful employment, they achieved to some extent the economic independence.

In nursery raising, the women have contributed right from filling of polythene bags upto the final stage of loading the saplings on trollies, in addition to other operations like weeding, hoeing, irrigating and shifting etc. The extent of participation of rural women in nursery have been studied in Kanaksinghpur PFFC in Uttar Pradesh where 8 lakh saplings were raised in the year 1988-89. Out of the total 8,987 workdays created in the nursery, 6,950 workdays were occupied by women only (around 75%). This motivated five women in raising nurseries on small piece of their own land in nearby areas.

In plantation and maintenance activities, rural women have taken up the job of filling of material i.e. FYM, gypsum, pesticides, etc. into pits.

They have planted saplings and took up the regular irrigation and maintenance work. The extent of involvement of women in these activities was a about 70 per cent.

During the year 1991-91, in Kankupur PFFC, in U.P., 40 ha. area was taken up under soil and water conservation works. The operations include construction of checkdams, contour bund, levelling and bunding. Total work days created for the above activities were 17,215 of which women were engaged for 9,603 workdays, which is about 56 per cent of the total employment.

Durry-weaving programme is being run in 4 societies in 9 villages where 220 rural women are regularly working on their own looms. The societies are selling 'durries' to the local people and to outstation parties as well, by charging Rs. 5 per durry as net margin. The programme has proved to be boon for the women members and the societies as well. In view of the regular production, the societies are thinking to open retail outlet points in the local market.

In the Kankupur Society, where broad leaves of *Butea minosperma* and teak are available in plenty. The women collect the leaves and bring upto the Centre where machines have been installed. With the help of these machines, leaf plates and cups are being prepared regularly the society ensures the marketing of the product.

The training programme for women on nursery raising, plantation, durry-weaving and *dona-pattal* making have been organised. In one of the such organised programme during August 1992, there were 120 women participants; out of 130 total trainees.

Indian Farm Forestry Development Cooperative Ltd.

Indian Farm Forestry Development Cooperative Limited (IFFDC) is a multi-State cooperative society registered on October 22, 1993. Its area of operation is in the States of Uttar Pradesh, Madhya Pradesh, Rajasthan, West Bengal, Orissa, Tamil Nadu, Gujarat, Andhra Pradesh, Karnataka, Maharashtra and Bihar. The broad objectives of the IFFDC are as follows:

- — To promote Farm Forestry on larger scale on Wastelands and also to develop forestry programmes under 'Integrated Farming System' for maximum economic gains to the members.
- — To promote PFFCS at Village Level and SFFDCS at State Level.
- — To provide Financial, technical, Marketing and extension services to the members of PFFCS and SFFDCS. The membership of IFFDC

is limited to IFFCO, PFFCS, SFFDC. Government of India, State Governments, NCDC and any other Co operative institution having interest for the promotion of Farm Forestry activities.

The management of IFFDC comprises of General Body, Board of Directors and Managing Director. It will be represented by 3 nominees of IFFCO and Government of India; 1 nominee of NCDC and Managing Director of IFFDC. Under the Transitory Bye-laws approved by Government of India, IFFCO has been authorised to nominate the Board and Managing Director of IFFDC for a period of initial 5 years.

IFFDC Project

Looking to the success of IFFCO's Farm Forestry Pilot Project, Canadian International Development Agency (CIDA) evinced interest in supporting the Farm Forestry Project. CIDA team visited Forestry sites during 1991 and 1994 and had prolonged discussions with the officials and executives of IFFCO responsible for implementing Forestry activities. The India-Canada Environment Facility (ICEF) is the project execution wing of CIDA in India. IFFDC project was approved by Joint Project Steering Committee (JPSC) in July 1994 and in April 1995 MOU was signed between IFFCO and ICEF.

The IFFDC Project is to be implemented initially by IFFCO and in due course it will be handed over to IFFDC. The Project activities have been undertaken in right earnest and the project is progressing well. The duration of the project is 5 years with a total out of Rs. 350 million of which Rs. 315 million will be contributed by ICEF and Rs. 35 million by IFFCO.

The target group will comprise of about 15,000 families of small and marginal farmers (men and women) owning less than two hectares and/or landless. The PFFCS will secure community or government lands and allot them to the landless. Each society will enroll, depending upon the size of the landholding, 100-300 members and create 200-250 ha. plantation. The size of the land holding of many members could be just about 0.5 ha; they are really poor families. Each plot will be a continuous piece of area of about 50 ha. area. The wasteland belonging to the farmers with larger landholding will also be taken for afforestation. The beneficiaries will be either members of the Primary Farm Forestry Cooperatives (PFFC) established already by IFFCO or the members of the proposed 90 PFFCS which IFFDC intends to establish. When the household is headed by a woman, she will be eligible for allotment of land, and also to become a member of the PFFC.

Project Components

Promote and Establish National, State and Village Level Farm Forestry Cooperative

The support activities will involve developing a legal structure of laws and Bye-laws, assisting in marketing of Farm Forestry products to ensure that the societies get the best return from their labour and providing technical guidance in the Farm Forestry activities. Linkages will be developed with other organisations such as State Forestry Departments that can assist in providing seeds, seedlings and forestry technologies.

Integrated Farm Forestry and Natural Resource Management

The activities under this component will involve enhancing skills required to develop village based and cooperative owned nurseries, assisting the PFFCS with the techniques and material for plantations and assisting in associated Farm Forestry activities like sericulture, agriculture, pisciculture, etc.

Training and Education

Sensitization workshops and training programmes will be held for the project staff and local leaders at all levels so as to be sensitive to gender, cultural and social issues. Developing in staff an "environmental perspective" will be an early activity. Extensionists will be trained so as to be able to effectively assist farmers in forming cooperatives, nursery and plantation development etc.

Socio-Economic and Planning/Monitoring/Activities

Baseline Survey, Cultural Analysis and Gender socio-economic studies will be undertaken. Participatory Rural Appraisal programmes will be organised and participatory monitoring and evaluation will be undertaken under this component.

Research and Development

A research plan will be developed related to multipurpose tree trials to know which species of trees and grasses, give the best yields. Research on rural energy conservation will be an important research activities and simple manuals will be developed to make research information available to farmer.

Project Finance

The project cost will be shared by ICEF and IFFCO on 90:10 basis. The Officer-in-Charge of the 'IFFDC Project' will be responsible for proper utilization of funds and maintenance of records. The total cost of the Project will be Rs. 35 crores.

Project Management

At the National Level, the IFFDC Project is headed by Jt. General Manager and he is supported by senior staff members. In the States of Uttar Pradesh, Madhya Pradesh and Rajasthan, the Project in the States is headed by the Project Executive with the supporting staff like Farm Forestors, Sr. Accountant etc. Besides, staff like Cooperative Specialist, Social Scientist and Extensionists (Male and Female) have been provided on Contract Basis in the Project. The Project Management Committee (PMC) at the National level; Project Technical Committee (PTC) at the State Level and the Project Implementation Committee (PIC) at the PFFC Level have been formed to guide the project officials in managing the IFFDC Project effectively. In these Committees, the officials of IFFCO, Government of India, State Government concerned and local representatives of PFFCS are represented. The meetings of these committees are organised regularly. Infrastructural facilities like Vehicles, Fax Machines, Personal Computers, Audio-Visual equipments etc. have been provided to educate the members for their maximum participation. The innovation like use of solar-energy operated water pumps are being provided at the PFFCS level to use the natural solar power for forestry activities.

The project has been in operation since April 1, 1995 and in this period significant progress has been made in terms of completion of plantation in 778.5 ha. in the 3 States of U.P., M.P. and Rajasthan, and 22 new PFFCS have been organised. The emphasis has been on participatory approaches to determine the species of the trees considered most beneficial by the members. Two Research Trials with the help of Forest Research Institute, Dehradun have been laid out at Sultanpur. The services of the experts in organising the training programmes have been utilised to motivate and educate the members on their role and responsibilities in farm forestry programmes through cooperatives. The agencies like 'Astha' of Udaipur and Association for stimulating know-how (ASK) of Delhi has been engaged to provide training to the PFFCS members of Cooperative societies, secretaries and Board members. Gender Sensitisation Workshops have been organised under the guidance of Gender Consultants who have been familiar with similar type of activities.

TWENTY-FIVE

FOOD PRODUCTION POTENTIAL OF JAMMU KANDI BELT (J&K STATE)

B.L. KAUL

In the Jammu region, the outer hills (Siwalik Hills) constitute the Kandi belt. This Kandi belt stretches between long. of 74°-21′ East to 75°-45′ E and lat. 32°-22′ N to 32°-55′ N, except in the western portion where it lies between the latitude of 32°-50′ N. to 33° North. Its southern boundary is Jammu-Pathankot National Highway, Ranbir canal and then along the Pratap canal to the line of actual control on the Munawar Tawi. The area is surrounded by River Ravi in the East and Munawar Tawi on the West. The Kandi area is not continuous with any administrative unit. It cuts across the districts of Jammu, Kathua and Udhampur. The total area of the Kandi belt has been estimated to be 4,89,266 hectares, out of which only 1,16,046 hectares (23.72%) is cultivated. The net sown area is 82,880 hectares.

The natural vegetation of the Kandi belt mostly consists of sub-tropical dry mixed forests of scrub type. Sharma and Kachroo (1981) have classified the forests of Kandi belt into five groups, which are as follows:

1. Acacia forests,
2. Bahuinia forests,
3. Dodonaea forests,
4. Mixed semi-deciduous, and
5. Chir forests.

The Kandi belt experiences sub-tropical climate, summers being very hot and winters cold and dry. The soils are coarse textured, mostly loamy sand to sandy loam, frequently covered by small to large boulders. The water holding capacity of the soil is very low and rainfall uncertain and poorly distributed, being usually less than 100 cm annually.

Topographically, the area is rugged and broken, intersected by a large number of dry rivulets.

Agriculture is the main occupation of the people living in the Kandi belt. 70 per cent of its population is dependent on land for its living. Majority of the farmers have small and marginal holdings. These holdings are scattered and uneconomic to cultivate. The main crops grown in the belt are bajra, jowar, maize, wheat and barley. Rice is grown in some areas which are located near the ravines and nallahas. Pulses like moth, cow pea, pigeon pea, gram, mash, moong and kulth are cultivated to some extent. Among the oilseed crops, til, sarson, toria and groundnut occupy a prominent place. Due to absence of any irrigation facilities, agriculture is dependent on the rains, which are unequal, irregular and show considerable variation. The major causes of water shortage and soil erosion are deforestation, denudation of the slopes and the rugged topography. The reckless cutting of trees and shrubs for fuel, fodder and wood has led to deforestation. Overgrazing of pastures and common grazing lands has made the whole landscape naked. Agriculture is uneconomic because of poor soils and low moisture content. Cultivation is done on unpermissible slopes and the methods of agriculture are conventional. A large number of people are poor and landless. There are no alternative employment opportunities for the people. There are no agriculture based industries in this belt. No infrastructural facilities are available in the Siwalik Hill Zone and the crop loan system is more or less non-functional. However, the crop production can be increased if adequate and corrective measures are taken with regard to land and crop management.

Recommendations

1. The Kandi soils are very poor in fertility. Continuous cropping without any periodical addition of organic matter leads to soil exhaustion. Areas receiving more than 70 cm of rain can be supplied with fertilizers with less risk under integrated nutrient management experimentation. In view of the increasing costs of fertilizers, integrated nutrient supply system should be introduced.
2. In a field having slope of even 2 per cent, lot of surface soil/ha is lost resulting in considerable loss of plant nutrients. Soil erosion can be checked by mechanical and biological measures.
3. High yielding varieties of seeds should be introduced to increase the crop production.
4. Much emphasis should be laid on water conservation measures.

In order to favour absorption of maximum moisture during rainfall in fields, the fields should be levelled, smoothed, terraced and graded for minimum earth work.

5. The Government should help the farmers in the storage of run off water in the catchment areas by proper watershed management. Subsidies should be provided to the farmers for the construction of water harvesting tanks, so as to provide life saving irrigation in the years of drought.
6. Sprinkle irrigation system should be introduced.
7. A suitable package of practices such as using improved seeds, timely sowing, judicious use of fertilizers, plant protection measures will help in achieving higher yield.

Since the Kandi lands owing to poor management practices are subjected to the processes of degradation and as such are not able to sustain arable crops, particularly during the drought periods, it becomes imperative to think about evolving certain alternate landuse systems for such lands. Adoption of agroforestry is one such system which constitutes the need of the day for the Kandi dwellers. An environmental and ecological balance is vital in fostering a healthy and progressive future for mankind.

A system for multipurpose uses of land in which trees and crops are planted, form an integrated approach to biological production within a certain area. Broadly speaking it also includes animal husbandry, fishery, apiculture and sericulture which can be arranged on the ecological principles and dynamics of energy flow.

Generally five main kinds of agroforestry systems have great potential for Kandi areas of Jammu. These are:

(a) Forestry-agronomy,
(b) Forestry-horticulture,
(c) Forestry-agronomy-animal husbandry,
(d) Forestry-agronomy-fishery,
(e) Forestry-agronomy-animal husbandry-fishery.

In conclusion it can be said that the Kandi belt possesses a higher production potential in respect of horticulture, forestry, animal husbandry etc., than what is realised by arable farming system.

TWENTY-SIX

FOOD SECURITY FOR LEPROSY PATIENTS THROUGH FAO ASSISTED PROJECT

PADMA VENKATARAMAN

Food security for the underprivileged sections of society needs special attention. The following project, funded by FAO is perhaps the only one of its kind addressed to leprosy patients.

The All India Women's Conference (AIWC) successfully completed project TCP/IND/2256 in December 1993. At the time when the project was terminated, a full crop of wheat and vegetables was growing on the farm in Tahirpur, Shahdara. Wheat gave a yield of over 6 tonnes per hectare, virtually the highest yield recorded in the country.

AIWC continued its support, with the technical back-up from the Indian association for the Advancement of Science (IAAS) and the impact of the same was assessed 18 months later in July 1995. The evaluation of the sustainability of the project revealed the following:

(i) Leprosy patients assimilated the knowledge and information as they were given the responsibility for cultivation of the farm on their own.

(ii) Total involvement of women in developing kitchen gardens.

(iii) Leprosy patients consumed far more leafy vegetables and fruits that supplied them with micronutrients.

(iv) Activities initiated under the project have become totally sustainable.

The World Food Summit which is to be convened from 13 to 19 November 1996 in Rome in its "A Call to Attention" mentions: "Achieving food security for today's hungry who constitute 20 per cent of the population of developing countries, requires policies that make it possible for them to grow or buy the food they need".

TCP/IND/2256 was based on this policy and AIWC is making further project proposals to assist this socially vulnerable group to grow their own food wherever cultivable land is available or to promote income generating activities in order to increase the purchasing power for nutritious food.

Because of the all-round phenomenal success of this pilot project, FAO in its Terminal Statement has recommended that this project should be replicated in other such leprosy patient colonies and plans prepared for their overall development covering not only health and nutrition, but also other social amenities like housing, sanitation, schooling, public awareness, etc.

As a follow-up of the recommendation, AIWC has initially prepared and submitted project proposals to FAO office in New Delhi for Tamil Nadu and Maharashtra which can be extended to other States like Uttar Pradesh, Bihar and Madhya Pradesh at the next stage.

We are very grateful to FAO Office in New Delhi, particularly the FAO representative to India and Bhutan for the earnest effort to get a donor for this noble endeavour. If we succeed in starting the work soon, this can be presented as a model working programme at the World Food Summit.

TWENTY-SEVEN

TOWARDS A VILLAGE FOOD SECURITY IN RAINFED AREAS: A Case Study

K.S. GOPAL* and M. SASHI KUMAR*

Introduction

Sugunamma is a semi-literate small farmer in Ibrahimpur village of Medak district. Today, she is the Sarpanch of her village Gram Panchayat to which she was elected unanimously. Her success in wresting the leadership of the village community is also attributed by the villagers to her role in building an innovative food security scheme for the poor with the help of a voluntary agency. Jaganatha Rao, a development worker in the agency, in an interview to the authors, explains the process of how the origin, problems and prospects as it is happening. They hope that delegates at the FAO conference on "Panchayati Raj—the key to food security and nutrition" will examine some issues and opportunities involved in promoting ideas in village level food security through community participation. This case is written as the programme enters the third year of implementation.

Background

Sugunamma is a poor widow living in Narayankhed taluk of Medak district in Andhra Pradesh. Medak is one of the poor regions of the State. Narayankhed is a recurringly drought prone area. It has low rainfall and agriculture is mostly dependent on rains. Some lands have irrigation facility from open wells and more recently from bore wells. Traditionally,

*The authors work for the Centre for Environment Concerns, 3-4-142/6, Barkatpura, Hyderabad - 500 027

irrigation was from village tanks but most are dysfunctional, silted and under cultivation. This absence of village tanks has effected the farmers as well as water available in the open wells.

Ibrahimpur village has no irrigation well. Even drinking water is supplied through pipes from a nearby tank. Sugunamma owns two acres of red soil land in her village. When her husband was alive every year they used to grow rainfed crops like yellow sorghum with an intercrop of red gram on their land. In some lands with good soils bearing water retention qualities a second crop with white sorghum was grown in a year. The produce, which included a lot of greens, were used for household consumption and the fodder for the bullocks. They also worked for wage labour in the fields of other people and received grain. The only cash incomes they got was when they work for road and other construction activities. In the years when they got a good crop food and fodder was assured of availability. Narsamma was happy and confident with the grain stored in her house.

Public Distribution System

In 1984 the Government announced a programme to supply 25 kgs of rice per family at a price of Rs. 2 per kg. in the village. Along with this the dealer was also to supply other commodities like vegetables oil, kerosene, sugar, etc. at less than market prices. But these came very rarely. The scheme is called as coupon rice as those with ration cards are eligible for the supplies under the scheme. So she applied for the ration card and got one. Some poor people in the village could not get the cards. While a few did not follow it up with the Sarpanch and other identification officials while a few others had gone in search of work to neighbouring sugar factories. When they came back and tried for the card they were told that the quota was over.

The coupon rice was beneficial to Narsamma. At least a part of her food requirement came at a low price. The price of rice was cheaper than the jowar that they were eating. Earlier rice was consumed by her family and the villagers only on occasions like festivals. Their regular food habit is jowar *roti* with some *dal*, onions and buttermilk. Most of the sorghum was grown under rainfed conditions with intercrops of pulses. Milk purchase centres were not in existence and milk in the form of butter milk was given free to neighbours. Fodder came from the straws of sorghum, leaf from the forests and grazing on community land of the village. When rains failed they had to buy sorghum from the market.

Farming Systems

Most poor peasants depend on the monsoon for getting a crop. They applied farmyard manure, undertook timely operations for ploughing, weeding, harvesting etc. These help them get regular and good yields of the sown crops even though they were low in productivity. Such farmers never use chemical fertilisers or pesticides. Upto a decade, most of them did not hear of it. It was known only when the State Agriculture Department and the Block Development office introduced these chemical fertiliser on subsidies provided the farmers cultivated certain hybrid varieties of sorghum. These hybrid varieties were not preferred for consumption by the people, also the straw was not liked by the cattle.

The richer people ate white jowar whose price was higher while the poor people consumed both the white and the yellow jowar. Many poor who did not have lands growing white jowar had access to it as the practice is to receive wages in kind. In this way even the wage labourer got a variety of food material which are necessary for a balanced diet.

Food Entitlement

Having got her card, every month Narasamma goes to the village shop and collects her entitlements of rice. She has some problems in purchasing the rice. Firstly, the dealer would bring the rice according to his convenience and Narsamma would not know this. So she has to retain the money and this was difficult or end up taking only part of the 25 kgs. Whenever she did not have the money she went to those without the cards, especially the rich people and borrowed money from them. As the landlords are also interested in buying the rice they were glad to help Narsamma. The arrangement is that half the quantity would be taken by the person lending the money. The practice is wide-spread in the village especially during seasons of low employment.

In this way even the rich benefited from the rice scheme and is acceptable to Sugunamma as no one else would come forward to give a loan and the dealer will not keep the stock for more than two or three days after arrival. When she asked the dealer as to why cannot bring the rice on specific day of the month, he complains that this is not possible because he has to collect the money and deposit it back to the government and wait to get the next monthly quota.

In recent months their is a talk that the government will increase the price of rice to Rs. 4 per kg and reduce the quantity of rice from 25 kgs to

15 kgs per card. Narasamma is worried that while 25 kgs per month was not enough for the family even for one meal of the day, the reduced 15 kgs, that too at a higher price would make it worse for her. Her dependence on rice purchases from the weekly market will increase.

A very low share of ration supplies in the consumption basket of the poor is detrimental to them. A poor person is worse off in a dual market system as the open market prices, from where they have to get the bulk of their requirement, would be higher in a dual market. They are worse off as they have to pay a higher price than they would have paid in the absence of the dual market. Narsamma also has doubts whether the scheme to make available essential commodities at low prices to the needy would continue.

Sugunamma finds that what started as a scheme to her benefit is likely to be harmful. Her anxieties increase as the wages now paid in her village nowadays are mostly in cash and very little food crops are grown. Another concern is that with coupon rice the family added rice to their food habits reducing their traditional cereals like sorghum. Rice has become a part of their family diet although she feels that for the hard working peasant jowar and ragi are more nutritious than rice. But cooking rice needs less fuelwood and is easier than making *rotis*.

Women's Sangham

A voluntary organisation is promoting women's Sanghams organisation in the villages. They are called Sangham and its purpose is to facilitate the economic and social development of women. In her village the Sangham has 62 members mostly from the poor communities and from different castes and communities. Thè Sangham meets every week in the evening to discuss matters. Sugunamma is a member of the Sangham and finds the women's meeting a source of relaxation and fellow feeling to which women do not have the facilities. Sangham members collect small savings from their members which is lent to needy members. The Sangham also helps the voluntary organisation in running a night school for adults and a balwadi (creche).

Jaganatha Rao works in the voluntary agency. Sometimes he attends the meetings of the village women's Sangham to supervise their working, look at the savings and loan accounts and talk on general issues. At one such village meeting in Ibrahimpur, he read an item from the newspaper. The newspaper article said that there has been a steep fall in sorghum production and that over the years the area coarse cereals has come down substantially. The newspaper said that this is due to a shift in the usage of lands to groundnut, sunflower and cotton cultivation.

When this news item was read to the Sangham members, Sugunamma said that the reasons mentioned in the newspaper for the decline in coarse cereal acreage is not the whole story. She said that in lands where irrigation is now available or in black and good soils this shift has occurred. But, on the other hand, she asserted that considerable land especially those growing rainfed kharif crop like sorghum and pearl millet have been left fallow.

Group Discussion—Food Security

The women felt that the most affected were lands growing minor millets consumed traditionally by poor people and grown on poor soils. In their estimation, over the last five years more than 200 acres of productive land is left fallow. When lands were given to the poor, under the land ceiling act, whatever may be the condition everyone worked hard and made it productive. After a few years those without irrigation sources or prospects for taking up two crops in a year, stopped cultivation of their lands. Thus while some of the land has shifted to remunerative crops they observe an increasing trend to leave poor and rain dependent cropping lands being left fallow. While traditionally land was left fallow for a certain period with a view to enable the soil to recoup nutrients, and arrest soil degradation, the fallows that are now emerging is due to desperation, neglect and lack of any institutional support.

Mr Rao expressed serious concern on the shifting cropping pattern in the country and about how farmers are moving away from growing food crops to cash crops. Ratnamma, a member of the Sangham said that at the way in which rice supplies are being reduced she was doubtful of the continuation of the rice scheme for the poor. Rao explained that the primary objective of the PDS is to build a food security for the people especially the vulnerable sections. Food security means the availability of sufficient food at all times for all people in order to ensure an active and healthy life. It refers to both quantity and quality needed for good health, he added.

The members felt that food access and security is vital for the poor people especially in these days of rising prices and purchases from the market. They felt that they must find a way out and not depend on the government. Susheela said that rice cannot be grown in Narayankhed as it requires large quantities of water. With sugarcane crops in the villages of the neighbouring Zaheerabad, drinking water has became scarce and rice cultivation would make it worse.

Rice Production

Susheela said that rice was no longer grown as in the olden days when farmers used to broadcast and grow rainfed rice. Now water and fertilisers are liberally used to grow huge quantities of fine and super fine rice. She said she saw this during her visit to the Krishna District with the animal husbandry officials when they went for purchase of milch cattle. She found the entire area was producing only rice and "you cannot see any other crop as far as the eye can see". She was happy to see so much of greenery while sitting at the window in her train journey. Not a inch of land is left uncultivated and every field gets abundant water, she added.

Rao said the places visited by Susheela are in the delta regions of the great Krishna and the Godavari rivers. These regions constitute the rich districts were the first in the country to introduce hybrid seeds, chemical fertilisers and tractors. Susheela interjected that the tractors are common like the cycles in our village. Rao said the water to these areas come from large storage dams built at huge cost across the river. Parvarthamma grumbled that her father's village was drowned in the construction of the Manjira dam for providing water to the city of Hyderabad. Many villages get submerged under these dams and the compensation paid is spent by the men folk drinking and frequent travel to the towns. She added that dams look beautiful but at the cost of huge suffering, displacement and new habits.

Rao said that more than seventy-five per cent water for agriculture comes from a few major irrigation projects and rice production uses up the bulk of these supplies. He added that although copious supply of scarce water is made available through large irrigation projects to these areas, the tax on water does not even meet a part of the maintenance cost of these projects leave alone their capital costs. Also, most of fertilizers consumed in the State is used in the production of rice. Several new and high yielding seeds have been introduced through research enabling a quantum leap in productivity. Pentamma complained why she was born in this land of rainfall dependent agriculture.

Susheela said all the farmers get loans for producing rice from the Banks unlike here where no Bank is willing to give crop loan except for cultivating sugarcane. She said that these loans are given to all and even the poor farmers are able to cultivate rice. Nirmala said that the people there must be very prosperous. Susheela said that while the wages in the area for women was high, she found that most of the earnings were spent on drinking and gambling. She found that even women and children were being encouraged to drinking. She observed that many women and children look weak and not healthy.

Rao said that apart from such assistance to rice growers even the loan waiver scheme meant for farmers caught in a vicious debt trap has benefited mostly farmers wth irrigation facilities. Rani said that not a single poor or deserving person got the waiver as only those having bank loans were extended this facility. Sakkubai said that no one lends to the poor with rainfed cultivation and they have no choice except the money lender. Even he does it with some other motive. She wanted Rao to find out why the bank loans for sewing machines given to women in her village were not included.

Yadamma suggested they go to the Collector and ask for irrigation facilities as provided in the places visited by Susheela. Ghousia Begum asked "how can all have abundant water as there is a limit to its availability". Rao said such copious water is not available in most parts of the State and most agriculture in rainfall dependent. Bujjamma enquired from Susheela if the price of rice was low in the areas visited by her. Susheela replied that even there the poor depend on the coupon rice. Some members "why the price of rice is high in those villages when all are growing it and getting high yields". Rao replied "it is so because lots of rice is purchased by the Government and then sold all over the State where it was not grown. This facilitates the sale of the balance at a higher price in the open market for the trader".

Sakku Bai felt that if anything goes wrong in those areas then their will be starvation all over the State. She felt that atleast crop rotation and intercropping should be done to reduce risk, improve soil and control pests. Susheela interjected that already many of the big farmers in the region have started growing fish by making large ponds on their lands as it is highly profitable. She added that many poor landowners want to grow fish but cannot afford the high costs.

Rao said that from what he has read the introduction of the rice scheme was facilitated and may even have been compelled by the increased production which came through high yielding seed and chemical fertiliser. He added that the subsidised rice scheme is only incidentally meant for the poor while the real benefit is for the big rice growers. He feels the situation is now drastically changing as the yields are falling and pests have increased and the plant response to fertiliser is not as it was earlier.

He expects major shifts in the cropping structure. He said that if the present subsidies on agriculture were spread equally in all the villages in India, each would receive over Rs. 3 lakhs per annum. He felt that with that money local food security can be built over few years.

Neglect of Rainfed Farming

Ratnamma said that if loans and crop insurance were given to rainfed farming then they do not have to depend on other areas for their food. She says nobody is bothered about drylands as they belong to the poor and cannot give the high and assured yields provided by irrigation. Sakku Bai interrupted that what is being done by the Government for dryland farmers is soil bunding which they also can do and have been doing. Papamma said that food can be grown only as long as their is soil and soil moisture and if these are absent seeds and fertilisers are helpless. "Instead of building bunds, they should provide crop loans, ploughing support and crop insurance which are the real problems facing those growing their owned food", shouted Sakku Bai. They joked that in the neighbouring hamlet all the lands were contour bunded last year although in recent years no crop is grown on these lands. Susheela said that these works are useful as soil is central to agriculture and cannot be allowed to wash away every monsoon. She added that many poors who could not have found work were able to get them in these programmes. Narsamma said that such works are taken as they are beneficial to the contractor and no one is worried of the problems of rainfed farmers. Sogunamma asked about food for the landless and Ratnamma replied they can go for wage labour and get grain and sometimes even fodder.

The discussion shifted to the reasons for the decline in rainfed cereal cultivation which is the only possible and real source for food security in rainfed areas. Papamma said that increasingly food growing lands are being left fallow and long fallows and the neglect of these lands has reduced the productivity of the soil. Sakku Bai said that investing in rainfed agriculture is risky and inputs are expensive whereas the incomes are low. Rajamani said that she will not do farming on drylands and instead work as wage labour. Rao asked her for the reasons to which she replied that her brother took loan from a money lender to cultivate the land he had purchased from his savings while working as a cycle rickshaw puller at Hyderabad. He lost the crop and could not pay back the loan. In two years the money lender took over the land to recover the principal and the interest and her brother is worse off and back to Hyderabad.

Endowment and Resources

Rojamma, the night school teacher, who reads newspaper said that in 1970s a sugar factory was established at Madhunagar village and to motivate farmers to grow sugarcane, the factory offered loans for cultivation of sugarcane and purchased of all the produce at assured prices. After the sugar factory was set up several banks came up competing to help the cultivation of sugarcane. Until then their was only a Cooperative Bank which had very little and often no funds. Many farmers benefited from this and sugarcane which was grown became a major crop and the only way to successful farming. Though less than five per cent of the cultivated land in the area grows sugarcane, it consumes all the ground water and the crop loans given by the banks. All inputs such as farmyard manure, bullocks and farm labour go to meet the needs of cane growers.

The endeavour of all farmers is to grow sugarcane, and indeed sugarcane cultivation is their only way to survival. But most farmers cannot grow sugarcane and the crops their lands could grow does not receive any support from the banks and other development agencies. Worse, sugarcane cultivation now determines the production costs of the other crops. Their influence on prices of inputs for farming has adversely affected farmers growing crops other than sugarcane forcing many of them to give up agriculture altogether. The worst affected are the small farmers growing dry crops and dependent on rainfed agriculture. Presently farmers find subsistence farming impractical and uneconomical, but they are unable to integrate into the sugarcane economy and benefit from it. This has led to the producers of food ending up as buyers of food. The change from food crops to cash crops and the problems facing the small land owning and rain dependent agriculturists forces them to leave their lands fallow. She concluded that sugarcane farming helped increase the incomes in the area but it has also increased fallows among the rainfed lands.

All the lands are not suitable for sugarcane crops nor is there sufficient water. The result is that, while the best lands with copious groundwater have joined the sugarcane bandwagon, the moderate is struggling to do so and the poor rain dependent lands have been left fallow. This has led to an explosive situation of increasing population, neglect of the resource base, soil erosion and widespread poverty. A process of silent desertification of arid lands is at work. Zaheerabad and Narayankhed taluks are a witness to this process.

Toward an Alternative

Rao suggested that the Sanghams must examine the livelihood of the rainfed agriculturist and develop resources that can assist them to be productive and independent. He added that such a analysis and a coupon system using fallows to cultivate cereals alone can give the food needed by the poor. The women said that it will be possible if support is provided to them in the form of tractor for ploughing, farmyard manure and small doses of chemical fertiliser. The women offered to work collectively in helping each other in undertaking farm activities which could be paid from the produce. Encouraged by the response of the women, Rao decided to present the conclusions of members of organisation's management and request them to write up a proposal and seek financial support from donar agencies.

The experts on the board of the voluntary agency drawn from academic institutions around Hyderabad welcomed the idea and the need to develop village level food security and traditional food habits. But it laid down two conditions:

— tractors should not be used as they would kill the microbes in the soils, and

— no chemical fertilisers should be used as they are harmful and against its philosophy.

Rao went to the Sangham and presented the conditions for support. The women said that tractors need to be used only for the first year and from the following years they would be undertaking ploughing by bullocks as it was cheaper and accessible to them. They needed tractors in the first year as the soils have become hard and bullocks are not be able to plough them. Further, they propose to use small doses of chemical fertilisers as currently their soil fertility is low and farmyard manure was very expensive and scarce. They said that a mix of farmyard manure with chemical fertiliser in small quantities will not cause any harm to the soil while ensuring reasonable productivity to their effort. Also, over the years fertiliser quantity can be reduced by regular application of farmyard manure.

The board was not acceptable to the pleadings of the women and held that the Sanghams suggestions were against their philosophy. They recommended that the practices of natural farming being taken up in their demonstration farm in a nearby village if practised by them will be supported. For two years the matter remained unresolved. The idea was gaining acceptance among some of the members of the Board as Rao arranged for some consultations with agricultural scientists. A "go-ahead" to the project was given to Rao.

But the donars had their anxieties. Many turned it down saying that the risk in rainfed agriculture was high as it depended on rains which were not dependable. At last one donar said that they could support the programme as a micro initiative and innovation for which they had funds which are small and the project must be completed in one year. Although Rao was not happy, he wanted the process of responding to the women should start. With Rs. 1,00,000, Rao and the village women's Sangham started the programme.

Getting Down to Work

The women calculated the minimum requirement of the village poor for sorghum. They found out that the rice card holders in the village were 110 families who collectively received 33 tonnes per year. They agreed that an equivalent quantity of sorghum should be made available under the scheme in the first phase of the project. They estimated that at the rate of 300 kgs. of sorghum procurement per acre, the project must cover about 200 acres of fallows. Of this every year half will have sorghum crop while the other half will be under pulses as annual crop rotation is vital for successful farming in such soils. Even at 200 acres, the land needed is less than half of the fallows available in their village. Crop rotation is preferred as it stabilizes yield at a level although it is unsuited for high productivity.

Traditionally sorghum is intercropped with redgram during kharif. But redgram has high pest problems. But profitability, nutrition supplement to the soil and harvesting schedules are the reasons for farmers choice of redgram. There are no biological pesticides to control pests in redgram and once chemicals are used the evidence is that while it does control the pests, the pests become resistant over a period of time. The Sangham discussed and agreed to intercrop sorghum with redgram and Pundi and Bebbarulu. Pundi seed is used for oil extraction and the stem for fibre in rope making. Bebbarulu offers lots of good quality fodder and the grain makes good pulse.

Scheme

In the first year forty-six women came forward to participate in the scheme with a total land of 60 acres. A five-member village committee was elected comprising of two women and three men to oversee the programme. The lands identified were fallow for the last ten to three years. The minimum land per farmer was one acre while the maximum was two acres. But the input support would be equal and on the basis of one acre per farmer. More than one acre had to be taken up due to land being contiguous, availability of bullocks and labour in the household.

Based on the land conditions ploughing by tractor/bullocks was taken up. Each acre of land was provided with two tractor loads of farm-yard manure which was procured from their village and the neighbouring Raghavapur village. Farmers were asked to procure their own traditional jowar seed while the seed of the intercrops are purchased from shops in Zaheerabad. A half bag of fertilizer was provided per farmer. Weeding was done on a collective basis by the women.

Certain aspects agreed by the sangham are:

(a) Crop rotation principle with sorghum every alternate year.
(b) No ploughing by tractor after the first year.
(c) Application of farmyard manure means the requirement of chemical fertilizers to be progressively reduced to zero levels without fall in productivity.
(d) In the first year the seeds of Pundi and Bebbarulu have to be purchased while sorghum seeds are got on the basis of seed exchange wherein double the quantity is returned on harvest.
(e) Harvesting wages and bullock ploughing share to be paid in kind.
(f) Loans given as per the condition of the fallow. The minimum was Rs. 1,300 and maximum Rs. 2,000 per farmer.
(g) Amounts spent towards ploughing, seed application, chemical fertilizer and weeding is a crop loan payable on harvest.
(h) Cost of tractor ploughing will be a term loan payable in two years and farmyard manure will be payable in three years.
(i) All loan repayments are in the form of grain which is purchased by the village PDS at the prevailing market prices.
(j) Automatic deferring of loan to the next year in case of crop loan and backlog to be collected in three annual instalments.

The Results

On an average the harvest was three bags of jowar and more. One farmer had an yield of one and half bags because he could not undertake the seed application in time. The yield of intercrops like redgram were poor. The village godown received a little over 14 tonnes of sorghum upon harvest (December) from the participating farmers at a procurement price of the prevailing market price of Rs. 2.70 per kg. The grain is supplied after sun drying to reduce the moisture content. An interesting aspect is that about 2.5 tonnes has already reached the poor as wage labour and an equal quantity to those offering the services of bullocks for ploughing. The Sangham has also collected five quintals of jowar seed which have been carefully chosen by the farmers and will be made available to farmers next year. Farmers are having dry fodder to feed their cattle.

The Sangham members decided that the periods from June to October is when the poor have the most need for food and the stored grain should be given only during these months. They identified the beneficiaries, fixed quota quantum, sale price, storage and the management of the programme. All the poor in the village are entitled to purchase the grain. In the first year itself the villagers see the programme as being very relevant as they were getting sorghum at Rs. 2.75 while the market price was Rs. 4.50 per kg. The sale proceeds of sorghum is given as crop loan for the next year.

Enthused by the success of the programme, the Sangham wants to develop all the fallow lands in the village and add pulses and firewood to the programme over the years. They propose leasing of fallow lands from bigger farmers so that landless women could also take up cultivation of food crops. "It is interesting", says Rao, "that these women are now talking of undertaking soil and water conservation measures—a programme I have been pushing for so long".

Delivery Mechanism

The visit of the district officials was organised by the voluntary agency. The Andhra Pradesh Scheduled Castes Finance Corporation included a scheme of loan for fallow land development in the Medak district annual plan. Rao submitted the duly filled in applications form taken from the farmers in the village. Although one year has passed the corporation has yet to release the funds. Therefore, further expansion has been delayed. The villager women are clear that such programmes cannot be taken up by government organisations. In such programmes timely help is as important as the providing of the loan. An NGO or the village Panchayat only will be able to manage the programme, says the Sarpanch, Sugunamma.

Inspite of constraints in the expansion of the programme to its full potential the villagers are carrying forward with the support received in the first year. They see the real viability of the scheme to depend on the productivity of their lands and want that new schemes must facilitate the constant improvement of the soil in terms of microbial action and supplementary nutrition of the soil using organic methods. It must have an inbuilt component of soil breeding to upgrade and maintain basic soil fertility under cereal-legume cropping patterns, and the use of indigenous manurial resources. Over a period of time this technique of soil management will increase the water absorption and retention capacities of these lands and build humus. In the long run chemical fertilizers can be withdrawn from the nutrition management of these lands as response to added chemical fertilizers will come down and micro nutrient deficiencies will be supplemented through organic manure. The availability of fodder will facilitate more cattle breeding leading to the increased availability of farm yard manure and bullock energy for ploughing work.

Distinguishing Features

In a discussion the women at Ibrahimpur the following were seen as the distinguishing features of the coupon rice and their model.

1. The existing system is based on intensive farming on good quality lands. It uses large quantities of expensive resources like water, chemical fertilizers and development of new varieties of hybrid seeds and pesticides. It is dependent on large dams which are harmful and have limited life span. These areas face problems of salinity and water logging leading to permanent and irrevocable loss of highly productive lands.
   The proposed scheme is based on extensive farming using poor quality lands. It uses local resources like farmyard manure, traditional good quality seeds and depends on rain water. It will give impetus to the badly needed multiplication and availability of diverse and good quality seed especially of minor millets. This scheme will enable neglected and soil eroding lands to be brought into the life of the people enthusing their involvement in conservation measures like watershed.
2. The scope of the existing system is restricted to areas with water potential. Even in such areas tapping, storage and supply of water is expensive. Large quantities of credit are needed and monocropping is the the practice. As the capital requirements are high such farming is of interest and benefit to the rich. Mechanisation is inevitable and such agriculture is male dominated. The new method is applicable in most regions in the country.

Credit requirements are small and crop diversity is central. This farming is within the reach of the poor people. This form of agriculture is done mostly by household labour which implies that women will continue to play an important part of agriculture production. These are *aada panta* .

3. The existing system is low on risk, and high on yields with substantial marketable surplus. It will face the problems of increasing costs and subsidies. It suppresses the potential of the people involved in dryland agriculture.

   The new system is high on risk, low on yields with potential to meet the village requirements. It would revive farming in these areas and make it viable. This will lead to increased availability of fodder, bullocks and organic manure leading to increasing productivity, prosperity and village self sufficiency. Subsidies can be progressively reduced and withdrawn in the long run. This relieves the pressures on irrigated lands and enables them to meet high margins such as those available in sugarcane. This system is more prone to fluctuations in production than irrigated agriculture and high buffers have to be maintained.

4. The existing system can operate only through a centralised mechanism like the State Government needing their constant intervention and management and is viewed as "their problem" without any scope of citizens initiative. It makes people dependent on the Government and needs huge infrastructure, massive storage and expensive transportation. It encourages people to move from their traditional foods for a low nutrition food.

   The proposed system operates effectively only when decentralised and managed by the village Sangham releasing the initiatives of the people and reducing dependence on the Government. Sorghum, pearl millet, cow pea etc. have high nutritive value.

5. The existing system creates growth centres in limited areas leading to uneven regional development. It takes the money from the poor areas and puts it into the hands of the richer areas encouraging wasteful and conspicuous consumption. It has lead to producers of food becoming consumers of food.

   The proposed system leads to development of the needy areas in most parts of the country and puts money into the local economy giving scope for the region to grow to its full potential. It encourages minimum food needs for all, encourages local production, and provides local employment.

DECENTRALIZED MICRO-LEVEL PLANNING AND ITS IMPLEMENTATION

TWENTY-EIGHT

DECENTRALIZED MICRO-LEVEL PLANNING AND ITS IMPLEMENTATION*

In an age of shifting paradigm of development from 'top down' to 'bottom up', recognition of local level realities is foremost on the agenda of development perspectives. Panchayati Raj Institutions (PRIs) is a way of projecting that reality through local institutional framework for progressing towards community-based sustainable development. PRI stands face to face with grassroot reality and hence is placed in a comparatively advantageous position than other development institutions to influence development from bottom and also generate waves of development from within. It is in this context that PRIs hold the key to progress towards food-livelihood security for its community members on a sustainable basis.

The first issue is learning about local community's perceptions on food-livelihood insecurity in a participatory framework. It is they who possess the knowledge to describe the problem best. Generally, it is most convenient for us (as outsiders to local community) to apply a definition of our own to understand the concept of food-livelihood security. By applying a simplistic definition to a multi-dimensional issue, we run the risk of missing vital aspects of such an issue and also distorting local facets of the problems at hand. It is important that we approach local communities who are exposed to considerable insecurity of food livelihood and ask them to explain the nature of such a multi-dimensional problem. Experience shows that they are not only able to explain the complex problem but also arrive at solutions and recommendations to the concerned problem. Such solutions and recommendations, emerging at the local level, can then become steps to identify effective ways to tackle the problem of food livelihood insecurity through local institutions.

The centrally sponsored schemes which are intended to meet certain

*On the basis of discussion at the National Conference.

national goals, need to be made only indicative, that is, the centre should define only the broad purpose and leave the detailed planning of the schemes as well as the mechanisms for implementations to the institutions at the district level. District planning by itself cannot be effective in removing regional disparities without a corresponding effort at the wider regional level, as 60 to 70 per cent of the total State plan outlays are still beyond the pale of district planning.

Political and bureaucratic resistance at the State level to sharing power and resources with the local-level institutions for planning from below, is often cited as the single most important reason for the failure of decentralized planning to strike roots. Therefore, those from the centre who advocate decentralized planning have been exhorting the State governments time and again to implement the agreed schemes and guidelines on decentralization. The Constitution (Seventy-third) Amendment Act 1993, mandates, among other things, periodic elections to Panchayati Raj Institutions, reservation of seats for Scheduled Castes and Scheduled Tribes in proportion to population, and reservation of not less than one-third of the elected seats in each Panchayat for women. Their powers include the preparation and implementation of plans for economic development and social justice; implementation of schemes entrusted to them by the State and Central governments; and exercising powers as delegated in subjects listed in the Eleventh Schedule (Annexure IV).

Some of the important issues which need to be coordinated at Panchayat level were identified as follows:

It is important to realise for the sake of participatory planning and action by Panchayats, that one set of key informants regarding food security are rural women. They perform host of activities which are mostly different from those of rural men. Such activities by tradition, include collecting fuel and fodder, gathering food from forests and commons, fetching drinking water, cooking, child rearing, household activities and farm operations. Though many of such activities may not be directly visible and tangible in terms of economic gains, it is well accepted that the rural women play a crucial role in food gathering.

Seasonal strategies for food-livelihood security are required to be intensified in consultation with the villagers especially during lean seasons with seasonal strategies to support livelihood, income and food of poor households of a community. Village community can be involved in raising nurseries for plantation of appropriate species. This would provide them with additional sources of revenues.

The fallow land and other selected areas can be planned jointly by the Panchayats with local villagers for eco-restoration. Species selection and plantation can be done by the village community for reforestation of degraded areas in the sanctuary. Such selection can be a mix of species, important to meet the immediate needs of the villagers.

Panchayati Raj Institutions, at all tiers, can effectively plan supply and distribution through the public distribution system. The emphasis needs to be on the critical periods in the concerned areas when supply of cheap food can be augmented. The local Panchayat can arrange for 'off-season' employment opportunities by vigorously implementing wage-employment generation schemes so that the poor people have greater access to pulses, rice and wheat especially during the critical periods.

The Panchayats can also plan a system of grain banks from where community members can borrow grains in times of deficit and repay them back when such situation improves. The other action by Panchayats can be in terms of encouraging formation of self-help groups amongst local community members.

The Panchayats can emphasize minor irrigation projects in local areas so as to increase opportunities for multiple cropping. This would lend its positive impact on locally available work opportunities.

It would be essential to raise the level of awareness of the beneficiaries (i.e. the poor) and their ability to take the initiative by organizing them into activity-specific groups, associations, and co-operatives and by using the mass media to disseminate useful information to them. The role of voluntary organizations is extremely important in this respect.

TRAINING REQUIREMENTS FOR MICRO-LEVEL PLANNING

TWENTY-NINE

TRAINING REQUIREMENTS FOR MICRO-LEVEL PLANNING*

The days of the green revolution as the only saviour for the hungry millions are over. From the time of a top-heavy model of agricultural growth, wherein technology along with essential inputs, were disseminated among farmers in the better endowed regions of the country, the 21st century will see a marked shift in agricultural growth--a growth that should possibly come from low-input agriculture based on location specific needs and appropriate technology drawing inspiration from the traditional farming practices. The development focus, therefore, has to shift to the grassroots. The new agricultural revolution, that is beginning to take roots, will follow the bottom-up approach. The Gram Panchayats, though not adequately equipped to transfer sustainable farm technologies, can certainly be the partners in the monumental task of agricultural reconstruction for which it is necessary to generate awareness and arrange intensive training to Panchayat functionaries and other local people involved in the process. An attitudinal change has to be brought in officials as well as the common people. There need to be strong linkages at the village, block, district and State level. The new micro-level planning concept has to emerge and then integrate with multi-layer planning. The ability to work as a planning team has to be developed, by changing the preconceived notions of the planners/leadership at the Panchayat level, especially for the Women Panchayat Presidents need to be developed and their ability to negotiate with officials and non-officials has to be strengthened.

District Planning: Lessons from India (FAO Planning Guide)

FAO has assisted the Government of India through the Lal Bahadur

*On the basis of discussion at the National Conference.

Shastri National Academy of Administration to prepare a manual entitled "District Planning: Lessons from India", which comprises a Planning Guide and a Trainers' Guide. The Planning Guide is a set of simple and self-combined guidelines for planning, and the Trainer's Guide is meant to help trainers plan and run courses on district planning using the Planning Guide as the main text. It is to provide district functionaries with concepts and simple tools of analysis for the preparation of 'district plans' according to the existing planning procedures and processes of consultation with the Panchayat bodies. It has been prepared through a joint collaboration effort of specialists from eight institutions in India thereby encompassing the experience in district planning and training which exists in the country. The Planning Guide Manual can be further extended to provide training to block level functionaries who have a key role to play in identification and implementation of plans at village, block and district levels. Measures relevant for developing food security plan at the village panchayat level will include the following:

(i) Identifying households which are genuinely insecure;
(ii) Linking Jawahar Rozgar Yojana and Food for Work Programme with Public Distribution System;
(iii) Supplying quality seeds and other inputs;
(iv) Providing vitamin and other micro-nutrients;
(v) Collecting local food samples to ensure food safety;
(vi) Maintaining 'grain banks' locally;
(vii) Organizing training in programme implementation for the local functionaries.

Training for Block Level Micro Planning Capabilities

Micro-level planning and its implementation calls for steps to identify village level needs clearly quantified together with resources, technologies, and implementation capabilities. India is blessed with NICNET (National Information Centre Network), wherein the Government of India has already invested over US $ 600 million, directly in hardware cost, besides the running cost. It has data available on different resources and applications for almost all the villages in the country. It also has on-line linkage to all the central ministries, State governments, and district headquarters. Having connected 520 district headquarters, its effectiveness is already seen as an information exchange highway at the government level.

NICNET is involved in issues relating to Food Security in terms of providing service to the Public Distribution System. In the expansion phase of NICNET, the hardware facilities are proposed to be extended from the District to the Block level. During this phase, training of trainers at the District level and functionaries and planning personnel for micro-level planning at the Block level can be undertaken. An outline of the On-line Network for Village Panchayat Institutions for Food Security was presented by Dr. N. Seshagiri, Director-General, NICNET. At the village level training is observed to be conspicuously missing. Also the type of training that would be required below the District level--at the Block and the Village levels would need a totally different approach from the already developed the training procedure/facility. It calls for a process of mass training in local language, (since English will not work there), and therefore, the training programme need to be developed in 14 different languages.

Training for the Block Level Panchayat Personnel for Micro-level Planning was termed as the "Last Mile Problem". In the first phase training of atleast 12,000 personnel was considered necessary to extend facilities to over 6000 Blocks.

National Informatics Centre (NIC) can also develop a low cost communication system utilising its 'Network' and use of CD-ROM player and Ku Van Satellite System. CD-ROM will help in more of illustrative demonstration necessary for training of village level functionaries.

Thus NIC can develop a 'Training Programme in Block Level Planning' by utilising NICNET facility.

(i) Training of the Trainers at the District level.
(ii) Training of Panchayat functionaries, NGOs, Cooperative functionaries in micro-level planning for food security at the Block Level.
(iii) Training 12,000 persons in over 6,000 Blocks through chain reaction phenomenon.
(iv) Developing CD-ROM based training material in 14 local languages.
(v) Training/arranging operational and maintenance staff at the Block Level.
(vi) Linking Block level training on micro-level planning on food security to the existing PDS.

THIRTY

INFORMATION SYSTEMS FOR SAFETY NET IMPLEMENTATION

N. SESHAGIRI

Introduction

Defining the food security as the capacity of a country, State, district or house-hold to meet the target levels of consumption on a year to year basis, information systems are required to quantify this capacity at periodic intervals. This in turn, would require databases for periodically estimating the adequacy of the aggregate food supply to meet the requirements of the population, factors and modalities required to assure uninterrupted food supply and to determine whether the food supply is amenable to various segments of the populace. The models for the target levels of consumption, may in turn, require quantification of the minimum recommended level on the basis of nutritional criteria. As food security can be regarded as a problem of short term variability, the database required for targetting this variability has to be more dynamic and updated very frequently. Short term variability of food supplies, may in turn, require information on the effect of the weather on the size of the harvest, effect of natural disasters, etc. In order to reduce the cost of importing adequate food for stabilising domestic supplies, world price information has to be periodically obtained. Despite stability in the aggregate for the country as a whole, certain segments of the population are facing insecurity of food supplies. This may be a local famine or it may the priority changes in distribution patterns for economies in transition to market systems. Another effect of liberalisation may be the fluctuation in real income within the country leading to consumption instability among weaker sections of the population. This will, in turn, alter the food consumption patterns of the vulnerable sections of the society. If fluctuations in the disposable income of the country could be smoothened, it is possible to attain stable food consumption at the national level and perhaps even for a large portion of the population. However the weaker sections may still require the benefits of the Public Distribution System (PDS) or market oriented safety-net arrangements with Government support.

Accelerated growth of the national economy can be accomplished by carefully worked out economic liberalisation. The process of liberalisation can be sustained in the long run only when appropriate safetynets are provided to safeguard the well being of the people who are affected in the short-term. Such people may be those who are below the poverty line or people who are displaced from their jobs due to increasing automation and modernisation. The variability in food supply described above as well as transportation bottlenecks tend to aggravate the insecurity caused by liberalisation. for sustainable liberalisation, the Government in particular and social and economic functionaries in general, will be required to carefully design and implement a food security system with local, State, national and international linkages. For example, the types of technologies for rain-fed crops that can reduce costs and increase yields, would require comprehensive information systems on such technologies and database of experience in using them in various parts of the country. Further, the infrastructure in agriculturally lagging regions have not improved adequately due to failure of policies. These two factors have resulted in a stagnant or declining per capita food production in several States except in Punjab, Haryana and Uttar Pradesh. Transportation bottlenecks and lack of movement optimisation has resulted in the failure of the PDS to transfer foodgrains from the surplus States like Punjab, Haryana and Uttar Pradesh to deficit States like Madhya Pradesh, Orissa and Bihar. As the poor in States like Kerala, Tamil Nadu and Gujarat have tended to depend on PDS supplies more and more, any variability in such supplies will cause considerable hardships. Certain constraints like non-availability of appropriate technologies, inadequate public investment in irrigation infrastructure and non-increasing private investment in agriculture in various districts, call for adoption of constrained optimisation models.

Pursell and Gulati[1] (1993) have argued that it is possible to limit the role of the Government to providing only the safetynet to the poor affected in the transition brought about by market reforms which eliminates controls on agriculture in domestic market and external trade. With the reforms resulting in 15 to 20 per cent increase in the overall level of agricultural prices and implementation of the Dunkel proposals by various food surplus countries further tending to increase these prices, it is likely that unstable world prices and increasing mal-adjustments may be felt by the weaker sections of the society. This would call for a highly optimised deployment of the safetynet in terms of the quantum of support, its distribution without transmission loss and information support for such optimisation. Hence, for the PDS to be fast reactive, the reaction time constant will have to be minimised by organising the PDS around a computer-communication network based information system spread throughout the country, especially linking the vulnerable areas. The NICNET Online Database supporting the PDS throughout the country has given a Management Information System (MIS) for demand for all allocation of, PDS commodities, PDS prices, details of Fair Price Shops, etc. Foodgrain Movement Operations Model developed along with multi object decision support system for PDS is described in Section IV. The special nature of the food security relief management require the development of a Distributed Control System Theoretic Model for Relief Management for maximising the food security of a population affected by variability in food supplies. This and associated GIS frame-work are highlighted in Sections V and VI.

Informatics Design of PDS/RPDS and Safetynets--Identification of Descriptors

The operational system efficiency of a PDS oriented towards price control and poverty alleviation is based on the following conditionalities:

(i) The consumption needs and typification of beneficiaries decides the commodity list.
(ii) With appreciable real income effect, the entitlement scale has to be at adequate levels.
(iii) To ensure adequate distribution, Government procurement of sufficient quantity should be comparable to net production of essential commodities.
(iv) A systemic approach to the identification of efficient procedure for issue of ration cards to targetted consumers should be ensured.
(v) PDS issue prices should be relatively well below the open market price.

The Information implication of the above five conditionalities are important. The information descriptors should include, commodity coverage, quantification of consumption needs, database of profile of beneficiaries, quantification of scale of entitlement, monitoring of rise in prices, competition of real costs underlying the utilisation of the distribution system, commodity supply position, net production of essential commodities, socio-economic status of various beneficiaries, database on ration cards issued, monitoring open market prices, database on location of retail outlets, etc.

Each of the above parameters identified, can in turn be broken up into the sub-descriptors. For example, for the database on retail outlet network, in turn, will have sub-descriptors like the following: Retail outlet locations, retail licences issued, stock position, re-ordering criteria, quality of comodities, profitability of the Fair Price Shops, etc.

The above descriptors are basically at the micro level. PDS modelling and analysis require databases on macro level factors also. For example, the supplies necessary for the PDS will depend on the population covered, their nutritional level requirements and inflation. Ensuring this would call for constantly updated information of macro level factors like entitlement of data on target populations, patterns of essential consumption of these targetted populations, tastes and food habits of the various target populations and the flow profile of essential commodities to those who are in real need of the subsidy.

Broad information descriptors for Administrative Data Processing (ADP) and Decision Support System (DSS) at the level of the Central Government, State/UT Governments, Districts and Sub-districts are given below:

LIST OF INFORMATION DESCRIPTORS

(Based on the PDS Model of Kabra & Ittyerah)[2]

Level	ADP	DSS
Central Government	1. Commodity procurement & Imports	1. Commodity coverage
	2. Procurement Price. Issue Price	2. Supply Inventories
	3. PDS Design parameters	3. Target Population details
	4. Allotments to States	4. Open Market price
		5. Subsidy details
State Governments	1. Receipts of Central Allocation	1. Estimates of Needs

(Contd.)

Level	ADP	DSS
	2. Procurement in the State	2. Warehousing details
	3. Purchases from other States	3. Intra-State procurement
	4. Warehousing/Silo status/ depot status etc.	4. Intra-state procurements
	5. FPS details	5. Open market price relative to issue price
	6. Consumer issue price	6. Commodity coverage
	7. Allotments to District	7. Periodicity & Regularity
	8. Transportation details	8. Ration scale
		9. Ration Cards database
		10. FPS details: Location, performance, margin, etc.
		11. Transportation Logistics and economics
District & Sub-district Administration	1. Warehousing/Lifting stocks	1. Quality & Quantity of delivery
	2. Issue of ration cards	2. Storage by FPS
	3. FPS details	3. Periodicity & regularity
	4. Offtake by FPS	4. Reserve Stocks & Inventories
	5. Enforcement, Inspection and vigilance	5. Monitoring of FPS

Information system implications of PDS and RPDS should also be designed in terms of those helping the design of delivery systems, estimating the supply trends, monitoring the buffer stocks, calculating the subsidies and supporting the evaluation and analysis studies for feed-back correction. These will be briefly touched upon below:

The Food Corporation of India (FCI) purchases, stores and transports the commodities to the Central Godowns. The State Governments, in turn, lift the commodities from the Central Godown and distribute them through Fair Price Shop networks. For efficient operation of such a delivery system, there is need for development of an online information system over computer-communication networks, topologically matching the trunk lines and arteries of distribution. The dynamic commodity flow information over this network, as a function of time, requires advance tools of distributed relational database management systems as is available over NICNET.

The supply trends will be both at the macro level and the micro level. The response of Government supply to fluctuations in production, so that it becomes higher in drought years than during normal years, is required to be consciously designed on the basis of information about the fluctuations as a time series and from computer-aided forecasts. Further, the Government supply should counter-compensate the inflation. An increase in inflation is required to be counter-compensated by a relative decrease in commodity prices. For this also, a network based online information system throughout the country is essential to be maintained in a distributed RDBMS.

Monitoring buffer stock position for creating a buffer stock database in various silos and godowns is an essential step in the distribution optimisation. Buffer stocks in a distribution network, play the same role as the capacitors in an electronic circuit. They store when in excess and discharge when there is deficit around. The PDS and RPDS distribution system is a clear example of a complex feedback control system. The lack of intuition concerning how feedback control systems work and how they can be modelled for system optimisation are possible partial reasons for failure of PDS systems in the past. Adhoc hunches, rather than characterisation of the system in terms of feedback control parameters and system optimisation, governed decision making in the past. With commodity movement of several thousands of crores of rupees involved every year, a well worked out feedback control system model is essential to save the PDS and RPDS from chronic failures in the future. Such models require regular information inputs, both deterministic and statistical. The present structure of FCI is not conducive to the implementation of such models. NIC has already developed such models for FCI, though however, the management of FCI inspite of their sincerity in implementation could not do so because of organisational structural deficiencies. A major overhaul of the FCI structure is essential before successful implementation of large scale feedback system models.

The optimum price policy is based on the following conflicting objectives:

(i) Provision of adequately remunerative price to producers.
(ii) Commodities are made available to various target groups at affordable prices.
(iii) Use of buffer stocks for the 'capacitor effect'.

For a systemic optimisation incorporating the above the three objectives in a weighted objective function subject to various constraints, the following subset variables are utilised: Administered consumer prices, irrigation charges, fertilizer price, electricity tariff, etc. which, in various combinations, help to keep the input price low. According to a paper by Hanumantha Rao[3] (1994), the total input subsidies on this increased from Rs. 10 billion in 1980-81 to about Rs. 75 billion towards the end of that decade. The input subsidies during the beginning of this period which amounted to about one-third of the total Plan expenditure on Agriculture, Irrigation and Sub-area programmes, increased to about 90 per cent towards the end of this decade. According to him, these input subsidies are responsible for the current trend of decline in real expenditure in agriculture and growing budgetary deficits. Such findings partly point to the paucity of information and modelling support to decision making in the past.

Evolution of studies of impact of PDS necessarily requires a good database. So far, the only database available was the National Sample Survey Organisation[4] (NSSO) data on PDS for the year 1986-87 along with the records available on Food and Civil Supplies. Whereas the NSS data is the best that can be culled out in the past, a number of new initiatives, especially by NIC, is under way which is likely to improve the situation in the future.

In addition to the above information descriptors, an elaborate exercise carried out by Y.K. Alagh[5,6] (1994, 1995) has brought out a preliminary illustrative list of indicators that are required for a national level food security information system. He has identified the following indicators for short run decisions:

(i) Estimate of Public Stocks of food items,
(ii) Price trends of food items and comparison with earlier years,
(iii) Estimate of private traders' stocks of food items,
(iv) Crop output expectations,
(v) International price trends,
(vi) Short run domestic demand trends/fluctuations in income and impact,
(vii) Weather fluctuations/disasters/food import indicators,
(viii) Estimates of infrastructure relating to food procurement,
(ix) Agricultural credit for trade and farm operations,
(x) Government decisions and support prices in relation to market trends/costs of production,
(xi) Trends in nutritionally risk segments of the population,
(xii) Tariff/quantity restrictions on food movement,

(xiii) Major technological achievements relating to food availability/ transport/processing,

(xiv) Food aid indicators.

The indicators at the national level for the medium term have been given by him as follows:

(i) Expected increase in agricultural potential in future,
(ii) Expected trends in food crops acreages,
(iii) Expected increase in demand for food items,
(iv) Expected change and price environment for agricultural sector,
(v) Expected policy adjustments in economic incentives to agriculture,
(vi) Expected development in agricultural markets/storage,
(vii) Impact of economic policies and food demand,
(viii) Likely trends in nutritionally risk populations,
(ix) International price trends,
(x) Major changes in regional demand/configurations.

NICNET Based PDS and RPDS Distributed Database

Keeping all the parameters described in the previous section in view, a distributed database is being evolved by NIC over its nation-wide computer-communication network, NICNET. The basic design of the system was carried out by the Civil Supplies Informatics Division of NIC[7] which has brought out a few divisional reports on this topic. A brief outline is given below.

Under the PDS, the Central Government procures and supplies six essential commodities--Wheat, Rice, Sugar, Edible Oil, Kerosene and Soft Coke. NIC has developed the following packages for supporting the decision making in the Ministry of Civil Supplies, Consumer Affairs and Public Distribution.

(i) *MIS for Demand and Allocation for PDS Commodities*-- This database maintains the demand information as proposed by the State Governments, allocation done by the Central pool and the quantity lifted by the State Governments. This database is updated monthly. Monthly reports are generated and sent to the Office of the Prime Minister. A number of other reports supporting decision making at various frequencies or on demand basis are also generated.

(ii) *MIS for Allocation and Offtake for RPDS*— This database maintains information on allocation system by the Central pool, quantity lifted by the State Governments, the number of Fair Price Shops for RPDS, the number of Ration Cards, additions/deletions information, de-hoarding information and the population covered under RPDS. Information on the assistance given by the Central Government for the construction of Godowns and Purchase of Mobile Vans are also maintained separately. The database is updated monthly for allocation and offtake while on a fortnightly basis the reports are generated and sent to PMO on Ration Cards, FPS, assistance etc.

(iii) *MIS on PDS Prices*— This database maintains State-wise information on the prices of Wheat and Rice for PDS and RPDS.

(iv) *MIS on FPS*— This database maintains information on State-wise FPS under various agencies and is updated monthly.

(v) *Procurement Database*— FCI and State Governments have field level agencies for undertaking procurement operations of foodgrains. About 8000 procurement centres for Wheat are operated by FCI and other agencies. Information on the following parameters are collected in every district unit overseeing the procurement operation.

— Quantity of grain arrived in the Mandi/Purchase Centre during the day
— Quantity procured by various agencies/traders
— Prevailing minimum/maximum prices for sale of grain during the day.

At present much of the Mandi figures are collated at the district FCI/State Government offices manually and thereafter sent to the Regional Office. Some of the field offices of FCI/State Government are using the NICNET facility available in various District Headquarters for entering their operational data.

(vii) *Storage Information System*— An elaborate information system has been planned by NIC for collecting information about the status of grains in silos, godowns and Cover and Plinth (CAP) deports. The quantity of storage space available at a point in time is a key information component apart from the type and quality of grains stored. Collection and storage of quality control information has also been attempted.

(viii) *Transportation Information System*— The grains procured/imported is required to be transported to target regions all through the year. About 190 lakh tonnes of grains costing Rs. 10,000 crores are moved every year by FCI alone mostly by Rail involving 0.6 million 4-wheeler equivalent wagons. The movement information is required to be correlated with the stock information for which pilot projects have been carried out over NICNET. Large scale correlation over the length and breadth of the country has been proposed by NIC to FCI. An elaborate software has been developed and structured and the correlated databases have been optimised.

(ix) *Stocks/Offtake Monitoring Information System*— Database on depotwise activity profile consisting of stock/offtake is found to be important. The broad parameters to be monitored for this database module are: Stocks of various grains, Inflows from other FCI/State depots, Issues to various schemes, Outflow to other FCI/State depots and Closing stocks. Release orders for Foodgrains/Sugar are issued by the Central Government and the State Governments take delivery from FCI depots against these release orders. Subject to other restrictions, transparency of FCI stock data would be helpful to the State Governments for planning their lifting/movement operations as well. It is for this reason that a distributed database on this has been designed and is proposed to be implemented nation-wide.

NIC has been providing active computerisation and NICNET support for monitoring PDS operations at the Centre. Since the Ministry of Food and the Ministry of Civil Supplies are both concerned with various aspects of PDS operations, common or correlatory databases are maintained wherever necessary, to provide uptodate information. Since NIC has developed the computer infrastructure from the District level upwards, it is feasible to undertake intensive but appropriate monitoring of PDS operations at the district, the State and the Central levels. The PDS monitoring System utilising NICNET for capture of the following basic data from the District to the State and the State to the Centre, consists of the following:

-- Demand, Allocation and Lifting of essential commodities
-- Number and coverage of Fair Price Shops
-- Number of Ration Cards issued, Units and Cards cancelled
-- End Retail Prices
-- Scale of rationing
-- Enforcement activities.

The State Governments are already utilising NICNET to send the fortnightly status reports and also the details from the blocks covered to the Centre. In addition, the State Governments are utilising NICNET for their own monitoring and implementation information between the districts and the State capitals.

Many of the NIC State Centres have been assisting the State Administration in the implementation of PDS and RPDS. Some of the typical State-wise databases developed by NIC which are in full scale operation are given below:

Arunachal Pradesh

-- Reports from Districts about storage of Essential Commodities
-- Messages regarding Truck requisitioning
-- Stocks of Foodgrains
-- Reports for Revamped PDS
-- Allotment and lifting of Essential commodities.

Himachal Pradesh

-- Fair Price Shops Monitoring
-- Godown Monitoring
-- Licences/Raids/Inspections monitoring
-- Open market rates monitoring

Kerala

-- Monitoring of PDS at District and Taluk level
-- Allocation, lifting and offtake details of Rice, Wheat, Sugar and Kerosene
-- Details of inspections/actions and confiscatioin details
-- Information on authorised dealers

- Information of licence details of Kerosene wholesalers

Madhya Pradesh

- Tehsilwise lifting position related to wheat, rice and sugar
- Inspection of Fair Price Shops
- Enforcement Activities
- Vigilance Activities
- Details of FPS
- Prices of essential commodities

Meghalaya

- Details of FPS
- Allocation of Foodgrains to FPS
- Elimination of Bogus Cards
- Monitoring price levels
- Enforcement activities
- Revamped PDS
- Stocks, Allocation and Lifting
- Scale of Rationing

Tamil Nadu

- Allocation and Lifting Taluk-wise/Week-wise
- Price Monitoring system
- Kerosene Distribution system
- Revamped PDS
- Enforcement activities
- MIS on PDS-Fair Price Shopwise details

Tripura

- Procurement and Distribution
- Distribution of essential commodities
- Prices of essential commodities

In the existing information system developed and operationlised by NIC with the cooperation of Central Government and State Governments, the following drawbacks have been noticed which are being rectified progressively.

-- Time lag in availability of data
-- Lack of aggregation and integration
-- Lack of analytical reports and good presentation
-- Excessive dependence on manual intervention and conventional modes of communication
-- Lack of exploration of cost-effective means for communications/ control.

For remedying the above deficiencies, the following course of action has been suggested by the NIC Division:

1. The information on crop prospects (Area/Production estimates) could be collected from the accredited statistical agency in every district and refined subject to availability of additional data.
2. To begin with, the primary data on stocks and issues from FCI/ State Governments depots could be collected each of the 450 and odd NIC district centres--the load on an NIC Centre on an average would work out to collection of data upon 10 depots on a daily basis. The distribution of FCI/State depots among the revenue districts being highly uneven, the above averages are representative only. This information will be collected by the District collectorate and passed on the NIC District Centre for transmission. Data on other modules of the Grain Management system could be added subsequently.
3. A mandate has to go from the office of the Chief Secretaries to all the District Collectors that they should make available the required data on Stocks/Offtake for FCI/State Government depots, in the prescribed proforma, to the NIC authorised agency in the district.
4. The data so collected has to be entered in the identified district Computer Centres and subsequently transferred to NICNET by the NIC accredited agency.
5. The data available throughNIC would be suitably processed and made available in an online MIS by the NIC Food and Civil Supplies Information Division.

Computer Network Based Models for PDS and RPDS

As mentioned in the foregoing Section, the problem of procurement and distribution optimisation is a highly complex optimal feedback control system. Without detailed enumeration of parameters and their interactions, accurate quantification and detailed characterisation of the feedback control system, there is no way by which integrated optimisation for increase of impact, consistent with decrease of overall costs, can be achieved in the PDS and RPDS schemes. NIC has made a beginning in this direction with the development of methodologies for three important modelling efforts.

1. Multi-objective Decision Support System
2. Distributed Optimum Feedback Control System Model
3. Geographic Information System (GIS) for Transportation Planning

While the detailed mathematical description of these three models is beyond the scope of the present paper, a brief outline of the approach is given here.

Multi Objective Decision Support System for PDS

The Operations Research and Modelling Division of NIC[8] has developed the methodology for a multi-objective decision support system for PDS and RPDS. Taking note of the reserve stocks in the central pool, the Ministry of Food allocates rice and wheat to the various States just a week in advance of each month. After the allocations are made, the demand projected by the various States, the available information and intuitive decision making, the documents highlighting the quantum to be supplied to the recipient States are passed to FCI for implementation. The actual movement decisions of source to destination are made by FCI again on the basis of urgency projected by various States, available information and intuitive decision making. The present movement planning of FCI is on a monthly basis. Based on the directional flows established by the FCI, the information of the movement is conveyed to the source as well as to the recipient depot. This forms the basis for the indents for wagons to be made at the originating stations with the Railways. Foodgrains for despatch are brought to a rail head, which is either a Railway owned or FCI owned siding and loaded manually into the wagons and at its destination is unloaded again at railway owned or FCI owned siding.

FCI expecting an exponential increase in procurement and arrival of stocks in the future. The present storage capacity with FCI and its agencies will not be sufficient to accommodate the entire procurement.

agencies will not be sufficient to accommodate the entire procurement. Procuring States like Punjab, Haryana, Uttar Pradesh, Andhra Pradesh have only limited capacity to accommodate grains and the surplus have to be moved to consuming States for storing and distribution. This has added a new dimension to the grain movement in PDS and RPDS.

To ensure optimal utilisation of the space at the existing warehouses, careful planning of the grain movement is necessary. For this, a computer aided model has been proposed to decide locations for creating additional storage capacities and also to determine the optimal monthly movement planning. The model developed is a multi-objective decision support system (MDSS).

Distributed Optimal Feedback Control System Model for PDS and RPD

The author has developed an Optimum Control system Theoretic Model for a Distributed Framework which can accommodate a Distributed Geographic Information System over a Computer-Communication Network which is in consonance with the framework in which the PDS and RPDS functions (Seshagiri, 1992). The Control theoretic Method suggested enables the contruction of models in terms of control objective functions and constraints as well as synthesis of control and realisation. The steps in the construction of the distributed system theoretic model of PDS and RPDS have been worked out with specific reference to the realisation of optimal distribution. GIS on NICNET takes input in the form of geo-reference data both in spatial and tabular forms. It provides efficient tools for inputting into the database, retrieval of selected data items for models and software modules for analysis. Both spatial (e.g. maps) and non-spatial (e.g. census data, field data) information can be integrated and spatially registered data layer can be analysed independently or in combination with a number of other layers. This enables to stitch together bundles of data and manipulate them for the management and planning of the PDS. The model is based on general theories of control systems earlier developed by Seshagiri[9] (1971), Rastrigin[10] (1974), Saluk Vadze[11] (1975) and Seshagiri[12] (1992).

Geographic Information System for PDS Transportation Planning

The Geographic Information System (GIS) software 'GISNIC' developed at NIC, can integrate multiple layers or vectors of maps with planning models intrinsically. Transportation planning in PDS is concerned with issues which are highly dynamic and temporal[13]. While applying geo-computing to transportation problems, one goes beyond spatial analysis, topologically indexed database structures or graphic display of geographic data. A geographic based information services strategy (GBISS) is found to be essential for regional planning under PDS.

Conclusion

The NICNET based online database supporting the Public Distribution System progressively being implemented throughout the country may give the Management Information System for Demand, Allocation and Offtake for PDS, RPDS, PDS Prices and details of Fair Price Shops. As support to the FCI, a Grain Management Information System concerning stocks/offtake monitoring is being developed and progressively implemented by NIC. The present Distributed Database developed by NIC for the Ministry of Food and Ministry of Civil Supplies and FCI require modifications in order to maximally benefit from the nation-wide network, NICNET. The next logical step in the evolution of the Food Security Information System is the implementation of the Distributed Database and Distributed Modelling over all the 500 District nodes of NICNET with local level optimisations reconciled with national level global optimisation on a dynamic basis. The exercises like this, when fully implemented, cannot only save, annually, thousands of crores of rupees by way of continuous integrated optimisation, but also ensures, through network-based monitoring, that the benefit of the thousands of crores of rupees of subsidies pumped in by the Central Government maximally reaches the poorer and the needy sections of the population with least 'transmission loss'.

NOTES

1. Purssel, G. and A. Gulati, 'Liberalizing Indian Agriculture: An Agenda for Reform', Policy Research Working Papers, World Bank, Washington D.C., September, 1993.
2. Kabra, K.N. and A.C. Ittyerah, *The Public Distribution System in India*, Eastern Books, New Delhi, 1992.
3. Hanumantha Rao, C.H., *Agricultural Growth, Rural Poverty and Environmental Degradation in India*, Oxford University Press, New Delhi, 1994.
4. National Sample Survey Organisation, "Utilisation of Public Distribution System: NSS 42nd Round", (July 1986-June 1987), *Sarvekshana*, 13(4), 1990.
5. Alagh, Y.K., *Indian Development Planning and Policy*, Vikas Publisher, Delhi, 2nd Edn., 1994.

the Workshop on Food Security and PDS in India, held at the Planning Commission, New Delhi, on 28-29 April, 1995.

7. 'NICNET-based National Grain Information System', Report prepared by Food and Civil Supplies Information Division, National Informatics Centre, New Delhi, 1995.
8. 'Computer-Aided Model for the Location, Selection of New Warehouses and Food Grains Movement', Report prepared by FCI and Analytics and Modelling Division, National Informatics Centre, New Delhi, 1994.
9. Seshagiri, N., 'Vectorial Flow Graph--A Concept for the Analysis of Generalized Feedback Systems', *International Journal of Systems Science* (UK). Vol. 1, No. 4, pp. 331-44, 1971.
10. Rastrigin, L.A., *Contemporary Principles to Control Complex Objects*, Mir Publishers, Russia, 1983.
11. Saluk, Vadze, *Problems of Vector Optimization in the Theory of Control*, Metsuiereba, Tbilisi, 1975.
12. Seshagiri, N., 'A Distributed Control System Theoretic Model of Natural Hazard Propagation and Reduction', World Congress on Natural Hazard Reduction, New Delhi, January 10-14, 1992, Published by The Institution of Engineers (India), 1992.
13. E.A. Harper & M.L. Manheim, ''Geographic Information Systems in Transportation Planning'', A Case for a Geographic-based Information.

CONCLUSIONS AND RECOMMENDATIONS

As a Preparatory Meeting to the World Food Summit the National Conference on "Panchayati Raj—The Key to Food Security and Nutrition was organized on July 2-3, 1996 at New Delhi by the Food and Agriculture Organization of the United Nations, Indian Association for the Advancement of Science, Indian Farmers' Fertilizer Cooperative and the UN Inter-Agency Group in India; under the auspices of Ministry of Food, Ministry of Agriculture and Cooperation, and Ministry of Rural Areas and Employment of the Government of India. The participants included officials of the Government of India, officials of State Governments, Representatives of Institutes involved in Panchayati Raj, Chiefs of Panchayats, and NGOs involved in Food Security issues.

Conclusions

The participants endorsed FAO's effort to organize the World Food Summit at Rome during November 13-17, 1996. The participants expressed the opinion that the expected commitment to be made by the Heads of Government/State has to be fully backed up by effective Action Plan for National Level implementation, as these emerge out of the National Preparatory Meetings in different countries. Whereas the World Food Summit will state as to 'What' should be done to deal with the identified issues relating to Food Security, the National Action Plan should place thrust on 'How' the action be initiated to effect the Commitment.

The Participants emphasised that the National Conference had played a crucial role in developing an option of actions that are relevant for India and other similar developing countries to attain Food Security. As the Chiefs of Village Panchayats and NGOs (involved in the preparatory process of the World Food Summit) were actively, involved in the discussion, the outcome has a direct relevance to the ground realities, and the recommendations will be workable solutions. The option of actions can be an important input for the World Food Summit, and should be sent for their considerations.

Food Security in India was considered to be best achieved by promoting decentralized local production and equitable distribution of food; and improving the capacity of the poor to access food. India has a well laid out Public Distribution System, but the offtake is reported to be low due to lack of purchasing power, resulting in certain incidents of malnutrition. This observation supports the need to promote local food production.

India is strengthening the Panchayati Raj Institution through the 73rd and 74th Constitution Amendments. The elected representatives of the people are being empowered to decentralise planning and administration of development programmes. Many of the programmes are having direct relation to ensuring food security including household and intra-household food security. Some of the food security areas for Panchayats to focus attention include convergence of services, monitoring of various services, nutrition garden at the community level, grain banks, production of low cost nutritious foods for children through women groups. Overall framework of legal, administrative and financial measures need be urgently developed so that Panchayats become effective delivery mechanism for Food Security.

Following specific recommendations emerged:

Recommendations

1. The World Food Summit provides an opportunity for seeking commitment for global action to fight hunger and malnutrition and to ensure Food Security for All. The Summit should clearly bring out that different approaches are required for food security for the urban poor and the rural poor in the developing countries. The Summit should also focus on food security for the valnerable groups, and woman and child, with particular mention of breast-feeding and supplementary foods.
2. The Panchayats and Local Self-government Institutions can play crucial role in ensuring 'household level' Food and Nutrition Security in India, as laid down in the National Nutrition Policy of 1993 and the National Plan of Action on Nutrition of 1995. This calls for Central and State Governments to undertake following steps:

(i) Empower Panchayats (and local self-government institutions) with appropriate and suitable allocation of financial resources to implement the programme of Food Security; and legislate land reforms for different situations.

(ii) Ensure effective involvement of all people, women and men, in decisions and actions that affect their food security, wherever appropriate by promoting cooperatives and NGOs.

(iii) Build capabilities in Panchayats for: (i) micro (village) level planning for Food Security, and (ii) implementation of the plans at village level through involvement of elected members; NGOs, cooperatives, and local entrepreneurs. Elected women members may be called upon to play a predominant role.

(iv) Education and training of elected representatives and functionaries of Panchayats and other Local Self Government Institutions, and NGOs be emphasised with the focus on sustainable food production through micro-level planning and implementation.

(v) Nutrition awareness creation should be made an integral part of various sectoral programmes with a view to ensure household and intra-household food security.

(vi) Develop appropriate cost effective Research, Development and Demonstration measures aimed at building/improving skills of small and marginal farmers and farm workers, from all sectors of agriculture including cereals, fruits and vegetables, fisheries, poultry and animal husbandry, leading to sustainable production. The emphasis should be on technology for improving agricultural productivity of rainfed agriculture and artisanal fisheries.

(vii) Develop appropriate (non-technical) measures to improve skills relating to managerial, operational, maintenance and marketing techniques to effect better returns from available local resources and produce.

(viii) Promote local off-farm income/employment generation activities to improve purchasing power of the rural poor, especially the artisans and landless labour.

3. A formal Agreement for creating 'Micro Level Planning Capacity in Panchayats' through assistance by the UN agencies is to be established, preferably on the World Food Day, 1996, i.e. October 16, 1996.

3.1 The UN Inter Agency Group will consider ways and means to strengthen the planning capabilities of the Panchayati Raj at district and block levels, by utilizing the existing NICNET hardware and software infrastructure and manpower. Whereas NICNET is in the process of expanding its network from district to block level through own resources, this opportunity should be utilized to train atleast two persons at each block level in micro-level planning process. This will call for training atleast 12,000 persons from over 6,000 development blocks in the country in one year.

3.2 A Working Group may be set up to develop the Programme Outline on Training for Micro-level Planning, to be considered for funding under the UN Programme on Food Security and Nutrition.

ANNEXURES

ANNEXURE - I

THE CONCEPT OF FOOD SECURITY IN INDIA

Background

The objective of Eradicating Hunger and Malnutrition and the consequent Human Suffering is within the reach of humanity. However, reaching this goal remains as great challenge today as in the past. Hunger and Malnutrition remains the most devastating problems facing the majority of the world's poors. Despite general improvement in food availability, health and social services, hunger and malnutrition exists in some form in almost all the countries. One out of five persons in the developing world is chronically undernourished, 192 million children suffer from protein-energy malnutrition and over 2,000 million experience micro-nutrient deficiencies. For the developing countries as a whole there has been a consistent decline during the decades of 70s and 80s in the proportion of chronically undernourished people. The current and achievable-challenge is to build upon and accelerate the progress that has occurred.

Understanding of Food Security

The food security is defined as a situation where everyone on the globe has access, at all times, to the food needed for an active and healthy life.

At the household level food security implies having physical and economic access to food that are adequate in terms of quantity, quality and safety.

The overall food security entails three basic issues viz.,

(i) availability;
(ii) stability; and
(iii) access.

Availability of enough food for all can be attained through efficient domestic production in each country and international trade. Appropriate use of natural resources can ensure universal food security sustainability.

Stability can be ensured by taking appropriate pre-empture steps. Harmful seasonal and inter-annual instability of supplies can be reduced. Natural and man made disasters can often be anticipated or even prevented, and reaction when they occur, can be timely, effective and constructive.

Access to adequate and safe food by all is possible. The vast majority of malnourished, either cannot produce or cannot afford to buy enough food. They have inadequate access to natural resources, jobs, incomes or social support. These factors can be and need to be addressed.

Thus, sustainability, efficiency and equitable availability of food require a comprehensive approach at the country level within the available infrastructure and traditional practices so that food is produced on a sustainable basis and is made available to the poor.

Root Causes for Lack of Food Security

Food security is affected by a wide range of factors that may lead to inadequate or excessive nutrient intake or may impair their optimum utilization. The factors most directly influencing nutrition are analyzed under the categories of food and health care. Development policies, though usually not included in the domain of the nutrition as such, can also affect nutritional well-being.

It should be stressed that poverty is the root cause of malnutrition leading to fragile food security. Acute and chronic undernutrition and most micro-nutrients deficiencies primarily affect the poor and deprived people who do not have access to adequate food, live in unsanitary environment without access to clean water and basic services, and lack access to appropriate education and information.

In developing countries, where approximately two-thirds of the population lives in rural areas, crop and animal production, fishery and forestry activities are direct sources of food and provide income with which to buy food. Increased production of food for family consumption or as a source of income helps to stabilise food prices and improve nutrition. Improved marketing facilities can also contribute to food security. In urban areas poverty and unemployment, as well as the poor quality of housing, health and education, are important factors affecting food availability. The degree to which increased income is transformed into improved food consumption and family care depends also on education and socio-cultural factors.

Strategies for Improving Household Food Security

In general, strategies for improving household food security should include:

(i) adopting overall development strategies and micro-economic policies that would create conditions for growth with equity;
(ii) accelerating growth in the food and agricultural sectors and promoting rural development that focusses on the poor;
(iii) improving access to land and other natural resources;
(iv) providing credit for poor household;
(v) increasing employment opportunities;
(vi) introducing income transfer schemes;
(vii) stabilising food supplies;
(viii) improving emergency preparedness planning, providing food aid, and strengthening the on-going mechanisms of household food security.

What Needs to be Done to Achieve Food Security?

There are two possibilities of achieving food security, as defined below:

(i) To produce own food needed to attain the food security; and
(ii) To have an access to food through food trade.

Having realised that the root cause of household food insecurity is poverty, actions to attain Food Security will be related to poverty alleviation. Household food security may be chronic, seasonal or transitory. The vulnerable groups include farmers living on marginal lands, landless or temporary labourers, small scale fishermen and forestry workers and the urban poors.

To overcome chronic, seasonal and transitory household food security and thereby to achieve food security, it is necessary to ensure sufficient food supply both at the national and at the household level; to have a reasonable degree of stability in food supplies throughout the year and also from one year to the other; and to ensure that each household is able to produce or procure the food that it needs.

The policies chosen to achieve food security must be at tuned to the characteristics of the country's food security problems, the nature of the food-insure groups, resource availability and infrastructural and institutional capabilities.

The seasonality of production in developing countries influences access to food. The pre-harvest season which is often characterized by food shortages usually coincides with the year's highest farm workload and greatest incidence of infectious diseases. Agricultural practices and technology can significantly affect food availability.

Suggested Approaches for the Food Security--Trade Based or Own Production Based

In the present context the trade-based supply stabilisation is being promoted under the Uruguay Round of GATT, wherein the risk for the low income food deficit country is very high. The developed countries supply essential food products to many of the developing countries which are anyhow protected under subsidised in the respective countries; but the low income food deficit countries supply the food that is of a secondary nature. As such the developed countries are correspondingly gaining much wider control through the tariff structure under GATT and the developing countries are facing an unfair trade situation.

Developed countries with fully grown market economy can adjust to the trade practices effeciently and ensure food supply, as in case of Japan. But, the low income food deficit countries may not be benefited by market economy to attain food security.

General perception of attaining food security in developing countries is through own production. Inspite of sufficient national food production and established public distribution system it does not lead to equitable availability of food for the poor in villages.

The important issue for consideration is the approach for attaining food security for the poors. Panchayati Raj institutions appear to be an option.

Food Security--Situation in India

For developing countries food availability on a national level is not sufficient as seen in case of India where food stocks to the tune of 36 million tonnes are available with the Food Corporation of India, but there are still a large number of persons who do not have an access for the minimum food requirement. Thus, for India, food security involves an overall rural development, agricultural development and corresponding poor man's development whereby he is able to either produce sufficient food in the decentralised form or else is able to earn to buy sufficient food. Equitable availability of food and equitable accessibility of food requires decentralised food production, decentralised storage and decentralised marketing.

Relevance of Panchayati Raj to Food Security

Considering the national administrative and governance practices, India has a unique Institution of Panchayati Raj which can ensure food security programme implementation at district, village and village levels. The 73rd Constitution Amendment of India envisages establishment of Panchayats as units of local self-government in all States and Union Territories of India. Adequate powers and responsibilities have been bestowed on these bodies at the appropriate levels to enable them to prepare and implement schemes for economic development and social justice as entrusted to them under the items listed in the Eleventh Schedule of the Constitution. Out of the 29 development items entrusted for the Panchayats, 17 have already been in place. The Tenth Finance Commission included a Chapter on financing the Panchayats and has gone into the principles governing the distribution and devolution of financial resources between the panchayats and the State/Centre.

Text of 73rd Constitution Amendment is given as Annexure-III.

Approach at the Proposed Conference

Thus, the effort at this Conference will be to identify an Action Plan whereby the Panchayati Raj Institution is effectively utilised for ensuring food security at the village level. Needless to add that the concept of food security, as being recommended for the Conference, is the one based on localised food production, its marketing and income generation for the poors. The decentralised approach at the micro-level, by involving the village Panchayats will lead to ensuring decentralised and equitable distribution and availability of essential foods either through own production or through income generation from rural development activities.

ANNEXURE - II

WORLD FOOD SUMMIT

13-17 NOV., 1996--ROME, ITALY

Background

The world leaders will assemble in Rome for making a public commitment to action to eliminate hunger. The World Food Summit will provide a historic opportunity for governments, international organisations and all sectors of civil society to join the forces in a concerted campaign to ensure food security--access of all time to the food required for healthy, active life--for all the world's peoples.

The idea of a world summit on food security was first raised in 1994 by FAO's Director General, Dr. Jacques Diouf. His proposal was unanimously accepted by the FAO Conference in October 1995 and supported by the United Nations General Assembly in December 1995.

The personal participation of national leaders is instrumental in mobilising all government ministries and agencies concerned with food security from agriculture, fisheries, forestry and environment to foreign affairs, trade, economy and development cooperation. This wide involvement, along with the active participation of NGOs, the private sector and other groups, is essential for developing a sound and realistic draft plan of action for the Summit and subsequently for ensuring achievement of the Summit's goals.

The high visibility of the Summit and its preparatory process also serves to draw public attention to the food security question and to stimulate debate in all sectors of society and in the media.

The agreements reached at the Summit will place food--the first and fundamental requirement for life--at the top of the global agenda alongside peace and stability.

The Summit will last for five days, 13 to 17 November, 1996. Heads of State and government will address the Summit from midday on Friday 15

November, through Sunday, 17 November.

Preparatory Meetings

Preparation for the World Food Summit has been designed to stimulate the broadest possible involvement at the lowest practical cost. The policies and actions for consideration at the Summit are being shaped through consultation among governments during sessions of FAO's Committee on World Food Security and its intersessional working group, and in this year's cycle of FAO's regional conferences.

As part of this process, FAO and governments are actively seeking inputs from:

— the United Nations system,
— inter-governmental organisations (IGOs),
— non-governmental organisations (NGOs),
— the private sector, and
— technical and scientific experts.

Analysis of the Issues

Preparations for the Summit are being supported by a series of analytical papers distilling the state of knowledge about the problem of hunger and ways of eliminating it.

Topics include:

— global development in food and agriculture,
— investment in agriculture,
— water and food production,
— food marketing, processing and distribution,
— lessons from the green revolution,
— problems of security and ethics,
— the socio-political and economic environment,
— food security assessment,
— success stories,
— food aid,
— food production and population growth,
— Impact of food production on the environment,
— food production and nutrition,
— food and international trade, and

— agricultural research.

The World Food Summit Seeks Commitment

The success of the Summit will be measured initially by the level of shared commitment it generates, and ultimately by the degree to which the absolute numbers of hungry around the world decline in the coming years. It is aimed at action, not the creation of new funding mechanism, institutions or bureaucracy.

Principal Areas of Post-Summit—Action

Participating nations have expressed their determination to agree on concrete, achievable food security goals, which they can attain individually or in partnership with others.

In the period following the Summit, actions, undertaken by governments, international organisations and civil society are expected to fall into the following principal areas:

— political, macro-economic and trade conditions needed to foster food security.
— policies and institutions that contribute to improving access to food for all.
— meeting transitory and emergency food needs in ways that encourage development.
— approaches to agricultural and rural development that encourage adequate, stable food supplies.
— equitable involvement of all people in decisions and actions that affect their food security.
— investment in research, extension, infrastructure and institutions for sustainable agriculture.
— international cooperation and assistance for food and agriculture.

ANNEXURE - III

WORLD FOOD SUMMIT PREPARATORY CONSULTATION IN INDIA
NATIONAL CONFERENCE ON 'PANCHAYATI RAJ— THE KEY TO FOOD SECURITY AND NUTRITION'

July 2-3, 1996, New Delhi

Explanatory Note on the Conduct of the Conference

Introduction

In consultation with the Ministry of Food, the focal point for World Food Summit in the Government of India, it was decided to organise preparatory meetings at the national level in India. The unique aspect of ensuring Food Security for the poors in India was identified as the route through the Panchayati Raj institution, which are elected bodies and are to ensure local self-governance at the district, block and village level. Consultations with the officials of Ministries of Rural Development and Food and various other experts helped to crystallise the concept of Panchayati Raj for Food Security for the Poors.

Concensus was arrived at organising a National Conference under the title "Panchayati Raj — the Key to Food Security and Nutrition" under the overall umbrella of the Ministries of Agriculture (the nodal point of the FAO in India), Ministry of Rural Development (the nodal point for the Panchayati Raj), and the Ministry of Food (the nodal point for the World Food Summit). The responsibility for organising such a national conference lies on the FAO, Delhi Office in collaboration with the Indian Association for the Advancement of Science—the Association, coordinating organising World Food Day programmes in India since its inception in 1981; Indian Farmers Fertilizer Cooperative; and the Inter UN Agency Group in India.

National Conference on Panchayati Raj—The Key to Food Security and Nutrition

The National Conference has been organised to focus on the need for ensuring food security for the poors in the rural areas. The solution to this problem is being looked in the local reference, i.e., ensuring food production capabilities locally so that food production centres are fairly distributed. Organising such spread-out system is considered feasible under the Panchayati Raj. The delivery mechanism of utilising the Panchayati Raj System has to evolve. Therefore, a need has been felt for organising the National Conference.

Objective

The objective of the Conference is to develop a strategy for micro-level food security and nutrition for the poors through the Panchayati Raj System; and to identify major areas crucial and requiring pioneering effort to develop the same.

Thrust

The thrust at the Conference will be on:

(i) Reasons for lack of Food Security; and
(ii) Potential of Village Panchayat system as an important mechanism for ensuring Food Security at the Village Level.

The Background Paper on Food Security elaborates on what needs to be done at the global, regional and national levels to attain Food Security. The only missing link is to how to do that.

The National Conference will therefore, focus on "how" and not on "what" to attain Food Security.

Since India has a unique Village Panchayat governance system, it is considered appropriate to focus on how the emerging system of Panchayati Raj can be made effective in attaining Food Security.

The first and the most important aspect is of micro-level (Village level) planning for attaining Food Security, the presentations are expected to suggest:

(i) instruments for establishing micro-level planning system;
(ii) delivery mechanism for ensuring implementation of the micro-level

plans; and

(iii) alternative routes for attaining village level Food Security.

Effort will be made to evolve suggestions aimed at optimum utilisation of the existing infrastructure; and work within the emerging national policies, thrust areas, financing mechanism.

The National Conference will be oriented to suggest an overall strategy for Food Security for the poors in India and one or two projects that can establish the micro-level planning system in the country.

One such area already identified is as follows:

The Last Mile Project—Fund Support for Training of Block Level Planning Personnel Using the Existing NICNET Infrastructure

One idea already gaining support during formal and informal, discussions, has been the capability and capacity building of Panchayati Raj Institutions at district, block and village levels. The micro-level planning is seen as an important element that will have a long term effect on sustained use of village Panchayat System for ensuring food security. Micro-level planning and implementation capability building requires effective information network that can be accessed in the shortest possible time. Fortunately India is blessed with NICNET (National Informatics Centre Network), wherein the Government of India has already invested over US $ 600 million, directly in hardware cost, besides the running cost. It has data available on different resources and applications for almost all the villages in the country. It also has on-line linkage to all the government ministries, State governments and district headquarters. Having connected 520 district headquarters, the effectiveness is already seen in information exchange at the government level. At present 520 districts are connected through this network. NICNET is in the process of extending the hardware on-line capability to block level, which is also the intermediary Panchayat level.

Thus NICNET will expand its network from 520 districts to 6,000 blocks in the country. This expansion is already being carried out under the normal programme for which finances are being arranged by NICNET through different agencies. After the hardware is in place, at the block level, that can certainly be utilised for other applications like the micro-level planning at the block level.

Creating, micro-level planning capability, at the block level, even at two persons per block, calls for training 12,000 persons in the first phase.

This exercise can be undertaken by NICNET in one to two years. However, funds for the same are required.

Panchayats being the local self-governance bodies will thus be empowered with the micro-level planning capability and the on line data network for effective communication. This will be a major step in ensuring involvement of village Panchayats in food security. Subsequently, it can be considered to extend this facility to Gram Sabhas, which is a body of the clusters of ten to fifteeen villages. At that stage, the system has to be extended to about 50,000 Gram Sabhas. But, will come in the long term.

Such a Project can be taken to the UN Inter Agency Group to consider collectively mobilising these funds and create micro-level planning capability in the Panchayats. This can appropriately be called bridging the last mile. The funding may be of the order of US $ 20 million and the coverage will be whole of rural India.

FAO is considering a TCP Proposal (for US $ 273,000) from the Planning Commission to execute a Pilot Project in three States of Maharashtra, Karnataka and Rajasthan. This project can be the fore-runner; and provide enough data and basis for the UN Inter Agency Group Support for the nation-wide Projects.

Outcome

The outcome is expected to be the following:

(i) Target and Approach for Food Security over the next 25 years, with emphasis on Action Plan for 2002, i.e., end of IX Five Year Plan.

(ii) One or two specific Projects covering activity, with wide reach, where technical knowhow and funding may be mobilised.

The Action Plan will aim at recommending policy measures and corresponding actions at the Central government level, State government level, and Panchayat level to strengthen the emerging Panchayati Raj governance system for ensuring food security, by the end of IX Five Year Plan.

The effort would be to evolve a long term strategy for planning at micro level (village Panchayat level) and integrating the micro plans to develop into the "National Plan for Food Security and Nutrition for the Poors through the Panchayati Raj System".

ANNEXURE - IV

THE CONSTITUTION (SEVENTY-THIRD AMENDMENT) ACT, 1992[1]

[20th April, 1993]

An Act further to amend the Constitution of India

Be it enacted by Parliament in the Forty-third Year of the Republic of India as follows—

1. **Short title and commencement**— (1) This Act may be called the Constitution (Seventy-third Amendment) Act, 1992.

   (2) It shall come into force on such date[2] as the Central Government may, by notification in the Official Gazette, appoint.
2. **Insertion of new Part IX**— After Part VIII of the Constitution, the following Part shall be *inserted*, namely—

   [*Pub. Note*: Part IX has been inserted in the text on pp. 101-107. There is no subsequent amendment to it.]

3. **Amendment of Article 280**— In clause (3) of Article 280 of the Constitution, after sub-clause (b), the following sub-clause shall be *inserted*, namely—

   "(*bb*) the measures needed to augment the Consolidated Fund of a State to supplement the resources of the Panchayats in the State on the basis of the recommendations made by the Finance Commission of the State;"
4. **Addition of Eleventh Schedule**— After the Tenth Schedule to the Constitution, the following Schedule shall be *added*, namely—

---

1. Received the assent of the President on April 20, 1993 and published in the Gazette of India, Extraordinary, Part II, Section 1, dated 20th April, 1993.
2. Came into force w.e.f. 24-4-1993 *vide* S.O. 267(E), dt. 24-4-1993.

[*Pub. Note*: The Eleventh Schedule has been inserted in the text on pp. 254-255. There is no subsequent amendment to it.]

[30a][PART IX

THE PANCHAYATS

243. Definitions.—In this Part unless the context otherwise requires,—

(a) "district" means a district in a State;

(b) "Gram Sabha" means a body consisting of persons registered in the electoral rolls relating to a village comprised within the area of Panchayat at the village level;

(c) "intermediate level" means a level between the village and district levels specified by the Governor of a State by public notification to be the intermediate level for purposes of this Part;

(d) "Panchayat" means an institution (by whatever name called) of self-government constituted under Article 243-B, for the rural areas;

(e) "Panchayat area" means the territorial area of a Panchayat;

(f) "population" means the population as ascertained at the last preceding census of which the relevant figures have been published;

(g) "village" means a village specified by the Governor by public notification to be a village for the purposes of this Part and includes a group of villages so specified.

243-A. Gram Sabha—A Gram Sabha may exercise such powers and perform such functions at the village level as the Legislature of a State may, by law, provide.

243-B. Constitution of Panchayats— (1) There shall be constituted in every State, Panchayats at the village, intermediate and district levels in accordance with the provisions of this Part.

(2) Notwithstanding anything in clause (1), Panchayats at the intermediate level may not be constituted in a State having a population not exceeding twenty lakhs.

30a. Part IX ins. by the Constitution (Seventy-third) Amendment Act, 1992, S. 2 (w.e.f. 24-4-1993). Earlier Part IX dealing with territories in Part D of the First Schedule was repealed by the Constitution (Seventh Amendment) Act, 1956, S. 29 and Sch.

243-C. Composition of Panchayats-- (1) Subject to the provisions of this Part, the Legislature of a State may, by law, make provisions with respect to the composition of Panchayats;

Provided that the ratio between the population of the territorial area of a Panchayat at any level and the number of seats in such Panchayat to be filled by election shall, so far as practicable, be the same throughout the State.

(2) All the seats in a Panchayat shall be filled by persons chosen by direct election from territorial constituencies in the Panchayat area and for this purpose, each Panchayat area shall be divided into territorial constituencies in such manner that the ratio between the population of each constituency and the number of seats allotted to it shall, so far as practicable, be the same throughout the Panchayat area.

(3) The Legislature of a State may, by law, provide for the representation--

(a) of the Chairpersons of the Panchayats at the village level, in the Panchayats at the intemediate level or, in the case of a State not having Panchayats at the intermediate level, in the Panchayats at the district level;

(b) of the Chairpersons of the Panchayats at the intermediate level, in the Panchayats at the district level;

(c) of the members of the House of the People and the members of the Legislative Assembly of the State representing constituencies which comprise wholly or partly a Panchayat area at a level other that the village level, in such Panchayat;

(d) of the members of the Council of States and the members of the Legislative Council of the State, where they are registered as electors within--

   (i) a Panchayat area at the intermediate level, in Panchayat at the intermediate level;

   (ii) a Panchayat area at the district level, in Panchayat at the district level.

(4) The Chairperson of a Panchayat and other members of a Panchayat whether or not chosen by direct election from territorial constituencies in the Panchayat area shall have the right to vote in the meetings of the Panchayats.

(5) The Chairpersons of--

(a) a Panchayat at the village level shall be elected in such manner as the Legislature of a State may, by law, provide, and

(b) a Panchayat at the intermediate level or district level shall be elected by, and from amongst, the elected members thereof.

243-D. Reservation of Seats-- (1) Seats shall be reserved for--

(a) the Scheduled Castes; and

(b) the Scheduled Tribes.

in every Panchayat and the number of seats so reserved shall bear, as nearly as may be, the same proportion to the total number of seats to be filled by direct election in that Panchayat as the population of the Scheduled Castes in that Panchayat area or of the Scheduled Tribes in that Panchayat area bears to the total population of that area and such seats may be allotted by rotation to different constituencies in a Panchayat.

(2) Not less than one-third of the total number of seats reserved under clause (1) shall be reserved for women belonging to the Scheduled Castes or, as the case may be, the Scheduled Tribes.

(3) Not less than one-third (including the number of seats reserved for women belonging to the Scheduled Castes and the Scheduled Tribes) of the total number of seats to be filled by direct election in every Panchayat shall be reserved for women and such seats may be allotted by rotation to different constituencies in a Panchayat.

(4) The offices of the Chairpersons in the Panchayats at the village or any other level shall be reserved for the Scheduled Castes, the Scheduled Tribes and women in such manner as the Legislature of a State may, by law, provide:

Provided that the number of offices of Chairpersons reserved for the Scheduled Castes and the Scheduled Tribes in the Panchayats at each level in any State shall bear, as nearly as may be, the same proportion to the total number of such offices in the Panchayats at each level as the population of the Scheduled Castes in the State or of the Scheduled Tribes in the State bears to the total population of the State:

Provided further that not less than one-third of the total number of offices of Chairpersons in the Panchayats at each level shall be reserved for women:

Provided also that the number of offices reserved under this clause shall be allotted by rotation to different Panchayats at each level.

(5) The reservation of seats under clauses (1) and (2) and the

reservation of office of Chairpersons (other than the reservation for women) under clause (4) shall cease to have effect on the expiration of the period specified in Article 334.

(6) Nothing in this Part shall prevent the Legislature of a State from making any provision for reservation of seats in any Panchayat or offices of Chairpersons in the Panchayats at any level in favour of backward class of citizens.

243-E. Duration of Panchayats etc.-- (1) Every Panchayat, unless sooner dissolved under any law for the time being in force, shall continue for five years from the date appointed for its first meeting and no longer.

(2) No amendment of any law for the time being in force shall have the effect of causing dissolution of a Panchayat at any level, which is functioning immediately before such amendment, till the expiration of its duration specified in clause (1).

(3) An election to constitute a Panchayat shall be completed--

(a) before the expiry of its duration specified in clause (1);
(b) before the expiration of a period of six months from the date of its dissolution:

Provided that where the remainder of the period for which the dissolved Panchayat would have continued is less than six months, it shall not be necessary to hold any election under this clause for constituting the Panchayat.

(4) A Panchayat constituted upon the dissolution of a Panchayat before the expiration of its duration shall continue only for the remainder of the period for which the dissolved Panchayat would have continued under clause (1) had it not been so dissolved.

243-F. Disqualifications for membership-- (1) A person shall be disqualified for being chosen as, and for being, a member of a Panchayat--

(a) if he is so disqualified by or under any law for the time being in force for the purposes of elections to the Legislature of the State concerned:
Provided that no person shall be disqualified on the ground that he is less than twenty-five years of age, if he has attained the age of twenty-one years;
(b) if he is so disqualified by or under any law made by the Legislature of the State.

(2) If any question arises as to whether a member of a Panchayat has become subject to any of the disqualifications mentioned in clause (1), the question shall be referred for the decision of such authority and in such manner as the Legislature of a State may, by law, provide.

243-G. Powers, authority and responsibilities of Panchayats--Subject to the provisions of the Constitution, the Legislature of a State may, by law, endow the Panchayats with such powers and authority as may be necessary to enable them to function as institutions of self-government and such law may contain provisions for the devolution of powers and responsibilities upon Panchayats at the appropriate level, subject to such conditions as may be specified therein, with respect to--

(a) the preparation of plans for economic development and social justice;
(b) the implementation of schemes for economic development and social justice as may be entrusted to them including those in relation to the matters listed in the Eleventh Schedule.

243-H. Powers to impose taxes by, and Funds of, the Panchayats-- The Legislature of a State may, by law, --

(a) authorise a Panchayat to levy, collect and appropriate such taxes, duties, tolls and fees in accordance with such procedure and subject to such limits;
(b) assign to a Panchayat such taxes, duties, tolls and fees levied and collected by the State Government for such purposes and subject to such conditions and limits;
(c) provide for making such grants-in-aid to the Panchayats from the Consolidated Fund of the State; and
(d) provide for constitution of such Funds for crediting all moneys received, respectively, by or on behalf of the Panchayats and also for the withdrawal of such moneys therefrom,

as may be specified in the law.

243-I. Constitution of Finance Commission to review financial position-- (1) The Governor of a State shall, as soon as may be within one year from the commencement of the Constitution (Seventy-third Amendment) Act, 1992 and thereafter at the expiration of every fifth year, constitute a Finance Commission to review the financial position of the Panchayats and to make recommendations to the Governor as to--

(a) the principles which should govern--

(i) the distribution between the State and Panchayats of the net proceeds of the taxes, duties, tolls and fees leviable by the State, which may be divided between them under this Part and the allocation between the Panchayats at all levels of their respective shares of such proceeds;

(ii) the determination of the taxes, duties, tolls and fees which may be assigned to, or appropriated by, the Panchayats;

(iii) the grants-in-aid to the Panchayats from the Consolidated Fund of the State;

(b) the measures needed to improve the financial position of the Panchayats;

(c) any other matter referred to the Finance Commission by the Governor in the interests of sound finance of the Panchayats.

(2) The Legislature of a State may, by law, provide for the composition of the Commission, the qualifications which shall be requisite for appointment as members thereof and the manner in which they shall be selected.

(3) The Commission shall determine their procedure and shall have such powers in the performance of their functions as the Legislature of the State may, by law, confer on them.

(4) The Governor shall cause every recommendation made by the Commission under this article together with an explanatory memorandum as to the action taken thereon to be laid before the Legislature of the State.

243-J. Audit of accounts of Panchayats--The Legislature of a State may, by law, make provisions with respect to the maintenance of accounts by the Panchayats and the auditing of such accounts.

243-K. Elections of the Panchayats--(1) The superintendence, direction and control of the preparation of electoral rolls for, and the conduct of, all elections to the Panchayats shall be vested in a State Election Commission consisting of a State Election Commissioner to be appointed by the Governor.

(2) Subject to the provisions of any law made by the Legislature of a State, the conditions of service and tenure of office of the State Election Commissioner shall be such as the Governor may by rule determine;

Provided that the State Election Commissioner shall not be removed from his office except in like manner and on the like grounds as a Judge of a High Court and the conditions of service of the State Election Commissioner shall not be varied to his disadvantage after his appointment.

(3) The Governor of a State shall, when so requested by the State Election Commission, make available to the State Election Commission such staff as may be necessary for the discharge of the functions conferred on the State Election Commission by clause (1).

(4) Subject to the provisions of this Constitution, the Legislature of a State may, by law, make provision with respect to all matters relating to, or in connection with, elections to the Panchayats.

243-L. Application to Union Territories--The provisions of this Part shall apply to the Union Territories and shall, in their application to a Union territory, have effect as if the references to the Governor of a State were references to the Administrator of the Union territory appointed under Article 239 and references to the Legislature or the Legislative Assembly of a State were references, in relation to a Union territory having a Legislative Assembly, to that Legislative Assembly:

Provided that the President may, by public notification, direct that the provisions of this Part shall apply to any Union territory or part thereof subject to such exceptions and modifications as he may specify in the notification.

243-M. Part not to apply to certain areas--(1) Nothing in this Part shall apply to the Scheduled Areas referred to in clause (1), and the tribal areas referred to in clause (2), of Article 244.

(2) Nothing in this Part shall apply to--

(a) the States of Nagaland, Meghalaya and Mizoram;

(b) the Hill Area in the State of Manipur for which District Council exist under any law for the time being in force.

(3) Nothing in this Part--

(a) relating to Panchayats at the district level shall apply to the hill areas of the District of Darjeeling in the State of West Bengal for which Darjeeling Gorkha Hill Council exists under any law for the time being in force;

(b) shall be construed to affect the functions and powers of the Darjeeling Gorkha Hill Council constituted under such law

(4) Notwithstanding anything in this Constitution,--

(a) the Legislature of a State referred to in sub-clause (a) of clause (2) may, by law, extend this Part to that State, except the areas, if any, referred to in clause (1), if the Legislative Assembly of that State passes a resolution to that effect by a majority of the total membership of that House and by a majority of not less than two-thirds of the members of that House present and voting;

(b) Parliament may, by law, extend the provisions of this Part to the Scheduled Areas and the tribal areas referred to in clause (1) subject to such exceptions and modifications as may be specified in such law, and no such law shall be deemed to be an amendment of this Constitution for the purposes of Article 368.

243-N. Continuance of existing laws and Panchayats--Notwithstanding anything in this Part, any provision of any law relating to Panchayats in force in a State immediately before the commencement of the Constitution (Seventy-second Amendment) Act, 1992, which is inconsistent with the provisions of this Part, shall continue to be in force until amended or repealed by a competent Legislature or other competent authority or until the expiration of one year from such commencement, whichever is earlier:

Provided that all the Panchayats existing immediately before such commencement shall continue till the expiration of their duration, unless sooner dissolved by a resolution passed to that effect by the Legislative Assembly of that State or, in the case of a State having a Legislative Council, by each House of the Legislature of that State.

243-O. Bar to inferference by courts in electoral matters--Notwithstanding anything in this Constitution,--

(a) the validity of any law relating to the delimitation of constituencies or the allotment of seats to such constituencies, made or purporting to be made under Article 243-K, shall not be called in question in any court;

(b) no election to any Panchayat shall be called in question except by an election petition presented to such authority and in such manner as is provided for by or under any law made by the Legislature of a State.]

[64][ELEVENTH SCHEDULE

(Article 243-G)

1. Agriculture, including agricultural extension.
2. Land improvement, implementation of land reforms, land consolidation and soil conservation.
3. Minor irrigation, water management and watershed development.
4. Animal husbandry, dairying and poultry.
5. Fisheries.
6. Social forestry and farm forestry.
7. Minor forest produce.
8. Small-scale industries, including food processing industries.
9. Khadi, village and cottage industries.
10. Rural housing.
11. Drinking water.
12. Fuel and fodder.
13. Roads, culverts, bridges, ferries, waterways and other means of communication.
14. Rural electrification, including distribution of electricity.
15. Non-conventional energy sources.
16. Poverty alleviation programme.
17. Education, including primary and secondary schools.
18. Technical training and vocational education.
19. Adult and non-formal education.
20. Libraries.
21. Cultural activities.
22. Markets and fairs.
23. Health and sanitation, including hospitals, primary health centres and dispensaries.
24. Family welfare.
25. Women and child development.
26. Social welfare, including welfare of the handicapped and mentally retarded.
27. Welfare of the weaker sections, and in particular, of the Scheduled Castes and Scheduled Tribes.
28. Public distribution system.
29. Maintenance of community assets.]

---

64. Sch. IX ins. by a Constitution (Seventy-third Amendment) Act, 1992, S. 4 (w e f 24-4-1993).

ANNEXURE - V

LIST OF PARTICIPANTS AT THE NATIONAL CONFERENCE

H.E. Dr. Surjya Kanta Mishra
Minister-in-Charge,
Land & Land Reforms,
Panchayats & Rural Development
Government of West Bengal
Writers Building
CALCUTTA 700 001.

Dr. M. Aram
Member of Parliament (MP)
11, Janpath
NEW DELHI.

Mr. Jayant Patil
Member
Planning Commission
Room No. 115,
Yojana Bhavan
NEW DELHI.

Mr. L.C. Jain
IDS
18, Barakhamba Road
NEW DELHI.

Mr. Vinay Shankar
Secretary
Ministry of Rural Development
Room No. 247, 'A' Wing,
Nirman Bhavan
NEW DELHI.

Mr. Arun Sinha
Secretary
Ministry of Food
Room No. 179,
Krishi Bhavan
NEW DELHI

Mr. S.P. Jakhanwal
Secretary
Ministry of Food
Room No. 173,
Krishi Bhavan
NEW DELHI.

Dr. (Mrs.) Sarla Gopalan
Secretary
Department of Women & Child Development
Government of India
Room No. 602,
Shastri Bhavan
NEW DELHI.

Dr. R.S. Paroda
Director-General, ICAR and Secretary,
Department of Agricultural Research & Education
Krishi Bhavan
NEW DELHI.

Dr. N. Seshagiri
Director-General
National Informatics Centre
Room No. 337, A Block,
CGO Complex, Lodi Road
NEW DELHI.

Ms. Sarita J. Das
Joint Secretary (IC)
Ministry of Agriculture
Room No. 123,
Krishi Bhavan
NEW DELHI.

Mr. Surendra Kumar
Joint Secretary
Ministry of Food
Krishi Bhavan
NEW DELHI.

Mr. Sunil Sud
Joint Secretary (Fisheries)
Ministry of Agriculture
Krishi Bhavan
NEW DELHI.

Mr. Pradeep Rao
Director (IC)
Ministry of Agriculture
Room No. 145A,
Krishi Bhavan
NEW DELHI.

Mrs. Shashi Prabha Gupta
Technical Adviser,
Food and Nutrition Board
Department of Women & Child Development,
Ministry of Human Resource Development
Room No. 390,
Krishi Bhavan
NEW DELHI 110001.

Mr. P. Venkatesan
Deputy Secretary
D/o. Consumer Affairs & Public Distribution System
305 'B' Wing,
Shastri Bhavan
NEW DELHI.

Dr. R.B. Singh
Director
Indian Agricultural Research Institute
Room No. 1, Pusa
NEW DELHI.

Dr. (Mrs.) Indira Chakravarty
Director Professor & Dean
All India Institute of Hygiene and Public Health
110, Chittaranjan Avenue
CALCUTTA 700 073

Mr. Dharmendra Nath
Secretary (Food)
Government of Madhya Pradesh
BHOPAL.

Mr. N. Das
Special Secretary
Food and Civil Supplies Department
Government of West Bengal
CALCUTTA.

Mr. Kamal Taori, I.A.S.
Chairman
U.P. State Textile Corporation
Vastar Bhavan, 1,
Smith Square,
Civil Lines
KANPUR
UTTAR PRADESH.

Mr. George Mathew
Director
Institute of Social Sciences
B-7/18, Safdarjung Enclave
NEW DELHI 110 029

Dr. P.S. Bhatnagar
Director
National Research Centre for Soybean (IARI)
Khandwa Road
INDORE (M.P.)

Mr. P. Michael Vetha Siromony
Deputy Director
Lal Bahadur National Academy of Administration
MUSSOORIE - 248 179
UTTAR PRADESH.

Mr. Abhijit Datta
Senior Fellow
Institute of Social Sciences
B-7/18, Safdarjung Enclave
NEW DELHI 110 029.

Mr. Manoj Saunik
Chief Executive Officer
Rural Development Department,
Government of Maharashtra,
CEO,
Pune Zilla Parishad,
Yashwantrao Chawan Bhavan
PUNE - 1.

Mr. Mihir Bhatt
Director
Disaster Mitigation Institute
25 Vasundhara Colony,
Gulbai Tekra,
AHMEDABAD 380 006

Mr. Dharamvir Singh
Extensionist
Sultanpur (U.P.)
V&PO - Akola
Distt. AGRA 283 102.

Mr. Swaraj Lata Goel
President
Braj Bhoomi Sewa Sansthan
Jaisinghpura
MATHURA 280 003
UTTAR PRADESH.

Mr. Laxmidass
Ex-Chairman, KVIC
Focus
Gandhi Seva Ashram
PO Oel,
Distt. Una
HIMACHAL PRADESH.

Dr. M.L. Dewan
Former Advisor, FAO
Advisor
Village & PO Ranichauri
Distt. Tehri Garhwal
UTTAR PRADESH.

Ms. Kunti Paul
President
All India Women's Conference
6, Bhagwan Dass Road
NEW DELHI 110 001

Dr. B. Mishra
Associate Secretary
Association of Voluntary Agencies for Rural Development (AVARD)
5 (FF), Institutional Area,
D.D.U. Marg
NEW DELHI 110 001.

Dr. Manorama Bawa
Secretary General
All India Women's Conference
6, Bhagwan Dass Road
NEW DELHI 110 001

Prof. R.K. Mohapatra
Chairman
Vision Foundation for Development Management
D-74, Amar Colony,
Lajpat Nagar
NEW DELHI 110 024

Dr. V. Balaji
Project Director
M.S. Swaminathan Research Foundation
3rd Cross Street, CPT Campus,
Taramani Institutional Area
MADRAS 600 113.

Ms. Geeta Mishra
Executive Secretary
All India Women's Conference
6, Bhagwan Dass Road
NEW DELHI 110 001.

Mr. Dhuleshwar Meena
Member
Consortium of Scientists
1-G-12, Vaishal Nagar
AJMER 425 862.

Mr. P.D. Bhatnagar
Secretary General
Consortium of Indian Scientists for Sustainable Development
M-7, Anasagar Link Road
AJMER.
RAJASTHAN

Mr. P.G. Menon
Advisor Programmes:
Indian Federation of UN Associates;
Convenor (Conf.) Consortium of Indian Scientists for Sustainable Development;
Executive Director,
Institute of Materials Management of India;
Res: D-409, Defence Colony
NEW DELHI 110 024.

Brig. N.L. Kapur
Indian Army (Retd.)
N-29, Green Park Extension
NEW DELHI 110 016

Mr. K.S. Gopal
Director
Centre for Environment Concerns
3-4-142/6, Barkatpura
HYDERABAD 500 027.

Dr. B.L. Kaul
President
Society for Popularisation of Science
517-A, Upper Lakshminagar
SARWAL JAMMU 180 005.

Mr. M.V. Rajasekharan
Executive Trustee & Coordinator
Asian Institute for Rural Development
7-A, Ratna Vilasa Road,
Basavangudi
BANGALORE 560 004.

Dr. Prashantak Routray
Programme Officer
Centre for Youth and Social Development (CYSD)

Plot No. 130, Saheed Nagar
BHUBANESWAR 751 007.

Mr. Padma Venkataraman
All India Women's Conference
37, Dr. Radhakrishnan Nagar,
Thiruvamiyur,
MADRAS 600 041.

Dr. G.K. Girish
Retired Joint Commissioner
Retired Scientist
6/2, Sector II, Rajendra Nagar
SAHIBABAD
GHAZIABAD.

Dr. J.D. Sharma
Associate Professor
School of Environmental Sciences
Jawaharlal Nehru University
NEW DELHI 110 067.

Ms. Poonam Sharma
Research Scholar
Jawahar Lal Nehru University
School of Environmental Sciences
Jawahar Lal Nehru University
NEW DELHI 110 067.

Mr. S. Ramachandran Pillai
Assistant Professor
Institute of Management in Government
Vikas Bhavan, P.O. Thiruvanthapuram 695 033
KERALA.

Dr. Fahimuddin
Fellow
Giri Institute of Development Studies
Sector - O, Aliganj
LUCKNOW.

Ms. Madhumita Chakravarty
Special Correspondent
Financial Express
Express Building
Bahadur Shah Zafar Marg
NEW DELHI.

Mr. Jayaraj
Editor (Agriculture)
United News of India
9, Rafi Marg
NEW DELHI 110 001.

Mr. Suresh Kumar
Newsreel, Correspondent
(Transmission Executive)
All India Radio (AIR)
Parliament Street
NEW DELHI 110 001.

Dr. Sudhirendar Sharma
Director
Energy Environment Group
PO Bag No. 4,
Lajpat Nagar
NEW DELHI 110 024.

Mr. Devendra Upadhyay
Correspondent
Deshbandhu
506, INS Building,
Rafi Marg
NEW DELHI.

Mr. Raj Kumar Gupta
Principal Correspondent
Observer of Business and Politics
13th Floor,
Vijaya Building,
Barakhambha Road
NEW DELHI.

Ms. Sunila Swaraj
Journalist
Press Trust of India (PTI)
4 Parliament Street
NEW DELHI.

Dr. Minnie Mathew
Programme Officer
World Food Programme (WFP)
53, Jor Bagh
NEW DELHI.

Ms. Chandni Joshi
Regional Programme Adviser
UNIFEM
40, Max Mueller Marg
India International Centre Building (2nd Floor)
NEW DELHI.

Mr. L.A. Mandalia
Programme Specialist in Water Resources
UNESCO
8, Poorvi Marg,
Vasant Vihar
NEW DELHI.

Dr. T. Walia
Consultant (PHA)
WHO
A-534, Nirman Bhavan
NEW DELHI.

Ms. Deepika Shrivastava
Project Officer (ECD & Disability),
Child Development
UNICEF
73, Lodi Estate
NEW DELHI.

Mr. Wasim Zaman
Representative
UNFPA
55, Max Mueller Marg
NEW DELHI.

Mr. Michael W. Ellis
Country Director
World Food Programme
53, Jor Bagh
NEW DELHI.

Mr. Thomas Lewinsty
Associate Expert
UNDCP
IIC Building, 40 Max Mueller Marg
NEW DELHI.

Mr. B. Radhakrishnan
Programme Officer
Integrated Rural/Area Development
UNDP
55, Max Mueller Marg
NEW DELHI.

Dr. S.P. Dhua
Regional Coordinator, RENPAP
UNDP/UNIDO
55, Max Mueller Marg
NEW DELHI.

Ms. Alison King
Inter-Agency Support Officer
IASU/UN
55, Max Mueller Marg
NEW DELHI.

Mr. Mahendra Pal
Senior Programme Officer
Royal Danish Embassy
11, Aurangzeb Road
NEW DELHI.

Mr. Manish Jain
Development Officer
British Development Cooperation Office
50-M Shantipath,
Chanakyapuri
NEW DELHI.

Mr. M. Christopher
Programme Manager
Natural Resources Projects
Overseas Development Administration
British Development Cooperation Office
Shantipath,
Niti Marg
NEW DELHI.

Ms. Hema Ramaswamy
Acting Office Director
Office of Social Development
USAID
28B, Institutional Area
Katwaria Sarai
NEW DELHI.

Dr. N.S. Randhawa
Ex FAO Staff Member
Chandigarh.

Dr. R.K. Malik
Ex Chief of Food Quality and Standard Service (FAO)
28, Feroze Shah Road
NEW DELHI.

Mr. R.K. Shukla
Ex. Agricultural Marketing Consultant (FAO)
283, Gulmohar Enclave
NEW DELHI. 110 049.

Mr. Dharmir Singh
Extensionist
IFFDC
Village & P.O. Akola
Distt. AGRA 283102.
(UTTAR PRADESH)

Mr. P.A. Dhananjaya Rao
Deputy Field Manager
IFFCO, No. 146,
Ist Floor,
2nd 'A' Cross,
Maruthi Nanagar
TUMKUR 572 102

Mr. Sudesh Kumar Singh
R.G.B. IFFCO Ranchi Constitution
Chairman Jinoriya FACS Ltd.
Jinoriya, PO Daudnagar
(Khaira Deep)
Distt. AURANGABAD 824 113.
(BIHAR)

Mr. Sudesh Kumar Singh
Jinoriya
PO Daudnagar
AMANABAD
BIHAR.

Mr. B.K. Gopal
Panchayat President
Baliganchalhi Gramaparishad
Malur Taluk,
Kolar Distt.
Karnataka State
Gramapanchayat Baligarakalhi
Chikllorrggullar village
Kudenoor Post,
Malin Taluk
KOLAR Distt.
KARNATAKA.

Mr. G.P. Singh
Field Officer
IFFCO
Lakhi Sarai
BIHAR.

Mr. Surender Singh Dalal
Field Officer
IFFCO
IFFCO-Hansi, Dist. Hisar
HARYANA.

Mr. Surendra Dalal
FO
IFFCO
Hansi
Hissar
HARYANA.

Mr. Amrik Singh
Sarpanch
Village Panchayat
Gram Panchayat Pali Teh. Narnand
Distt. HISAR. (HARYANA)

Mr. Ramesh Chander
Member, Panchayat
Gram Panchayat
Garhi Moth, Th: Narmand
Dist. HISAR.
(HARYANA)

Mr. Romesh Kumar
Member Panchayat
VPO-Garhi (Moth)
Tehsil - Narnaund
Distt. HISSAR.

Ms. Nishatai Namdeorao Chauhan
Chairman
Panchayat Sammittee Ghatanji
P.O. Ghatanji
Distt. YAVATMAL (MAH.).

Mr. Sudhir Ghatak
Sabhapati
Panchayat Samiti
Kalna II Block,
P.O. Singerkone,
BURDWAN
(WEST BENGAL)

Mr. Nikhil Dutta
Sabhapati
Panchayat Smiti
Memari - II Block
P.O. Paharhati
BURDWAN
(WEST BENGAL)

Mr. Parthasarathi Bhattacharya
IFO
IFFCO
Area Office-Burdwan
Distt. BURDWAN.
(WEST BENGAL)

Mr. Parmanand Tyagi
Pradhan
Village Bayana
P.O. Dasna
GHAZIABAD.
(UTTAR PRADESH)

Mr. Raisa Bano
Pradhan
Panchayat Raj,
V & PO Sikandra
Distt. ALLAHABAD.
(UTTAR PRADESH)

Mr. Dharamvir Singh
Extensionist
Sultanpur
V&PO - Akola
Distt. AGRA 283 102. (U.P.)

Mr. D.V.V. Satyanarayana
President, Primary Rural Bank
Chebrolu, Unguturu Mandel
West Godavari
ANDHRA PRADESH

Mr. B.K. Gopal
Iggalur, Panchayat
Malur Taluk
Kolar
KARNATAKA.

Mr. P.A. Dhananjaya Rao
Dy. Field Manager
IFFCO
Tumkur
KARNATAKA

Mr. Parmanand Tyagi
Pradhan
Village Bayana
Ghaziabad (U.P.)

Mr. Vikram Prashad
Field Officer
IFFCO
GHAZIABAD (U.P.)

Mrs. Nishatai Namdeorao Chavan
President
Ghatanji Panchayat Samiti
P.O. Ghatanji
Yavatmal (MAHARASHTRA)

Mr. V.L. Shende
Field Officer
IFFCO
8, Sai Shradha Apartment
Sarswat Chowk
Tilakwadi,
Yavatmal
MAHARASHTRA.

Mr. Gajendra Prasad Singh
Field Officer
IFFCO, C/o Shri. Rajniti Pal Yadav
Nayatola,
Purani Bazar
LAKSHMISARAI 811 311.
(BIHAR)

Dr. S.V. Kaore
Deputy Area Manager
IFFCO, 53-54,
Govardhan,
Nehru Place
NEW DELHI.

Dr. O.P. Gaur
Joint General Manager
(IFFDC & PR)
IFFCO
53-54, Govardhan Building,
Nehru Place
NEW DELHI.

ORGANISING AGENCIES

Mr. Peter Rosenegger
FAO Representative in India and Bhutan
FAO/UN
55, Max Mueller Marg
NEW DELHI.

Dr. V. Kumar
Marketing Director
IFFCO
53-54, Govardhan Building
Nehru Place
NEW DELHI.

Dr. B.P. Govil
Joint General Manager (Agricultural Sciences)
IFFCO
53-54, Nehru Place
NEW DELHI. 110 019.

Dr. K.P.A. Menon
215, Kailash Hills
NEW DELHI.

Mr. Pradeep Chaturvedi
Indian Association for the Advancement of Science
D-11/55, Kaka Nagar
NEW DELHI.

Mr. O.P. Dewan
Information Officer
FAO/UN
55, Max Mueller Marg
NEW DELHI.

Mr. V. Kumar
Consultant
FAO/UN
55, Max Mueller Marg
NEW DELHI.

INDEX